Democracy, Security, Peace

Series Editor Prof Dr Michael Brzoska

DSP   Volume 221

A publication of the Institute for Peace Research and Security Policy at the University of Hamburg

Wolfgang Zellner (ed.)

Security Narratives in Europe

A Wide Range of Views

Nomos

Die Deutsche Nationalbibliothek lists this publication in the
Deutsche Nationalbibliografie; detailed bibliographic data
is available in the Internet at http://dnb.d-nb.de

ISBN   978-3-8487-4507-4 (Print)
        978-3-8452-8750-8 (ePDF)

British Library Cataloguing-in-Publication Data
A catalogue record for this book is available from the British Library.

ISBN   978-3-8487-4507-4 (Print)
        978-3-8452-8750-8 (ePDF)

Library of Congress Cataloging-in-Publication Data
Zellner, Wolfgang
Security Narratives in Europe
A Wide Range of Views
Wolfgang Zellner (ed.)
218 p.

ISBN   978-3-8487-4507-4 (Print)
        978-3-8452-8750-8 (ePDF)

1st Edition 2017
© Nomos Verlagsgesellschaft, Baden-Baden, Germany 2017. Printed and bound in Germany.

Contents

Foreword

This volume represents both the raw material and a by-product of the 2016 OSCE Network of Think Tanks and Academic Institutions' project and report "European Security – Challenges at the Societal Level"[1]. This project differed in two respects from other projects dealing with Russian-Western relations: *First*, it seriously strove to overcome the limitations of comparable reports, which focused solely on state action, and to include societal actors and factors, only to find out that this was not as easy as one would imagine. And *second*, it used more than a dozen national security narratives as the starting point for the report, which embedded the discussion into a much broader and much more differentiated context than the usual Russian-Western dichotomy. Originally, the publication of these country narrative reports was not planned. However, after we had realized how valuable and useful they were, we decided to publish at least most of them. This volume contains 13 country narrative reports in the order provided by the English alphabet. We have also decided to reprint the report, which was published in late 2016 on the website of the OSCE Network and as a printed brochure in a limited number of copies, as an annex to this book.

Both the notion of "narratives" and the finding that more than two of them exist, go back to the report "Back to Diplomacy" compiled by the "Panel of Eminent Persons on European Security as a Common Project" under the Chairmanship of Ambassador Wolfgang Ischinger. In his foreword to the report, Ischinger wrote: "For governments and other institutions, as well as for the OSCE as a whole, it might be worth considering a research project on these different narratives, on our common history, bringing together scholars from different countries, and aiming to set out more systematically our divergent views of the past, and how and why they developed."[2] Precisely this was done by the OSCE Network project.

The term "narrative" has currently reached a certain prominence in political discussions. It is borrowed from an equally fashionable strand of political science, discourse analysis, without necessarily taking on board the whole theoretical construction connected with the latter.

This volume is not based on a specific theory or uniform understanding of "narratives". For our purposes, it is sufficient to understand narratives as a complex of interconnected tales on different aspects of security and security policy: perceptions of threats, challenges and chances, assessments of the

---

1   Wolfgang Zellner (principal drafter), Irina Chernyk, Alain Délétroz, Frank Evers, Barbara Kunz, Christian Nünlist, Philip Remler, Oleksiy Semeniy, Andrei Zagorski, European Security – Challenges at the Societal Level (OSCE Network of Think Tanks and Academic Institutions), Hamburg 2016.

2   Final Report and Recommendations of the Panel of Eminent Persons on European Security as a Common Project, November 2015.

beliefs of one's self and others, positions, interests and objectives, assessments of the international environment and its developments, and so on.

Security policy narratives serve a number of political purposes: Domestically, narratives unify actors behind certain positions, provide legitimacy and prepare action. *Vice versa*, counter-narratives block action by diminishing legitimacy and disputing certain positions. Internationally, narratives display the positions of states or other actors, dispose predictability or unpredictability, depending on certain actors' preferences, draw "red lines" or point to opportunities for compromise and negotiation.

There are long-term and short-term narratives. Long-term narratives can persist over decades and even centuries, can gain and lose in prominence over these periods and change their form, structure and parts of their substance. Political conditions decide which narratives gain or lose relevance at a certain time. We were particularly interested in the longer-term features of security-related narratives that frame actors' behaviour substantially over time. Significant changes in narratives are typical for times of crisis and transformation or even historical turning points. In this respect, the increasing referral to the narratives, which can currently be observed, is an indication of more profound crises.

One of the greatest rewards of dealing with security-related narratives is the observation that the different country-specific tales are much more complex and diversified than the binary Russia-Western pattern would suggest. On the one hand, security-related perceptions, positions and objectives within what is usually called the "West" cover a much broader spectrum than anyone of us would have believed before this project. On the other hand, in addition to shared positions, there are also a great many disputes and disagreement between Russia and its partners in the Collective Security Treaty Organization (CSTO) and the Eurasian Economic Union (EEU). If treated responsibly, the knowledge of these commonalities and differences opens up substantially more possibilities for co-operative policy approaches.

I want to thank all authors of this volume for their contributions and all their efforts to bring them into good shape. My very special thanks go to Christiane Fröhlich who spared no effort in seeking to harmonize essays that originally differed substantially in terms of language and style. My sincere gratitude goes also to Susanne Bund and Elizabeth Hormann who edited all of the texts in their highly professional manner. I also want to express my gratitude to the members of the project's reflection group – Nadezhda Arbatova, Hüseyin Bağci, Serena Giusti, William Hill, Kornely Kakachia, Dzianis Melyantsou, Kari Möttölä, Barend ter Haar, Marcin Terlikowski and Monika Wohlfeld – who discussed the country narrative reports at a workshop at the Geneva Centre for Security Policy (GCSP) in May 2016. I am grateful to the GCSP, the Friedrich Ebert Foundation and to Naida Mehmedbegović Dreilich for organizing two workshops in Geneva and Moscow. And I warmly thank the sponsors who made the overall project possible: the Austrian Federal Ministry for Europe, Integration and Foreign Affairs, the Finnish Ministry for Foreign Affairs, the German Federal Foreign Office, the Swiss Federal Department of Foreign Affairs and the Friedrich Ebert Foundation.

Finally, I would like to express my special thanks to Gernot Erler, the Special Representative of the German Federal Government for the 2016 OSCE Chairmanship. He is the father of the idea of devoting special attention and a specific project to the different and opposing security policy narratives in the OSCE area. Without his intellectual stimulation and his support the "European Security" project would not have been possible.

Wolfgang Zellner

Kari Möttölä

Finland between the Practice and the Idea: the Significance and Change of Narrative in the Post-Cold War Era

Abstract

Faced with an unsettled and fractured situation in European security, Finland continues to rely on a foreign policy reflecting a guarded attitude and combining long-term doctrines of small-state national realism, liberal Euroatlantism and normative globalism.

Concerning the strained relationship between Russia and the West, the Finnish elite and public narration views Russian power politics as challenging the foundation of European security, but stops short of giving up on the order as broken.

Adjusting a common OSCE-framed security order through a process of redefinition (*Paris II*) would avoid a unilateral great-power deal (*Yalta II*) and an open-ended, multilateral renegotiation of norms and principles (*Helsinki II*) as alternatives with severe geostrategic difficulties for Finland.

The confidence of alert public opinion in the foreign policy remains high and calls for change are limited compared with the significance of events in Europe at large and in the strategic space of the Baltic Sea region. In the welfare domain, economics is markedly securitized due to Finland's halting performance in European and global markets.

While the geopolitics of Russia's military power is a familiar challenge for Finnish narration, responding to the information war, cyber attacks and hybrid war as active social technologies calls for new kinds of tools and strategies to control and guarantee the confidence-building nature of the Finnish territory.

Enhanced attention is focused on regimes closely linked to economic welfare and societal security, stronger agency for the European Union and effective Nordic co-operation. While a bid for NATO membership is not in sight, the possibility remains a means of influence, together with a closer security relationship with the United States, calling for requisite narration.

Introduction: Narratives for a Europe in Crisis

The role of narratives on the current crisis of European security is emphasized by a 'competition of narratives' within the European order, shaken by "a return of geopolitics" and "a resurgence of geo-economics" driven by

Russia and the West (as organized politically within NATO and the European Union), with participation by in-between actors.

As a concept for analysis and policy, narrative may refer to material, institutional and ideational drivers of actorness.[1]

From the strategic point of view, narrative is a means used by policy makers to construct a shared meaning of the past, present and future of international politics in order to shape the behaviour of domestic and international actors. Publics regularly internalize and rationalize the world in the form of narrative and the media may exert a greater impact on public perceptions than government does.

From the discursive point of view, narrative is an identity-driven and identity-reproducing process, whereby nations, leaders or people strive to connect their roles and destinies with internal and external developments. As a result, narrative tends to be a widely used and recognized story of the past.

Narrative and policy belong together and proceed in parallel. Narrative is used to validate or legitimate policy for domestic and international audiences and those messages may not necessarily be identical, but are tailored to serve a function or purpose. The need for narrative within governments and societies is at its greatest when there is a change in policy underway or expected. As interpretations of developments in the Euro-Atlantic and Eurasian regions, narratives serve to rationalize and validate strategies and actions in a formative period of international security.[2]

The crisis in and around Ukraine has brought the situation to a head, with narratives commenting upon the status and future of a unifying "security community" within the framework of the norms, principles, and institutions of the Organization for Security and Co-operation in Europe (OSCE) and its area of responsibility.

Both the initial Russian narrative and the Western counter-narrative characterize the current situation as a rupture of the established order based on post-Cold War commitments and understanding. For Russia, the breakdown is a cause for and for the West it is an effect of recent negative developments. A political settlement on a renewed common security order remains uncertain or out of reach.

Russia has been more assertive in the game of narration over a long period of time. The aggravated Western response has raised the question of whether Russia's actions should be treated as violations of fundamental commitments or interpreted as a rejection of the post-Cold War security governance. Similarly, Russia's implications for the adoption of spheres of interest and calls for a European security treaty represent for NATO and the EU

---

1   Cf. Ronald R. Krebs, Narrative and the Making of US National Security, Cambridge 2015.

2   Interviewees consulted by the author in preparing the article: Tuomas Forsberg (University of Tampere); Marko Lehti (Tampere Peace Research Institute); Hanna Ojanen (University of Tampere); Johanna Rainio-Niemi (University of Helsinki); Pekka Visuri (Finnish National Defence University).

an unacceptable overturning of the OSCE-framed security regime, with mutually reinforcing institutions and organizations, each with its own area of action and responsibility.

It is significant that narratives used to shape policies and impact outcomes embrace an unsettling or potentially fractured situation, in which a formerly common narrative related to the Helsinki/Paris regime is being contested, complemented or supplanted. At the same time, the ongoing situation testifies to a broader set of underlying and conflicting issues beyond the Russian-Western relationship, in particular the rise of socioeconomic narratives securitizing the consequences within regional and global change, caused by globalization and the financial and economic crisis of 2008 and onwards.

While country-to-country circumstances vary, national narratives are playing a two-level game by addressing domestic and external (regional or international) situations and audiences. While expected to be a key item in most narratives, the representation and significance of the role of the Russian-Western relationship reflect a varied set of values and interests. Not all national narratives evaluate the great-power relations with identical attention or intensity.

Finland as a Narrator: Setting the Background

The Legacy of the Cold War: Russia and the Fault Line

Finland entered the post-Cold War era with a legacy of practical or pragmatic national realism underpinning a dominant narrative of the workings of the world order, with great-power politics at its core. A by-product of the past experience was the idea of Finnish exceptionalism reproduced by the forces of history and geopolitics in intermittent association with one of the powers in the Moscow-Berlin-Stockholm triangle.

Having been the overriding issue in the bipolar Cold-War milieu, an eastern relationship with Russia was to retain a primary but adaptable status for Finnish foreign policy in the post-Cold War trajectory. While Finland's ability to deal with Russia bilaterally is a key part of the narrative, with variable attention to Nordic and European directions, as well as an inevitable response to global change, Russia's role in the Finnish strategic agenda has been proportioned in sync with changes in the European and world orders.

A leading driver in the Finnish experience has been the effect of the country's location at a *fault line* of contested policies and narratives in Europe. While signifying a geopolitical and ideological borderline in the Cold War, a crucial question since has been the extent to which the division is supplanted by a normatively and institutionally unifying European order, with Russia as an integral contributor, or regenerated by Russia's challenge as a status-seeking revisionist power.

Alongside the Russian factor, since the Cold War, Finland's international position has been reshaped and strengthened by joining the western forces of liberalism and acceding to economic and political integration in European, transatlantic and global order-building. The advent of a 'post-post-Cold War' era continues to be coloured by the future of a normative and institutional fault line. Russia has a role in the Finnish narration, not only as a great-power neighbour, but also as a key factor in the unification or division of Europe at large.

Finland in the Cold War: Eastern and Neutrality Policies

Never occupied, and a sovereign Nordic democracy, Finland was placed in a Soviet zone of privileged influence by the great-power Yalta arrangement (1945) and the bilateral treaty of friendship (1948) with security and defence implications. Drawn from the experience of military overextension, together with political survival in the war, Finland was determined to guarantee, by its own policy and action, that it would not again land in a situation in which the eastern great power would have cause or an excuse to claim being militarily threatened through the Finnish territory.

Termed in hindsight, Finnish small-state realism, the policy of survival embraced statecraft as the art of maintaining domestic democratic order, while not provoking the Soviet Union/Russia as a neighbour with what could be perceived as its legitimate security interests and accommodating ideationally to the world of power politics.[3] For an influential geopolitical school in the Finnish polity, the lesson learnt and adopted in 1944 has remained a consistent argumentative narrative, being challenged, but not overturned by schemes of defence integration within the European Union or closer partnership with NATO.

While constraints flowing from the prioritized eastern policy varied with the east-west tension, Finland's room for manoeuvre was enlarged and utilized by an active policy of neutrality, associated and strengthened with the Helsinki order of the 1975 Final Act. Finland maintained – although with a less permanent or visible profile – a working relationship in the security policy area with Washington, which valued its stability-promoting neutral role in the sub-region and wider Europe.

The policy of neutrality allowed the opening of another consistent strand in the Finnish narrative, driven by idealist or liberalist thought, on participation in the normative and institutional process of multilateralism and western integration, shaped by globalization in the longer term, as a welfare- and security-promoting and influence-creating strategy of foreign policy. The

---

3   Tuomas Forsberg and Matti Pesu, The "Finlandisation" of Finland: The Ideal Type, the Historical Model, and the Lessons Learnt, in: Diplomacy & Statecraft 27(3)2016, pp. 473-495; Johanna Rainio-Niemi, The Ideological Cold War: The Politics of Neutrality in Austria and Finland, New York 2014.

neutrality policy was also embraced by the realist school as an instrument for managing Finland's relations with great powers. With universal conscription and the mobilization-based military capability, designed to cover the entire territory of the country as its leading principles, an indigenous defence solution was sustained to serve armed neutrality - in practice, though not formally called so.[4]

In line with the ending of the Cold War, through the restored sovereignty and unification of Germany and the dissolution of the Soviet Union, Finland unilaterally nullified (1990) the 1947 Paris peace treaty-related military limitations on its sovereignty. Finland's neutrality was embraced by Mikhail Gorbachev's "new thinking", which dislodged Russia's interest in controlling Finnish domestic politics and the bilateral treaty relationship with Russia was renewed with a new treaty to comply with the practices based on the common norms and principles of the Paris Charter for a new Europe (1992).

With the breadth and rapidity of change testing the capability for intelligence, foresight and planning, Finland had to take decisions unaware or uncertain of their implications in the newly permissive milieu. To avoid undue pressure on the Gorbachev regime, which might endanger its reforms, and in view of uncertainty which might otherwise follow in European change, Finland was cautious about moving to rectify the bilateral relationship with the Soviet Union/Russia (1991/92) and apply for membership in the European Community/Union (1992). Driven by economic rationality, with security justification significant, albeit less prominent in the public discourse, Finland attached no legal or *de facto* opt-outs to EU membership, while ascertaining that accession did not require or embrace military alignment with collective defence obligations.

In the end, the transition phase from the Cold War was not a particularly taxing time for Finland compared with the pressures experienced during the heyday of Soviet power in bipolarity. In the Finnish narrative, the Gorbachev regime is recognized to have occupied a key role in ending the Cold War. The timely and successful adaptation of the eastern and neutrality policies, both of which had strong public support, showed that the country was going to address the emergent European order as a competent and capable actor with full sovereignty in form and practice.

Managing the Onset and Course of the Post-Cold War Order

Facing the onset of the post-Cold War era (1989-92), Finland's narrative of its place and policy was reflective of a combination of uncertainty, unification and integration as drivers of a new Europe.

---

4   Harto Hakovirta, East-West Conflict and European Neutrality, Oxford 1988; Kari Möttölä, The Politics of Neutrality and Defence: Finnish Security Policy Since the Early 1970s, Cooperation and Conflict XVII/1982, pp. 287-313.

Although there were fundamental layers of continuity, the incoming post-Cold War narrative entailed a transition in policy and identity, from marginality by Cold-War neutrality to centrality by European integration. The narrative of a "security state" coping with power politics was to be coupled with one of a competitive "welfare state" capable of a top performance in European and global markets. At the same time, marginality has remained an historic element and an alternative or opt-out position in the narrative battles over Finnish identity, driven by uncertainties in geopolitical and geo-economic futures.

While the configuration of the United States as a sole superpower and a weakened Russia on the European scene was recognized as an unknown and unpredictable premise for international ordering, the great-power relations at the time were seen to be mainstreamed by co-operation in regional conflict management and arms control, trends traditionally perceived as serving Finnish security interests.

While a Europe without dividing lines or socioeconomic gaps was taken as a legitimate promise, the new Russia and other former constituent parts of the Soviet Union, together with the Western Balkans and adjacent regions, were seen as posing an arc of instability, potentially causing indirect or "new" risks and threats. At the same time, within an all-European security order in flux, Finland was treading on a path to unprecedented political integration within the European Union.

The puzzlement of dealing with a weak Russia in transition did not drive Finland to underestimating the sensitivity of a bilateral eastern relationship, however normalized or generic it might become in a unifying Europe. Whether transposed in substance or geography, there was the possibility of a Russian-driven fault line remaining or resurging in Europe, albeit shaped with new forms of security risks and threats. Despite the asymmetry with the West in non-military and conventional military power, Russia, as a neighbouring nuclear-weapons power, retained a key place in Finnish security threat assessments.

The geopolitically retreating, institutionally dissolving and domestically reforming Soviet Union/Russia was transferred to the category of unstable or fragile states and societies to be addressed with engagement in dialogue and support for reform, while enhancing societal resilience at home. Scenarios on security and safety risks concerned nuclear power and other environmental catastrophes in adjacent areas as well as refugees, driven by the chaos of civil war, crossing Finland's eastern border. Redeployment of Soviet/Russian forces from Central-Eastern European and Baltic states to bases too close for comfort led to Finnish enquiries for clarification. None of these concerns were to materialize in a serious way as the era of the Yeltsin regime unfolded in the 1990s.

Nightmares of geopolitics, such as spheres of influence or interest-based arrangements imposed by great powers over small states, remained in the background of a narrative in which a renewed great-power confrontation was not viewed as an overarching factor or as a separate concern for Finland. A model example of the promising atmosphere was the US-Russian co-operation on threat reduction by the dismantling of nuclear weapons. With NATO in search of a mission and a potential membership not on the active Finnish agenda, Finland was not a party to the Russian-Western great game, which engendered the dispute over NATO enlargement.

In the context of CSCE-based order building, Finland focused on the institutionalization of the process and conventional arms control. No peace dividend was envisaged as maintaining territorial defence and remaining militarily non-allied were retained as residual "cores" of neutrality. Diplomatic efforts as a non-party actor were directed at preventing armament build-up in flanks as a consequence of the treaty on Conventional Forces in Europe (CFE). Confidence- and security-building measures were promoted as tools of transparency on a transforming politico-military playing field among states with different postures of military defence and alignment.

In the Finnish narrative, a functioning CSCE/OSCE-framed security community, with all states bound by common norms in dispute settlement and conflict resolution, would make neutrality superfluous. In a more definite manner, neutrality as a term defining the foreign policy line was discarded during the accession period of 1992-95, as Finland committed itself to a common foreign policy in a deepening and enlarging European Community/ Union.

Going forward in embracing the post-Cold War Europe in the 1990s and beyond, in a newly permissive milieu, as realism was complemented by normative and liberal features in the foreign policy narrative, Finland invested in the enlarging role of the EU in supporting and managing political and economic transition eastwards as a key structural means for unifying the continent, although viewed as an uneven and uncertain process. An instrumental objective of strategic value for Finland, a proponent of support for Russian "modernization", the EU-Russian partnership was troubled with uncertainty and frustration. The positive and confidential narrative of the 1990s on European integration and multilateralism was to include growing security concerns from the early 2000s on.[5]

Russia's emergent effort under the Putin regime, from the late 1990s and into the following decade, to regain a great-power status, remained an ambiguous and protracted security concern, complicated by its failing reform, domestic instability and ethnic conflict within the country and the wider post-Soviet space. Although there were initial concerns about sub-regional stability in the Baltic Sea rim, NATO's openness for enlargement and partnership was taken in the Finnish narrative as legitimate follow-up to the freedom of choice principle in the Helsinki *acquis*. At the same time, the implications of

---

5   Tuomas Forsberg and Hiski Haukkala, The European Union and Russia, London 2016.

a sensitive Russia-NATO relationship were felt in the growing US attention to the security of the Baltic States in the context of NATO enlargement, although the dispute did not militarize at the time. The Finnish response was an active promotion of stability-enhancing and institutionalized sub-regionalism around the rims of the Baltic, Barents and Arctic Seas.

As an interim conclusion, throughout the post-Cold War era and into the pre-Ukraine crisis 2010s, the dominant Finnish narrative had seen an all-European situation being largely settled in the OSCE framework, albeit with worrisome trends of fragmentation producing signs of brittleness in the common order. In tune with internal and external developments, Finland has been an active and model student of the concept of comprehensive security, adopted as a mode of action by the countries and international institutions driving multilateralism within the OSCE and the United Nations.

Public confidence has sustained a foreign and security policy line towards wider Europe, consisting of stability and transition support, co-operative crisis management and participation in the EU's common security and defence policy, in parallel with participation in NATO's partnership for peace. In the politico-military sphere, Finland has not experienced a security deficit separate from overall European and global developments. With growing attention to strengthening societal security, institutionally and materially, completing the strategic approach, elite and public support for the posture of military defence by denial and non-alliance has remained robust, including preparedness for the possibility of power politics as a matter of doctrine.[6]

Back to the Future: European Security Becoming Unsettled

Europe on a Descent to Multiple Crises

The post-Cold War trajectory of European security has turned during the 2010s into a prolonged process of indeterminate complications, driven by a geopolitical and geo-economic competition, a deficit of domestic and international governance and a complex socio-economic crisis. With a presumptive rupture of the European order and despite the concept of security community reconfirmed in the Astana declaration of 2010, no clarity prevails on the significance or consequences of the violation of the established rules of conduct by Russia over Ukraine, as argued by a broad majority of OSCE participating States, or the use of force by the West in the series of other regional conflicts, as argued in the Russian narrative.

While references to a "new Cold War" have not gained critical support among politicians or experts, there are two main reasons for ambiguity around the assessments of the transformation underway.

---

6   Kari Möttölä, Finland's Comprehensive Security: Challenges and Responses, Network for European Studies, Helsinki 2014.

On one hand, as a predominantly Russian-Western dispute, the crisis in and around Ukraine has long roots in rhetoric and substance. The contestation of narratives is driven by the political use of history, reaching as far back as the incomplete digestion of the dissolution of the Soviet Union by Russia and the revitalized critical historiography of Western policies towards the Gorbachev and Yeltsin regimes in the defining period of ending the Cold War and immediately thereafter.

On the other hand, the Ukraine crisis is not the sole defining turn in the turbulence underway in the European and global order. An undeniable game-changer is the economic and financial crisis of 2008 and its political and social consequences, not least within the European Union and its member-states.

Amidst integrated and advanced western countries, struggling with stagnation or recession and coping with a lingering Euro-crisis and runaway globalization, both of them feeding Euro-scepticism, the rise of populism and extremism, as well as the threat of transnational terrorism and the migration and refugee crises, are dominating the agenda in most polities, shaking the confidence of established market democracies and not only transit or failing societies and countries. Consequently, the ideational, institutional and material future of the European order has been seen to hang in the balance in the contest between liberalist and populist forces in the elections in several key European countries, in the wake of Brexit and in the face of the uncertainty created by the ascent of Donald Trump in the United States.

Finnish Narration on Europe at a Political and Economic Crossroads

The Finnish narration is faced with providing answers to a number of serious and formative questions on Finnish agency. Are the contours of Finnish foreign and security policy as formed in the Cold War and post-Cold War eras under stress or duress? Does the current situation represent the end of an era or the breakdown of an order?

Even while recognizing that international relations are characterized by rising tensions and serious and intractable crises, Finnish narrators would not be apt to conclude that the Helsinki/Paris order is necessarily broken. Were that the case, a renewed European order would be imposed by power politics (Yalta II) or constructed through a renegotiated political settlement on basic norms and principles (Helsinki II) – both geostrategic dilemmas for Finnish planning and, at best, severe challenges for foreign policy.

Consequently, and not unexpectedly in the long historic tradition, a search for redefining stability and continuity in a pragmatic and multilateral mode (which could, analogically and analytically, constitute a Paris II process)[7] is articulated for the core philosophy of the Finnish course of action in

---

7   Yalta II, Helsinki II, and Paris II are here used for illustrative and analytical purposes; they are not quotes from any official Finnish narrative.

the dominant leadership narrative supported by parliamentary and party-political consensus and the largely sympathetic or non-challenging public opinion. Calls for adjustments with a direct or tangible impact on the foreign policy line are minor or marginal, keeping in mind the range of accelerating external events and trends of relevance for the Finnish foreign, security and defence policies.

The economic and financial crisis has shaken Finnish self-confidence and societal stability more deeply than the Ukraine crisis with its run-up and aftermath, while it is admitted that a precarious phase in the great-power relations is at hand, instigated by actions of a resurgent and assertive Russia and correspondingly shaped by a revitalized NATO's response of reassurance with direct and regional impacts for Finnish security.

During the post-Cold War era, the relative positions of economics and security have switched in Finnish narrative, driven by events and reproducing identity. Economics has been securitized, as the dynamic European and global markets have called for a competitive state to perform at the highest level to sustain the benefits of social welfare.

While the maelstrom of global crisis continues to be leading to a loss of confidence in the field of economics, the effects of the Georgian and Ukraine wars and other indications of instability and disunity filtering and spreading over the political management of the European order have returned back to traditional security a great deal of its relative priority – although its signifi-cance had never been forgotten in Finnish narration.

Although the multilateral institutions in which Finland has consistently invested strategic capital for sustaining comprehensive security, the Organi-zation for Security and Co-operation in Europe (OSCE) and the European Union (EU), have suffered and lost in credibility and effectiveness in the across-the-board, but differentiated fragmentation underway, they have re-tained legitimacy as foci in the Finnish narrative.

In the context of the comprehensive concept of security, the Finnish re-sponse has targeted the respect for a normative principle: Ukraine's freedom of choice in domestic and foreign policies must be respected and restored. The issue came up internationally with the discussion on a Finnish (or, alter-natively, Austrian) model or example for Ukraine's future external orienta-tion, presumptively through a great-power arrangement. Finnish debaters noted that it is only Finland's past Cold-War combination of eastern, neutral-ity and integration aspirations, which could be haltingly comparable to Ukraine, although with conditions. There was no will to offer Finland, with its exceptional history and trajectory as a present-day model or to engage in a discussion on limiting or conditioning a fundamental principle in interna-tional politics and law.[8]

---

8   For the 'parachronistic' use of the concept and policy of finlandization related to the
     current situation in European security, see Tapio Juntunen, Helsinki Syndrome: The
     Parachronistic Renaissance of Finlandization in International Politics, in: New Perspec-

Drawn from authoritative surveys, Finnish public opinion emerges in which alertness is mixed with continuity in security perception. In an opinion survey, conducted in autumn 2016[9] on issues causing concern among citizens, the international situation with refugees, employment and Europe's economic outlook topped (from 85 to 75 per cent respectively) the list, followed by international terrorism, political extremism, Syria, the situation in Russia and climate change, with the growth of immigration (61%) and asylum seekers (61%) in Finland, as well as cyber threats and Ukraine, further down in the list. On the other hand, the share of people who considered the military situation in the Baltic Sea region more threatening doubled in 2014-15 from the time before the Ukraine crisis, while the share of those who saw Russian actions negatively affecting Finnish security was slightly reduced in 2015 (57%) and in 2016 (59%) from the peak in 2014. Altogether, the share of those who looked to a less secure world for the next five years rose considerably in 2014-15 to 65 per cent and remained at 59 per cent in late 2016, with close to a similar peak in 1993-94, caused at the time by recession at home and political chaos in Russia.

As for policy solutions to alleviate security and safety concerns, specifically with respect to the handling of the Ukraine conflict, a slight majority in late 2015 graded EU actions negatively, whereas a slight majority viewed Finnish actions upon the outbreak of the crisis positively. When asked about security-enhancing factors in late 2016, the list was topped by participation in Nordic defence policy co-operation (79%) followed by EU common defence (62%), EU membership (54%), international economic co-operation and participation in international crisis management. Favourable views on military non-alliance (45%) and a possible NATO membership (32%) sent mixed signals.

At the same time, as an indication of the will to defend the nation, the share of those who think the Finns should take up arms in all situations, even if the outcome seemed uncertain, has remained high (71%) as has the support for general (compulsory male, voluntary female) conscription (79%). At the same time, after 2013 (32%) there was a significant increase of the share of those in favour of increasing defence spending to 2014 (56%), 2015 (47%) and 2016 (47%) respectively.

While the surveys show a realization and knowledge of change taking place in the international environment, the greater public sees developments

---

tives 25(1)2017, pp.1-19; Hans Mouritzen, Small States and Finlandization in the Age of Trump, in: Survival 59(2)2017, pp.67-84.

9   Finns' opinions on foreign and security policy with a special focus on defense-related issues have been surveyed systematically since the 1970s by the Advisory Board for Defence Information (ABDI), a permanent parliamentary committee administratively part of the MOD. For the report (02/2016) issued late 2016, see http://www.defmin.fi/files/3579/ABDI_(MTS)_December_2016_Report_in_english.pdf.

as confirming the established foreign and security policy line. The defence policy was viewed among the population as being conducted extremely (7%) or fairly well (72%) and the foreign policy as well (70%) in the late 2016 survey.

Support for possible Finnish membership in NATO has served as a closely followed thermometer as well as a potential game-changer in the impact of public opinion on the fundamentals of foreign and security policy. Although the measured support for membership peaked at 30% in 2014 and has slightly decreased since, the share of those opposed to the idea of membership is also going somewhat downwards. In three different surveys in 2015, those in favour of membership numbered 25, 22 and 27 per cent, whereas those against reached 43, 55 and 58 per cent, respectively, while in late 2016, the shares for and against were 25 and 61. Figures from earlier surveys tell the same story: 30-60 (2014), 21-70 (2013) and, more than a decade ago, 28-63 (2005). The overall variation in the last twelve years has remained between 18 and 30 percentage points for those *for* and between 58 to 71 percent for those *against* a NATO membership.

On the whole, while the present official line enjoys broad consensus, the Finnish public is becoming more fragmented and divided, politically and socially, on the issue of military non-alliance. While support for membership grows towards the right and decreases towards the left, no party is unanimous on the NATO issue. While the state leadership takes guidance from public opinion, actors across the political spectrum are keeping their options open. Although no Finnish government or political party has – so far – taken actual political steps or called for immediate action to accede to NATO membership, the political decision-makers are keen to keep their options open and not to become forced into taking a clear-cut or binding final stand on the issue. At the same time, the NATO question remains a formative issue, related to fundamental choices in Finnish security policy.

Consequently, the Russia-NATO-Finland contingency has, on occasion, presented competing narrations, especially when the borderline between advisory analysis or foresight and official government or public policy becomes blurred or contested. As a MFA futures report prepared by the policy planning unit noted that NATO membership would clarify Finland's position in many ways, the authors were criticized by the foreign minister for stepping overboard and not consulting the political masters.[10] When a think tank report commissioned by the government identified, in dire terms, the consequences of Russian power politics towards Finland as part of a foreign policy driven by the Putin regime's ("system") preoccupation with survival, the analysis of the Russian domestic situation was widely commended for its straight talk, commensurate with open public discussion, but the conclusions on potential

---

10   Finland's position, security and welfare in an increasingly complex world, Futures Outlook of the Ministry for Foreign Affairs, Publications of the Ministry for Foreign Affairs 10, Helsinki 2014.

Russian transgressions and pressures endangering Finnish sovereignty and security were rejected by prominent opposition politicians as overly deterministic or unfounded scaremongering.[11]

2016 Government Report on Finnish Foreign and Security Policy

The opinion surveys cited above were conducted prior to the activation of public and elite discussion and narration in connection with the government's report on Finnish foreign and security policy (issued on 17 June 2016)[12], a document prepared, as a rule, during a government's four-year tenure, and an assessment of the effects of Finland's possible NATO membership by an independent group of experts commissioned by the MFA (published in April 2016)[13].

In the narrative of the government report, in the context of broader and global changes in the international security environment, "the return of Russia to thinking in terms of power politics, including its internal development, the growth of its military potential and increasing military activity challenge the very foundation of the European security regime and create instability in Finland's operating environment."

As for the situation in Finland's strategic neighbourhood, the report laments that "during the past ten years or so", "the essence of the security regime", based on co-operation, shared security and arms reduction, as well as confidence-building, has been challenged "to an extent", and "destabilized" by Russia through its actions and interpretations. The report goes on to note that the West and Russia have starkly different opinions on how to restore stability in the region.

In connection with the deterioration of security in Europe and regionally, the annexation of the Crimea by Russia and its complicity in the conflict in eastern Ukraine have led to a vicious circle of tension and military activity in the Baltic Sea region. The tense security situation has a direct impact on Finland, "a member of the western community", and the use of threat of military force against Finland "cannot be excluded."

Referring to the contrasting narratives of Russia and the West about the post-Cold War era and to Russia's perception of international relations as a geopolitical zero-sum game, the report asserts that, in its quest for a stronger great-power status, Russia has "mostly abandoned" co-operation-based security and is challenging the European security order. Moreover, Russia has promoted its goal of a sphere-of-influence-based security regime and demon-

---

11 Venäjän muuttuva rooli Suomen lähialueilla [Russia's changing role in Finland's neighbourhood], Publications of the Government's analysis, assessment and research activities 34, Helsinki 2016.

12 Government Report on Finnish Foreign and Security Policy, Prime Minister's Office Publications 9, Helsinki 2016.

13 The Effects of Finland's Possible NATO Membership: an Assessment, Ministry for Foreign Affairs, Helsinki 2016.

strated the will and capacity to employ military force in attaining such an objective.

While noting that active participation in international co-operation advances Finland's interests as a part of global burden-sharing, with respect to the basic line of action of Finnish foreign and security policy, the report defines Finland as "a country which does not belong to any military alliance. Finland actively and extensively intensifies its international networking. Finland maintains the option to seek membership in a military alliance."

More specifically, in asserting that Finland maintains the option to seek NATO membership, the report refers to the independent assessment – commissioned by the MFA as an intellectual expert work not binding on the government – when charting the conditions for and consequences of possible Finnish NATO membership: Finland and Sweden share a security environment with NATO and their choices are closely connected. NATO membership would fundamentally impact the regional security policy situation in the Baltic Sea region and would be "a fundamental and far-reaching decision in Finland's foreign and security policy, and would, therefore, require wideranging debate and careful consideration."

The independent report goes deeper in envisaging a potentially "strong, even harsh" response by Russia, notably during the transition phase, to a Finnish bid for and adoption of NATO membership, including the use of the ethnic Russian card, and adversely affecting bilateral trade and political relations. Russian representatives, including President Putin, have, as a rule, warned that Finnish NATO membership would force Russia to redeploy its forces closer to the Finnish border, presumably as a hedge against any hostile use of Finnish territory.

While the Finnish independent report stressed the benefits of coordinated and parallel Finnish and Swedish moves on the NATO issue, within the context of sovereign decisions, the corresponding Swedish report, commissioned by the government, took note of the risks involved in the geopolitical differences between the two neighbours and the necessity for a broad regional perspective in potential Swedish decisions.[14]

Based on the public and political response to the independent assessment, in which NATO membership is called a sea change in Finnish security strategy and its relationship with Russia, and to the 2016 government report, no policy change in the government or parliamentary sphere is to be expected at least until after the next general elections due in 2019.

At the same time, in the defence policy report, issued by the government in early 2017, Finland will actively and extensively continue and strengthen its international defence co-operation and networking with the aim of developing the capabilities and enacting the appropriate legislation to provide and

---

14   Säkerhet i ny tid [Security in a new era], Statens offentliga utredningar 57, Stockholm 2016. In the late 2016 survey, 34% of Finns thought Finland should join NATO if Sweden took the step while 54% did not see the link as necessary.

receive international assistance as outlined in and required by the Lisbon Treaty, which guides the EU common security and defence policy, and in the partnership between NATO and Finland, together with Sweden, involved in the Enhanced Opportunity Programme (EOP). In the bilateral framework, Sweden retains a special status with no predetermined limits set on how far joint planning and preparation may extend beyond peacetime situations. Partnership with the United States has progressed rapidly beyond materiel co-operation to the areas of readiness and interoperability as well as training and exercise, including on Finnish territory, driven and underpinned by the growing US and NATO interest in and concern about the stability and security of the Baltic Sea region.[15]

In a capsule-like summary, the goal-setting of Finnish foreign and security policy is presented in the 2016 government report as a corrective response to "degrading co-operation-based security in Europe and the development towards a balance-of-power regime, the deteriorating security situation in the Baltic Sea region and Russia's unpredictable internal and foreign policy development as well as the threats and possibilities included in global trends."

In characterizing the international environment more generally as a challenge to foreign and security policy, the report stresses the need for Finland to anticipate change and to employ its strengths efficiently and flexibly. The report asserts that Finland can strengthen its international position and even act as a trailblazer in a transforming environment where the hallmark is rapid and unpredictable change.

As for the introduction of priorities and goals in Finnish foreign and security policy, the report lists focal areas into the mid-2020s in the following order: strengthening the European Union as a value and security community; deepening co-operation with Sweden, which "enjoys a special status" in bilateral relations, and with which Finland pursues wide-ranging foreign and security policy co-operation based on shared interests and "without any limitations"; together with co-operation with the other Nordic countries; deepening co-operation with the United States as "an important partner" whose commitment to NATO and military presence in Europe is "essential" to Finland's security; promoting co-operation and maintaining a dialogue with Russia aimed at stable and well-functioning bilateral relations; and developing the relationship with NATO as the key actor in advancing transatlantic and European security and stability; together with other bilateral, regional and global issue-areas, stressing rules-based action in international relations in security, human rights and co-operation as well as in trade.

---

15   Government's Defence Report, Prime Minister's Office Publications 2, Helsinki 2017.

Contestation among Narratives

Although the Ukraine crisis, with its run-up and consequences, has been a strategic surprise, calling for critical reassessment of the way the international order works, and affects Finland and Europe at large, the Finnish narrative, as a comprehensive public and private discourse, has yet to overturn the established policy line for something fundamentally new.

Narrative is a mode of power and testifies to the power of language in politics, whether as a product of events and interests or as a presentation of causality to underpin strategies and policies. As a rule, societal structures resist changes, but the logic of the theory submits that narratives become contested when the external milieu transforms from a settled to an unsettled one. [16]

Finland is used to being guided by a dominant *argument* as a rhetorical mode of narrative, which refers to the normative correctness or the instrumental rationality of the policy pursued, as in the structured Cold War environment. When, at the ending of the Cold War, *storytelling* seized the opportunity to explain the opening of western integration and bring the new experience to the public-at-large, a new combined narrative emerged, which would remain dominant through the post-Cold War era.

The question at hand is whether the dominant argument will survive the challenge of the unsettled situation or be contested and ultimately replaced by a new or retrospective storytelling narrative as a result of change in external or domestic conditions or a failure in leadership. The outcome could be a turning point in Finnish security policy, comparable in significance only with those made at the onset of the Cold War and the opening of the post-Cold War order.

A primary challenge for Finland is how to interpret the implications of the return of geopolitics and the resurgence of geo-economics as concomitant factors in the evolving European order in its wider and immediate strategic space: in bilateral relations with Russia; the special relationship with Sweden and multilateral Nordic co-operation; and as a member-state within the European Union; as well as in partnership with NATO and bilaterally with the United States in the Baltic Sea region.

Russia as a European and Neighbouring Power

The Finnish narrative was Russia-focused even before the outbreak of the Ukraine crisis, whereby Russia, as an unsatisfied power, was – and is – seen

---

16   Krebs, cited above, p. 42.

questioning and breaking *modus vivendi* as a culmination of an adversarial process underway for a decade or longer.

While the Finnish government narrative leaves no doubt that Russia's actions in Crimea and eastern Ukraine have caused the current tension and degradation in regional and European security, it stops short of concluding or making accusations that the outcome would – in an irreversible fashion – be a breakdown or the aim would be a replacement of the European security order as established since the end of the Cold War. Hence the 2016 white book narrative on the security regime being challenged "to an extent" and "destabilized" and noting that Russia has "mostly abandoned" the co-operative security order.

While Russia has made NATO enlargement a question of principle in European security ordering, Finland has not perceived military pressure targeted or tailored against itself. It is recognized, however, that Finland's immediate security environment has witnessed continued military tension due to Russian activities and NATO responses in intelligence, air policing, exercises, troop deployments and command and control basing since the outbreak of the Ukraine crisis.

Despite the unpredictability of Russian behaviour as a growing threat and the direct effects in Finland's strategic vicinity, flowing from Russian actions in and around Ukraine on security, Russian policy is not seen to encompass a specific or separate military threat against Finland. At the same time, in the Finnish narration, a return to a balance-of-power regime and Russia's promotion of a sphere-of-influence-based order are anathema to the rules-based and co-operative order based on the freedom of choice principle in the foreign and security policy orientation of states, which remains essential for Finland's international position and security.

While based on the EU's common positions and staying within the confines of the EU sanctions regime, a course of action followed by the Finnish leadership has included maintaining high-level bilateral contacts with Russia – albeit with scant visible results – with broad domestic elite and public support. Referring to unpublicized US-Russian contacts and a broad – if not unanimous – European willingness and interest in conducting dialogues with Russian representatives, the Finnish leaders argue for the benefits of such contacts, both for efforts at searching a way out of the European-wide crisis, despite the stalemate in the Minsk-based process, and for Finnish national strategic and practical interests. A Finnish initiative for improving civilian and military air safety over the Baltic Sea has gained particular publicity.

The strategic significance of the long common border became evident in late 2015 when the Russian Border Guards, in an unexpected and uncharacteristic incident, let asylum-seekers cross the Finnish border in the North, although that matter was solved and the stream stopped rather quickly as a result of agreement at a high political level to restore border security. Moreover, with a long history of trade and economic relations with Russia and suffering disproportionally from the targeted sanctions and countersanctions, Finland has continued to practice bilateral co-operation in trade, business and energy as far as possible, within the confines of the sanctions regime, although the collateral damage in trade with and investment inside of Russia and agriculture and tourism in Finland is serious.

While in the political and normative sphere of Europe at large, Finland is responding to a revisionist but largely isolated Russia, in the area of security and defence, Finland is faced with a relatively strengthened Russia, which is using unpredictability and rapid action as a tactical and strategic tool, and demonstrating, and engaging in hybrid war and cyber power, not only in Eastern Europe, but also in the common strategic space with Finland in Northern Europe. An active information war conducted by Russia and its proxies in the media and social media has become part of the new normal in the Finnish public perspective, albeit with scant direct influence on authentic Finnish media practices.[17]

The Russian mode of political-military operation around Ukraine and Georgia represents for Finnish narrators a familiar geopolitical dilemma from post war, Cold War and even earlier post-Cold War conditions, in which a great power's need for deep forward defence is set against a smaller state's right to sovereign self-defence. The situation is different in an information war or a cyber operation and even in the case of a hybrid war, in which officials from lower levels of government or non-state players, such as trolls or otherwise non-identified or non-recognizable actors, enter the scene. In such cases, it is more complicated to prevent or deny external pressure while, on the other hand, guaranteeing its co-operative mode of action as a neighbour or maintaining control over the 'non-threatening' nature of its territory is not in Finnish hands as before. Various social technologies of deception provide Russia with a new and enlarged spectrum of causes or excuses to raise bilateral issues with security implications even if they are related to identity or societal conditions rather than territorial defence.

The European Union and Management of the Fall-out from the Ukraine Crisis

For Finland, with a societal agenda focused on economic problems, the "Russian-Western" crisis is embodied in the relationship between Russia and the European Union. Finland had expressed concern about the internal course in Russia towards illiberal authoritarianism causing a stagnating and conflictual relationship with the European Union. As the malfunctioning relationship broke out into a full-scale crisis as a result of Russia's geo-economic-to-geopolitical power play over Ukraine's western engagement, the Union turned out to be unprepared for Russian unpredictability, and was barely

---

17 Katri Pynnöniemi and Andras Rácz (eds.) Fog of Falsehood: Russian Strategy of Deception and the Conflict in Ukraine, FIIA Report 45, Helsinki, 2016.

cognizant of the geopolitical connotations of its policy of outreach, even though the dispute had long roots in the stalemate of the EU-Russian partnership.

Joining in the collective response of the EU to Russia's annexation of Crimea as a breach of international law and its involvement in the use of force in eastern Ukraine as a violation of Ukraine's sovereignty and territorial integrity, Finland is a participant in an asymmetrical power struggle in which both the EU and Russia have made false assessments and miscalculations. Although the conflict has not been militarized, it has the combined contours of geopolitics and geo-economics, which the Union has not experienced before and for which it has a skewed pool of instruments, with the unanimous introduction of economic sanctions against Russia being the principal geo-economic tool.

The unsettling situation is testing EU unity, as the combined force of economic and political interests may be pulling member-countries in different directions over the issue of sanctions. For Finland, the stakes in both areas are high. This is reflected in troubled public opinion, although no significant segment has voiced support for a Finnish walkout from the united front in sanctions and other responses. The leadership is catering to the conflicting atmosphere by combining strict adherence to the EU common line of conditionality with a consistent use of bilateral tools of contact with Russia, within the allowed sphere.

While the political contention around Ukraine seems to stagnate any progress towards resolution, Finnish attention is focused on preventing further division within the European Union under stress from economic and migration crises. While no definitive break-up of the rules-based order as a consequence of Russian revisionism and unilateralism is envisioned or declared, there is a growing concern in the Finnish narration over the risk of the crisis-driven atmosphere and illegitimate activity emanating from its core around Ukraine and other intractable conflicts over further issues and other sub-regions, with the Baltic Sea region as a prime case.

A further concern is a divide within the EU between those for whom transnational terrorism is the dominant threat and those who stress the challenge of Russian conduct. While for Finland, terrorism is not securitized to the same degree as in the countries with experience of serious attacks, Finland is also not joining with the Baltic States and Poland in public narration of the acuteness of the Russian threat. In Finnish policy, supplementary stability-promoting activity has focused on supporting and stressing innovative sub-regionalism in Northern Europe and the Baltic Sea region as well as in the Arctic sphere.

Altogether, the post-Cold War developments have altered the mode of rationale in Finland's narrative, as an EU member-state, of relations with Russia. The focus in Finland's eastern policy has shifted from support for and trust in Russia's modernizing reform as a strategic objective into a policy of hedging against Russia's geo-economic and geopolitical encroachment in its neighbourhood and, more widely, in Europe and further on to adopting a policy of conditionality calling for the implementation of the Minsk agreements and Russia's compliance with the common norms and principles of the Helsinki and Paris documents with respect to the war in eastern Ukraine and also the annexation of Crimea as a longer-term issue.

The "principled pragmatism", introduced in the new EU global strategy as a guiding approach to the common actorness and leadership of the European Union, points to a long-term response to the Russian challenge. Strengthening resilience has replaced direct democracy promotion as the instrumental objective for eastern partnership countries in the common neighbourhood between Russia and the Union.[18]

The Strategic Rise of the Baltic Sea Rim

The paralysis of all-European co-operation in conventional arms control and military security has turned attention not only to the NATO-Russian dimension, but also to (sub-) regional security complexes. Nordic and Baltic Europe, as a strategic space of allied, non-allied, EU and non-EU states, has turned into an area of increased Western interest, leading to steps in NATO's response policy in an action-reaction spiral with Russia.

In the context of Finnish policy aimed at stability promotion and conflict prevention, the narration calls for efforts to save the sphere of sustained progress in pragmatic co-operation in the Baltic Sea and Arctic sub-regions and to initiate dispute settlement and arms control over problematic patterns in the political-military sphere.

Recognizing the opposing stands between Russia and NATO on the culprit for the increased tension in the Baltic Sea region, the government views the presence and action of NATO as bringing stability to the security situation and notes that the Finnish-Swedish joint action in strengthening their defence capabilities is aimed at raising the threshold against incidents and attacks.

At the same time, stark threat perceptions in the government report and escalating military activities by Russia and NATO have enlivened a set of competing narratives promoting disengagement and de-escalation as models for Finnish response. Even though critics might support a NATO option in principle, they stress the priority goal of keeping Finnish territory outside of any military conflicts and warn against taking up plans or timetables for enacting NATO membership.

Joint assessments by the five kindred neighbours of Russia's actions with European and sub-regional developments have brought Nordic co-operation and coordination back to the sphere of core issues in security. Of

---

18   Shared Vision, Common Action: A Stronger Europe. A Global Strategy for the European Union's Foreign and Security Policy, Brussels 2016.

special and tangible significance is the wide-ranging Finnish-Swedish bilateral defence co-operation. While covering, in addition to procurement and technological issues and joint exercises, operational planning for situations beyond peacetime, the pattern of Finnish-Swedish co-operation falls short of, but does not rule out a defence alliance in the longer term.

The increased US interest and geopolitical presence in the Northern European and Baltic Sea region has become a focal point in security and defence assessments in Washington and the Nordic capitals. While connected with the NATO/US reassurance policy on the security of the Baltic States, the turn is welcomed by Helsinki and Stockholm for promoting not only regional security, but also their bilateral security and defence relations with the US. A US-Nordic summit in the 1+5 (instead of 1+3) format in Washington DC in May 2016 expressed the participants' joint commitment to upholding the European security order with the established principles. As asserted by a US representative, the summit signified the position of the Nordic countries, irrespective of their military alignment, within the core security interests of the US in Europe.

A Triangle of Doctrines Tested

Faced with change in the international situation and the challenge of overcoming the political, military and normative gaps in European and wider security, the Finnish narration from the leadership argues that "Finland is therefore reacting, but not overreacting."[19] National defence and security, western integration, relations with Russia and international law constitute the pillars of stability-oriented foreign policy and an active defence.

While the Finnish media and public discourse writ large have adopted the narrative of a rupture in the European security order, the realist school of thought views the Ukraine crisis rather as a stage in the great-power geopolitical competition, whereas liberalist and identity-based approaches look for potential changes in the future. Although the European crisis is significant enough to have initiated a competition among accommodating, pragmatist and activist narratives, it is too early to call the situation a watershed in Finland's orientation towards Russia or international relations at large.

The response of narrative and policy to the current crisis testifies to the evolution of long-term traits in the Finnish strategic doctrine since the adoption of national realism as a strategic conclusion from the outcome of the war and through enlarging and deepening liberal aspirations, initiated in the course of the Cold War and matured in integration and globalization, with consequences for identity formation within the post-Cold War order. The

---

19   President Sauli Niinistö, in Helsinki 5 April 2016.

dynamics of Finland's security policy have been explained in recent scholarship by a triangle contingent of three schools of thought.[20]

The core goal of small-state realism is survival under the pressures of Russian power politics and negotiating a sovereign course of action in a world order dominated by a permanent military and security competition among great powers. While smallness has been a generic feature since independence, hardened by lessons of history and geopolitics, realism for Finnish thinking is a practical approach towards the political laws governing world politics, even if the outcome may not be the best possible one.

A liberal trait, reliant on international co-operation as an initial way of distancing from the Russian sphere of influence, has taken shape in the operationalization and institutionalization of membership in the EU and partnership with NATO as Euroatlantism, where strengthened western commitments frame and underpin liberal democratic domestic politics.

As an overtly normative extension of the liberalist conception, globalism looks at a world order where identity-shaping values, rules and institutions, as inescapably global features, shackle power politics over the long perspective.

As an adjustment and response to the external environment, Finnish foreign policy is shaped by the relative weight of the three schools of thought in decision-making and public narration, as inferred at each turn from the nature of change in Russia's position and international relations. The Ukraine crisis seems to verify the small-state realist conception of great-power confrontation, but excessive bilateralism or a retreat to hedging is supplanted by the commitment to a common EU stand. The key role of the European Union in managing and resolving the Russian-Western conflict verifies the value of belonging to an inclusive western group, although deepening security integration towards NATO may not be pertinent in the evolving situation. For globalism, the European crisis may seem to be a step backwards in inevitable multilateral change, leaving the doctrine short of tangible short-term guidance in the play of power politics underway.

As an interim conclusion, in an unsettled international crisis of the highest relevance, Finland's foreign policy seems to be driven by a combination of long-term doctrinal traits and narratives. It is indicative of the guarded and ambiguous Finnish attitude towards unravelling events that realist, liberalist and constructivist theories – largely corresponding to small-state realism, Euroatlantism and globalism as schools of thought in policy – can all be applied to argue both in favour and against Finnish NATO membership as a critical choice in the current and future foreign policy.[21]

---

20   Hiski Haukkala & Tapani Vaahtoranta, Suomen turvallisuuspolitiikan linjat ja koulukunnat [Lines and schools of thought in Finnish security policy], in: Fred Blombergs (ed) Suomen turvallisuuspoliittisen ratkaisun lähtökohtia [Points of departure for the Finnish security policy solution], Helsinki 2016, pp. 55-76.

21   Cf. various articles in Blombergs (ed.), cited above.

Finnish narration is faced with the task of constructing an argument or a story for a nation acting in an unsettled and potentially fractured international situation. A perspective is required for narrating on the question between the transactional and the transformational: whether we are experiencing a new era or looking into a new order in European security.

Finland is used to having a dominant and argumentative narrative on a country located in a precarious geopolitical situation and capable of using the opportunities and benefits of a co-operative and liberal international order. While the dominant narrative, combining realist and liberal teachings and guidelines from the post-Cold War era, is not contested by an alert, but confident public opinion, there is a potential need for creative storytelling as pressures mount on policy adjustment over several issues.

For Finnish planning and foresight, it is awkward to be faced with a great-power (Russian-US) relationship so skewed and asymmetrical in terms of ambition, intention and capability, with respect to the Ukraine issue and beyond. This may constitute the harbinger of a new division or fault line in Europe.

While the outcome of a great game, such as a Yalta II, would be dangerous and a multilateral ordering overhaul, such as a Helsinki II, unpredictable and uncertain, Finnish narration speaks for continuity, adjustment and restoration of a security community in the OSCE framework - a process of redefinition which might lead to a Paris II.

For Finnish narrators, the Russian mode of power politics around Ukraine and Georgia represents a familiar geopolitical dilemma, whereas social technologies of deception, such as an information war, cyber operations or hybrid war, produce a new kind of challenge for managing neighbourly relations.

In the trajectory of dispersing self-help policies, Finland continues to focus on the European Union and sub-regionalism in Northern Europe as regimes which are directly connected to the success of the domestic polity and economy.

A Nordic country and a dedicated EU member-state will be drawing on the freedom of choice principle and pursuing a responsible and co-operative role. Although a bid for NATO membership is not in sight, the possibility remains as a tool of influence. For the near future, a closer security and defence relationship with the United States over the northern strategic space will call for a requisite adjustment in narrative.

Barbara Kunz

French Discourses on Russia: the End of a Foreign Policy Consensus?

Introduction: Two Major Strands within the French Debate

This chapter aims at providing a general overview of French discourses on Putin's Russia. As will be shown, there is no single discourse, but several competing ones covering almost the full spectrum, ranging from what may be labelled pro-Putinism to extremely critical stances. This was obvious not least in the run-up to the 2017 French Presidential elections, when eleven candidates with very different attitudes vis-à-vis Russia fought for the presidency eventually won by Emmanuel Macron. The chapter is, in large part, based on an analysis of public statements by politicians and media reports (yet deliberately leaving out sources, such as Sputnik News or RT) as well as a number of background briefings with officials. It also relies on statements made during events under Chatham House rules, which can, consequently, not be quoted with full attribution. Not all statements leave written traces and this chapter should, thus, be understood primarily as an attempt to capture the mood of French debates on Russia during 2016 and the first half of 2017.

In the general French debate, Eastern Europe has been of relatively little importance since the demise of the Soviet empire. This holds true for Russia itself, but even more so for the countries "in between" Russia and the West.[1] In France, "the East" is traditionally less important than "the South" – a fact which has again come to be more pronounced since the recent terrorist attacks in Paris, Nice and elsewhere. Even after the annexation of Crimea, Russia has, thus, long been none of the truly predominant topics in the French public debate. France has simply been more focused on the terrorist threat, the Middle East and domestic issues. Throughout the 2017 presidential campaign, however, the question of how Paris should deal with Moscow moved up on the political agenda as one of the polarizing matters. Arguably still not of primary relevance *per se*, this development was due, in part, to the increasingly obvious nexus between Syria, the fight against terrorist attacks perpetrated by the Islamic State and Moscow's policies in the Middle East. A growing number of Frenchmen – and a number of politicians, especially in the conservative camp – asked whether it would not be worth paying the price of co-operating with Putin (and even Bashar al-Assad) in order to fight the main enemy. This stance is, thus, only indirectly about Russia, but it greatly affects public opinion, given that terrorism is a key issue in the cur-

---

1   The exception being Armenia due to the large diaspora community.

rent French debate and the single most important security threat.[2] It even seems fair to assume that the "work with Putin against Daesh"-approach constitutes a majority opinion. This latter idea was briefly the official approach after the November 2015 terrorist attacks in Paris, when the French president sought to build an alliance against Daesh.[3] Different objectives pursued on the ground, however, made French leaders realize that any such idea was illusionary for the time being. The series of vetoes on resolutions pertaining to Syria in the United Nations Security Council may serve as an illustration of these difficulties. Moreover, at a more fundamental level, the 2017 campaign revealed that France no longer has a mainstream foreign policy discourse shared across the political spectrum. Attitudes towards Russia in particular may be used as an indicator for this observation: ideas on what France's relations with Russia ought to be always also carry more general ideas on France's position in Europe and in the world and on who its allies should be.

When it comes to views on Russia, the general public is, by and large, sceptical of the country as well as Vladimir Putin and his foreign policy. In a poll carried out by the Pew Research Center in 2015, 70 per cent of French respondents said that they held a "largely unfavourable" view of Russia.[4] The same poll finds that 85 per cent have "no confidence" in Vladimir Putin.[5] More recent results confirm these findings: in May 2017, 63 per cent of respondents held "negative views" of Russia; 73 per cent held "negative views" of Vladimir Putin.[6] Moreover, according to an October 2016 poll, 61 per cent of French respondents believed that "France was right to sanction Russia" and that the "embargo" should remain in place. The same poll also reveals that 18 per cent want to see "diplomatic rapprochement" with Russia.[7]

Among the political class, Russia and the matter of bilateral and European relations with Russia are of greater importance. French elites traditionally lean toward Russia-friendly stances, and the idea that Russia and France are united by special, historical bonds lingers on. Nevertheless, such posi-

2   A September 2016 poll thus finds that 97 per cent of respondents say that the risk of an attack is "high." Ifop, L'évaluation de la menace terroriste. Poll for Midi Libre and La Dépêche, September 2016, at: https://fr.scribd.com/document/324154147/Enquete-Ifop-sur-la-menace-terroriste.

3   Cf. French Presidency, Discours du Président de la République devant le Parlement réuni en Congrès, Versailles, 16 November 2015, at: www.elysee.fr/declarations/article/discours-du-president-de-la-republique-devant-le-parlement-reuni-en-congres-3/.

4   Pew Research Center, Russia, Putin Held in Low Regard around the World. Russia's Image Trails U.S Across All Regions, Washington, 5 August 2015, p. 2.

5   Ibid., p. 5.

6   Jannick Alimi, Pour les Français, Vladimir Poutine plombe l'image de la Russie, Le Parisien, 29 May 2017, at: www.leparisien.fr/international/pour-les-francais-vladimir-poutine-plombe-l-image-de-la-russie-19-05-2017-6962484.php.

7   Harris Interactive, Perceptions des priorités de la France dans le monde. Comment les Français perçoivent-ils les priorités et le positionnement de la France dans le monde ?, October 2016, at: http://choiseul.info/wp-content/uploads/2016/11/Rapport-Harris-Perceptions-des-priorit%C3%A9s-de-la-France-dans-le-monde-Institut-Choiseul.pdf.

tions are not necessarily accompanied by in-depth knowledge of evolutions in Russia, let alone language skills or first-hand experience in the country. Reasons for this historical affinity differ and range from the 1892 Franco-Russian alliance, "traditional" Gaullist foreign policy convictions, anti-Americanism and the remnants of a Cold War dichotomous world view to admiration for strong leadership and a country ready to re-establish its great power status. Some still pursue the idea of a "*grande alliance*" between Russia and France.[8]

During the 2017 presidential campaign, much was said about "globalists" opposing "sovereignists" (sometimes also referred to as "neo-Gaullists" or "gaullo-mittérrandéens"). In a nutshell, the globalists (essentially Benoît Hamon and Emmanuel Macron) argued in favour of globalization and European integration, open borders and markets. The "sovereignists", on the other hand, portrayed globalization and the EU as the enemy, offering "solutions," such as renationalization of policy fields and closed borders (Marine Le Pen, Jean-Luc Mélenchon, and, to some extent, also François Fillon). This distinction also marked the dividing line in the debate on Russia: on the one hand a "European mainstream" approach which in essence seeks continuity with the Hollande position and, on the other hand, the "neo-Gaullist" sovereignist approach, with a much softer stance on Russia. The two strands should, of course, be understood as ideal-types; distinctions are often not as clear-cut in reality. Nevertheless, most statements on Russia and Russian-Western relations can be subsumed under one of the two labels.

The French version of the official mainstream European approach up to May 2017 was the Hollande position and the view held by most officials, generally buying into the official discourses at the EU and NATO levels (to whose shaping France of course contributes). Emmanuel Macron's statements throughout the campaign, as well as his first steps as head of state (including during Vladimir Putin's 29 May visit to Versailles)[9] clearly indicate his ambition to continue along that line. This approach is very critical of Russia's actions in Ukraine and considers the annexation of Crimea illegal. It is in favour of keeping sanctions in place as long as the Minsk agreements are not implemented and seeks to contribute to a solution to the Ukraine conflict through its engagement in the Normandy framework.[10] The narrative pre-

---

8   For a concise overview of the five key candidates' positions on foreign policy, see Thomas Gomart and Marc Hecker (eds.), Foreign Policy Challenges for the Next French President, Notes de l'Ifri, 2017. For an excellent in-depth analysis of French pro-Russia discourses, see Olivier Schmitt, Pourquoi Poutine est notre allié? Anatomie d'une passion française, Hikari Editions, Paris, 2017. See also: Alain Besançon, Sainte Russie, Editions de Fallois, Paris, 2012.

9   On 29 May, 2017, Vladimir Putin attended the opening of an exhibition in commemoration of diplomatic relations between France and Russia established three centuries earlier on the occasion of Tsar Peter the Great's visit to France.

10   I.e. France and Germany negotiating with Russia and Ukraine in order to find a solution to the conflict between the two latter countries.

sented in the French mainstream media outlets, such as Le Monde, Le Figaro or French Public Radio fits, by and large, into this approach. That said, calls for "pragmatism" and compartmentalized co-operation with Russia are also a rather frequent phenomenon (and notably so as far as terrorism is concerned), placing French discourses on the somewhat "softer" end of discourses on Russia in the European Union and NATO. Staunch anti-Russian attitudes are rare in France, just as Russophobia is not part of the picture.

The neo-Gaullist approach can be found among some strands of the centre right *Les Républicains* party, as well as with the extreme right-wing populists from *Front National* and with the "sovereignist" extreme left. Neo-Gaullists are rather apologetic vis-à-vis Putin – or even openly supportive. In a nutshell, their discourse may be summarized as follows: they call for the end of the sanctions regime and/or view Russia as a "humiliated" great power that deserves better treatment by the West. Russia is considered to be a historical ally of France, and working together (against the Americans) is often viewed as a possibility to avoid Paris' loss of great power status, just as "emancipation" from the United States and NATO is considered necessary. Putin is admired by some adherents of this strand for his patriotism and strong leadership. Islamophobia and the fear of Europe's cultural decline also play a role, especially among traditionalist, Catholic segments of society opposing, for example, same-sex marriage.[11] Ever since 2014 and clearly prior to the 2017 electoral campaign, Hollande's approach was at times heavily criticized by his neo-Gaullist opponents: notably for the cancelled Mistral deal in the fall of 2015[12] or Putin's "postponed" visit to France to inaugurate Paris' new orthodox cathedral in October 2016.[13] Among the more spectacular manifestations of the neo-Gaullist approach are visits to Crimea by members of the French National Assembly or calls for the abolishment of economic sanctions against Russia – even officially demanded by the *Assemblée Nationale* after a – non-binding – late-night vote driven by Thierry Mariani, a well-known member of the "pro-Putin lobby," for which only 101 MPs (out

---

11 Demonstrations against same-sex marriage have mobilized hundreds of thousands in recent years.

12 Nicolas Sarkozy was against cancelling the Mistral deal, just as François Fillon, who accused Hollande of having taken that decision only "because M Obama or Ms Merkel asked him to do so," judging that France should have an "independent voice" in the conflict between Russia and Ukraine. RTL Radio, Vente des Mistral à la Russie: Sarkozy critique la 'décision démagogique' de François Hollande, 4 November 2015, at: www.rtl.fr/actu/politique/vente-des-mistral-a-la-russie-nicolas-sarkozy-critique-la-decision-dema-gogique-de-francois-hollande-7780365015; Fillon fustige l'annulation du contrat de vente des Mistral à la Russie, Le Point, 5 September 2015, www.lepoint.fr/politique/fillon-fusti-ge-l-annulation-du-contrat-de-vente-des-mistral-a-la-russie-05-09-2014-1860268_20. php.

13 Cf. Coup de froid diplomatique entre Moscou et Paris, La Croix, 11 October 2016, at: www.la-croix.com/Monde/Coup-froid-diplomatique-entre-Moscou-Paris-2016-10-11-1300795410.

of 574) were present.[14] A non-negligible portion of such discourses is also directly addressed to French farmers, arguing that they pay the price for sanctions against Russia. Within the centre-right *Les Républicains*, the neo-Gaullist approach is the majority approach. The most notable exception was party primaries' runner-up, Alain Juppé. Among the other candidates for the presidential ticket, positions varied: while Alain Juppé's views were, by and large, in line with the Hollande approach, Nicolas Sarkozy and François Fillon clearly belonged to the sovereignist camp (despite the fact that Sarkozy was formerly known to be an "Atlanticist," notably having initiated France's "return" to NATO during his presidency). In the primaries, Fillon frequently argued for closer relations with Moscow and is known to be a long-standing "friend" of Putin[15], while Sarkozy has met with Putin on several occasions in recent months, and has called for an end to EU sanctions.[16]

All of these tendencies are even more pronounced toward the fringes of the political spectrum. For instance, in 2011, the 2017 presidential runner-up, Marine Le Pen, declared that she "admired" Putin"[17]; in 2014, she said she "shared values" with Putin on the "defence of the European civilization's Christian heritage."[18] The extreme left is also arguing in favour of Russia, albeit not on cultural grounds. The bracket that keeps the extreme right and the extreme left together on this matter is essentially the idea that France would be better off without outside (read: U.S.) interference and constraints resulting from the country's membership in the EU and NATO. On the fringes of the political spectrum (and in portions of the centre-right), pro-Russian attitudes are thus often a direct consequence of deeply rooted anti-Americanism, which is simply a matter of principle. In March 2014, Jean-Luc Mélenchon of the far-left *La France insoumise* (fourth with 19.58 % in the presidential election's first round) was, for instance, quoted as saying that he supported, "without sympathy," the "enemy of the United States" – while

---

14   This vote took place on 28 April, 2016. Among the 55 "yes" votes, 44 came from Les Républicains, two from the Front National (= all FN members of parliament).

15   See e.g. Benjamin Sportouch, "François Fillon et son ami Poutine," L'Express, 29 January 2014, at: www.lexpress.fr/actualite/politique/francois-fillon-et-son-ami-poutine_1318016. html.

16   See e.g. his speech: Discours de Nicolas Sarkozy à l'Institut des Relations Internationales de Moscou, 29 October 2015, at : www.republicains.fr/actualites_discours_nicolas_ sar-kozy_moscou_20151029. See also Jean-Baptiste Garat, Sarkozy chez Poutine: la question russe divise Les Républicains, Le Figaro, 29 October 2015, at : www.lefigaro.fr/politique/ 2015/10/28/01002-20151028ARTFIG00345-la-question-russe-divise-les-republicains.php

17   Marine Le Pen dit 'admirer' Poutine, Le Point, 13 October 2011, at: www.lepoint.fr/ politique/election-presidentielle-2012/marine-le-pen-dit-admirer-vladimir-poutine-13-10-2011-1384085_324.php.

18   Marine Le Pen assure partager des 'valeurs communes' avec Poutine, La Chaine Parle-mentaire, 18 May 2014, at: www.lcp.fr/afp/marine-le-pen-assure-partager-des-valeurs-communes-avec-poutine.

also accusing Washington of paying people tasked to "destabilize this insurrection [in Crimea]."[19]

The extreme-right *Front National* also has proven financial ties with Russia as it received loans from Russia. According to Marine Le Pen, this is because no French bank was willing to fund the party.[20] Le Pen was also the only presidential candidate to be received in Moscow, where she met with Putin in late March 2017.[21] As far as centre right-wing parties are concerned, rumour has it that links to Moscow are very tight too. On a general note, Russian influence on French politicians and its soft power has become a matter that is dealt with in books that have received considerable attention, most notably so in Nicolas Hénin's La France russe ["Russian France"] and Cécile Vaissié's Les réseaux du Kremlin en France ["The Kremlin's networks in France"].[22]

Threats Perceived

This sub-chapter intends to analyze the extent to which Russia is perceived as a threat in the French discourse. Looking at France's recent White Papers on Defence – the current version was published in 2013 –, Paris has been taking a close look at developments in Russia for some time. This 2013 White Paper contains an analysis of the "state of the world", based on the distinction of "threats related to power" and "threats of weakness." Quite in line with the earlier assessment of 2008, Russia is dealt with under the first header. The White Paper Commission's authors describe, inter alia, how Russia is heavily investing in its military – including nuclear – capabilities, which they qualify as "rearmament," and assess that the "energy issue has become a key plank in Russia's foreign policy." Their conclusion is that

> [t]hese developments show that Russia is equipping itself with the economic and military clout that will enable it to engage in power politics. The outcome of this plan, however, remains uncertain.[23]

---

19   Vivien Vergnaud, Pourquoi ces politiques français soutiennent Poutine, Le Journal du Dimanche, 4 March 2014, at: www.lejdd.fr/Politique/Pourquoi-ces-politiques-francais-soutiennent-Poutine-655726.

20   For more information, see Médiapart's webpage dedicated to the matter (Médiapart's journalists uncovered the issue in 2015), at: www.mediapart.fr/journal/france/dossier/ dossier-largent-russe-du-front-national.

21   Cf. Isabelle Mandraud, A Moscou, Vladimir Poutine adoube Marine Le Pen, Le Monde, 24 March 2017, at: www.lemonde.fr/election-presidentielle-2017/article/2017/03/24/marine-le-pen-recue-par-vladimir-poutine-a-moscou_5100247_4854003.html.

22   Nicolas Hénin, La France russe. Enquête sur les réseaux Poutine, Paris, 2016 ; Cécile Vaissié, Les réseaux du Kremlin en France, Paris, 2016.

23   French Ministry of Defence, White Paper on Defence, Paris, 2013, p. 36, at: www.defense.gouv.fr/actualites/la-reforme/livre-blanc-2013.

At the same time, Russia is clearly not a vital threat to the nation's security from a French perspective. Similarly, although many agree that Moscow's actions need to be followed very carefully, Russia is not really considered to be a threat to NATO member states. Behind closed doors, the discourse on Russia to be heard in the Baltic States, for instance, is, consequently, largely seen in Paris as exaggerated (and annoying). France nevertheless participates in NATO's reassurance measures, e.g. sending troops within the framework of the Alliance's Enhanced Forward Presence.

Other threats are considered to be of higher relevance to protecting the country's security, especially terrorist attacks. But cyber warfare, (nuclear) proliferation or developments in Asia are also high on the agenda.

Responsibility for the Current Tensions

Unsurprisingly, when it comes to explaining what factors led to renewed conflict between Western Europe and Russia and, notably, the Ukraine crisis, points of view differ among the adherents of the two strands.

Adherents of the mainstream/government approach consider Russia to be largely responsible for the current situation. That said, almost nobody claims that "the West" – i.e. mainly the EU and NATO – has acted flawlessly ever since 1991. Thus, although NATO enlargement, for instance, is not considered to be a mistake, some argue that Russian concerns could and should have been taken more seriously.

From a neo-Gaullist perspective, the West – and first and foremost the United States – is largely responsible for the current situation. It is seen as the result of the West's humiliating of Russia[24], or at least of a neglect of Russia's interests[25]. Notably, the enlargement of NATO, but also the European Union's Eastern Partnership, are considered to be major mistakes and acts of unnecessary disrespect of Russia's interests. François Fillon, for instance, claimed in March 2017 that if Russia "has gone astray," this is because "we had a bad policy toward Russia in the first place."[26] Some – notably within the *Front National*, but also the extreme left (see Mélenchon quoted above) – go as far as to directly blame the United States: according to that approach, not only were Russia's interests disregarded, but also those of France (or perhaps Europe). Quite logically, Marine Le Pen calls for France to leave

24 See e.g. French Senate, Rapport d'information fait au nom de la commission des affaires étrangères, de la défense et des forces armées par le groupe de travail sur les relations avec la Russie : comment sortir de l'impasse ?, N°21, Paris, 7 October 2015, at: www.senat.fr/rap/r15-021/r15-0211.pdf.

25 See e.g. Nicolas Sarkozy, Discours de Nicolas Sarkozy à l'Institut des Relations Internationales de Moscou.

26 La matinale d'Europe 1 radio show on 13 March, 2017 (Russia is being discussed starting at about 1:25:00). See also Marine Pennetier, Fillon impute la 'dérive' de la Russie aux sanctions européennes, Reuters, 13 March, 2017.

NATO's integrated command structure, which is considered to be a vehicle for American influence and detrimental to French national interests. But the EU is also believed to carry part of the responsibility, especially by the *Front National* which argues, for instance, that the Deep and Comprehensive Free Trade Agreement (DCFTA) with Ukraine was "in nobody's interest."[27]

Russian-Western Relations: Turning Points and Decisive Factors

The objective of this sub-chapter is to analyze the factors that are said to influence the development of Russian-Western relations according to the various discourses. What were the milestones that led from 1991 to where we are today and what alternatives would there have been to the choices actually made? There is little disagreement within the two strands of French discourse as to whether "the West" was the winner of the Cold War or not. The fact that NATO survived and that the Warsaw Pact did not, with several of its former members or Soviet republics joining the Western alliance, speaks for itself. Another question, however, is whether this Western victory is considered to be a good thing or not and whether the West treated Russia in a fair manner.

Similarly, the major turning points during the post-Cold War era are the same for adherents of both strands: (potential) NATO enlargements, Kosovo, the 2008 war in Georgia and, most importantly so, the 2014 annexation of Crimea (with some rare voices refuting the term "annexation," instead e.g. calling it "reunification").

Again, what differs is the reading. While NATO enlargement is interpreted by large segments of the French political establishment as sovereign nations' decisions to join a military alliance, others view it as an instance of U.S. imperialism. The Bush junior administration's declared objective to make both Georgia and Ukraine, in particular, join NATO is widely considered to have been a major mistake – in line with France's (together with Germany) decision to block these countries' accession to the alliance at the 2008 Bucharest summit. The *Front National* continues to accuse the United States of wanting to "NATOize" Ukraine.[28]

Overall, the idea of "missed opportunities" is shared across the board, arguing that the damaged relationship with Russia is the result of mistakes made in the past. For many adherents of the neo-Gaullist strand, the first and, perhaps, most important one of these missed opportunities is the West's un-

---

27   Marine Le Pen, L'accord de libre-échange avec l'Ukraine n'est dans l'intérêt de personne, press release, 27 June 2014, at: www.frontnational.com/2014/06/laccord-de-libre-echange-avec-lukraine-nest-dans-linteret-de-personne/.

28   Front National, L'Ukraine de l'Ouest désormais 'ouvertement' vassalisée par Washington, press release, 5 December 2014, at: www.frontnational.com/2014/12/lukraine-de-louest-desormais-ouvertement-vassalisee-par-washington/.

willingness to reconsider the European security architecture after the Soviet Union's demise. Had Gorbachev's "common European home" become reality, the current situation would not have developed. All subsequent missed opportunities derived from this first one: diverging views on NATO enlargement and the EU's actions – notably the Eastern Partnership – in its Eastern neighbourhood (sometimes described as "awkward" or "clumsy")[29], but also, e.g., EU energy policies considered to be disadvantageous from a Moscow perspective (referring in particular to the EU Commission's 2009 third Energy Package and its "Gazprom clause" – an assessment, of course, also shared outside of France)[30]. As far as the Eastern Partnership is concerned, many deplore the absence of a true "strategic vision." And some argue – as can also be heard occasionally – that, due to disinterest in the matter among the Western European EU member states, managing the relations with the Union's Eastern neighbourhood was left to the (anti-Russian) Central European countries and Germany.

Others – arguably the majority of observers – are more critical when it comes to the possibility, back in the early 1990s, of establishing a truly pan-European security order. Almost no one denies that mistakes were made by "the West" and that the EU in particular could have acted in a less naïve or awkward way, with greater attention devoted to the Russian perspective.

The mainstream approach essentially sees Moscow's decisions and acts as the factor currently shaping Russian-Western relations. Criteria for improved relations having been set within a number of multilateral frameworks, it is up to Russia to comply with the principles of international law.

For many adherents of the neo-Gaullist perspective, in turn, the main factor influencing French-Russian relations is the United States. As some would put it, it is the U.S. which prevents France (or sometimes Europe) from having relations with Russia as they should be, based on common interests on the international stage (and perhaps a shared understanding of each other's great power status). For example, Nicolas Sarkozy stated in early 2015 that "the separation between Europe and Russia is a tragedy. That the Americans want this, they have the right to do this and it's their problem [...]."[31] Fillon explained in July 2016 that France should engage in a "dialogue with Vladimir Putin that is not distorted by the prism of American or

---

29   French Senate, Rapport d'information fait au nom de la commission des affaires étrangères, de la défense et des forces armées par le groupe de travail sur les relations avec la Russie : comment sortir de l'impasse ?, 7 October 2015, p. 58 (cf. fn. 24).

30   This is of course no exclusively French view. For an analysis, see Céline Bayou, Russie: Gazprom dans la ligne de mire de l'Union européenne, La Documentation Française, 12 August 2011, at: www.ladocumentationfrancaise.fr/pages-europe/d000411-russie.gazprom-dans-la-ligne-de-mire-de-l-union-europeenne-par-celine-bayou/article.

31   Benoît Vitkine, Crise ukrainienne : Nicolas Sarkozy reprend la rhétorique du Kremlin, Le Monde, 9 February, 2015, at: www.lemonde.fr/europe/article/2015/02/09/crise-ukrainienne-nicolas-sarkozy-reprend-la-rhetorique-du-kremlin_4572863_3214.html.

NATO views of the relationship with Russia."[32] Within that context, some also deplore increased French "alignment" with the U.S., as for instance translated into the French return to NATO's integrated command in 2009. As outlined above, the *Front National* and the extreme left argue along the same line.

Some also directly accuse Ukraine of having led "multi-vectoral" policies that alienated Moscow, while others argue that, historically speaking, Ukraine is not a "real" nation state anyway – i.e., Russia's Ukraine policies should, consequently, be considered as intra-Russian affairs. Still others simply think that the Crimea issue is settled. Thierry Mariani (a *Les Républicains* member of the National Assembly who has led several controversial trips to the peninsula), for instance, argues that "Crimea is Russian. Let's move on to something else."[33]

Factors Conducive to Russian-Western Co-operation and Shared Interests

The following paragraphs are intended to identify and discuss the factors that are said to be conducive to Russian-Western co-operation. Wherein lie common interests, according to the French discourses? And in which fields would both sides benefit from co-operation? In line with the general French realpolitik approach, based on national interests, factors perceived as conducive to Russian-Western co-operation are, first and foremost, shared interests. Both strands emphasize the existence of shared interests. What is more, France and Russia share a number of features: both are permanent members of the United Nations Security Council and both are nuclear powers.

For many, there simply is no alternative to co-operating with Russia, at least on selected issues. Western-Russian co-operation should, in particular, cover matters where interests pertaining to international security converge: combating (Islamist) terrorism, but also preventing nuclear proliferation and organized crime.

This, first and foremost, concerns Syria and the fight against the Islamic State, a point notably made by a number of the right-wing politicians with presidential ambitions (Sarkozy, Fillon, see above). Yet, while both "the West" and Russia are viewed as having an interest in a stable and peaceful Middle East (and in particular Libya and Syria), the identified causes for the current turmoil are not necessarily the same. For that reason, actual co-operation proves difficult – as the French government so notably came to

---

32   François Fillon on 12 July 2016 during the "Télématin – Les 4 vérités" TV show on France 2.

33   'La Crimée est russe. Passons à autre chose.' (Mariani), Le Figaro, 31 July 2016, at: www.lefigaro.fr/flash-actu/2016/07/31/97001-20160731FILWWW00119-la-crimee-est-russe-passons-a-autre-chose-mariani.php.

realize in the aftermath of the November 2015 terrorist attacks in Paris and as is still obvious with respect to Syria.

Moreover, logically, both France and Russia would benefit from economic co-operation. The deepening of Franco-Russian relations that occurred after 2008 was primarily driven by the economy and French companies "discovering" the Russian market. French exports to Russia quadrupled between 2000 and 2013.[34] This applies to the civilian sector, but also to armament deals between Russia and the (state-owned) French defence industry. The most widely known example is, of course, the 2011 Mistral deal. Contrary to other European countries, the energy issue is further down on the agenda in France due to the country's lesser dependence on imports from Russia. Some argue, nevertheless, that there is also potential for co-operation in the field of civilian nuclear energy.[35]

The notion of "the West" may, however, be particularly problematic in this context. For many, France/Europe and the United States are not necessarily to be subsumed under the same category. According to a more anti-American (or at least: America-sceptic) logic, there is, in fact, a Russian-European interest which consists of balancing the United States and containing U.S. influence in Europe. Unsurprisingly, Franco-German-Russian rejection of the 2003 U.S. invasion in Iraq is often mentioned as an instance of ideal congruence of interests, a moment of unity in opposition vis-à-vis Washington. Both Russia and France are said to favour a "multipolar world" (as opposed to a U.S.-dominated unipolar international system), with France often having an approach that differs from that of its European partners.

Returning to a Co-operative Russia-West Relationship

Overall, French interlocutors privilege engaging Russia over containing it. "Hawkish" stances are a scarce phenomenon in France. In line with the EU's five principles[36], "selective engagement" and compartmentalized co-opera-

---

34 Cf. French Ministry of Foreign Affairs, La France et la Russie, at: www.diplomatie.gouv.fr/fr/dossiers-pays/russie/la-france-et-la-russie/.

35 Cf. Laurence Daziano, Développer les relations économiques avec la Russie, La Tribune, 25 January 2016, at: www.latribune.fr/opinions/tribunes/developper-les-relations-econo-miques-avec-la-russie-545544.html.

36 The March 2016 EU Foreign Affairs Council agreed on five principles that would henceforth guide the EU policy towards Russia: (1) Implementation of the Minsk agreement as the key condition for any substantial change in the EU's stance towards Russia. (2) Strengthened relations with the EU's Eastern Partners and other neighbors, in particular in Central Asia. (3)Strengthening the resilience of the EU (for example energy security, hybrid threats, or strategic communication). (4) Need for selective engagement with Russia on issues of interest to the EU. (5) Need to engage in people-to-people contacts and support Russian civil society. Foreign Affairs Council, 14/03/2016, Main Results, at: www.consilium.europa.eu/en/meetings/fac/2016/03/14/.

tion is the preferred scenario for most. Engagement may cover a number of areas.

A 2015 report by the French Senate[37] (the report being more on the neo-Gaullist side overall), for instance, suggests a pan-European conference on security and economic development in Europe, modelled after the 1975 Helsinki CSCE, potentially within an OSCE framework.[38] The idea of such a conference reappeared in the 2017 presidential campaign – yet not in the Macron camp. For Jean-Luc Mélenchon, it was linked to the question of borders in Europe as he explained during the televised debate between all candidates: "In Europe, the first thing to do, that's a conference on security from the Atlantic to the Ural, because all of the tensions come from the fact that, when the Soviet Empire crumbled, nobody has negotiated borders with anybody."[39] Mélenchon also argued that "we need to talk again about all borders. The border between Russia and Ukraine, is it at the end of Crimea or before? I don't know. We need to talk about it."[40] François Fillon – contrary to Benoît Hamon, who vehemently opposed Mélenchon's statements – seemed to agree with the idea of renegotiating borders in Europe. He explained that that question "needs to be asked in light of international law and the right to [national] self-determination," also saying that "there are borders that were drawn under conditions nations cannot accept, that separated nations and this debate, we cannot refuse to see it take place."[41] Overall, however, the possible recognition of the annexation of Crimea is not one of the defining topics in the French foreign policy debate, and Mélenchon and Fillon were criticized for their statements the day after.[42]

Other areas include security issues or energy. Nicolas Sarkozy called for the construction "between the European Union and Russia, of a new and true 'human and economic space', which needs to be invented, on equal terms, by

---

37 French Senate, Rapport d'information fait au nom de la commission des affaires étrangères, de la défense et des forces armées par le groupe de travail sur 'les relations avec la Russie : comment sortir de l'impasse ?, 7 October 2015.

38 Ibid., p. 94.

39 See the full video of the debate at www.youtube.com/watch?v=VYXhy7Om0gs. For a transcript, see Présidentielle: vif échange entre Mélenchon et Hamon sur la Russie, France Soir, 21 March, 2017, at: www.francesoir.fr/actualites-elections/presidentielle-vif-echange-entre-hamon-et-melenchon-sur-la-russie.

40 Again, see the video of the debate. A transcript of the quote may be found at: www.lci.fr/elections/video-grand-debat-poutine-et-la-russie-le-sujet-qui-rapproche-melen-chon-et-fillon-2029732.html.

41 Again, see the video of the debate and a transcript at www.francesoir.fr/actualites-elections/presidentielle-vif-echange-entre-hamon-et-melenchon-sur-la-russie.

42 E.g. the interview with political scientist Frédéric Charillon: "Estimer que la paix passe par la redéfinition des frontières est surprenant," Le Monde, 23 March, 2017, at : www.lemonde.fr/idees/article/2017/03/23/estimer-que-la-paix-passe-par-la-redefinition-des-frontieres-est-surprenant_5099276_3232.html. See also J.S. Mongrenier, Conférence sur les frontières de l'Atlantique à l'Oural: la dangereuse idée de Mélencon, Challenges, 28 March 2017, at: www.challenges.fr/monde/europe/conference-sur-les-frontieres-de-l-atlantique-a-l-oural-la-dangereuse-idee-de-melenchon_463259.

Russians and Europeans".[43] Likewise, Sarkozy and others argued for the progressive ending of economic sanctions against Russia (while still emphasizing the Minsk II agreements). And although French business representatives are remarkably silent on the matter, it seems self-evident that tighter economic relations are on many companies' wish lists.

Within the mainstream/government approach (and sometimes even beyond, see the above-mentioned Senate report), the implementation of Minsk II is still the condition *sine qua non* for true and full-fledged co-operation between the West and Russia, in line with the five principles adopted at EU level. At the other end of the spectrum, ending sanctions is considered to be a necessary first step toward better relations, and there is at least some understanding for Russia's approach to Ukraine. Leaving NATO and beginning to follow policies "independent from U.S. interference" are also measures considered necessary by some on the fringes of the political spectrum. Another minority position consists of calling for Ukraine to declare its neutrality in order to "ease tensions."[44]

Conclusions

As this essay has intended to show, merely looking at government positions is insufficient in order to grasp the full spectrum of French approaches to Russia. These approaches are, in fact, multidimensional and are fed from many sources – many of which are not even directly linked to Russia as such. Putin's actions matter, but other factors can be at least equally important: visions of France's role in the world, the relationship it should have with the United States, or simply France's national interests. Thus, unlike in many other European countries, attitudes towards Russia must not necessarily be considered an independent variable shaping the discourse. Rather, they can also be dependent variables shaped by other factors. This is especially true when the "Russia-Syria nexus" comes to the fore: given that the most prominent French concern these days is terrorist attacks, fighting the Islamic State is a top priority. The role Russia may or may not play in that context is likely to shape many Frenchmen's views on Moscow and the necessity of co-operating with Putin.

It is for these reasons that French approaches to Russia may also be qualified as potentially volatile beyond Emmanuel Macron's presidency. This is not only a matter of party politics, but also a matter of possible future events, especially terrorist attacks and evolutions in the Middle East. France

---

43 Nicolas Sarkozy, "Discours de Nicolas Sarkozy à l'Institut des Relations Internationales de Moscou." (29 October 2015, cf. fn. 16 and 25).

44 See French Senate, Rapport d'information fait au nom de la commission des affaires étrangères, de la défense et des forces armées par le groupe de travail sur 'les relations avec la Russie : comment sortir de l'impasse ?, 7 October 2015.

is perhaps the country where the Russia-Syria nexus has the greatest domestic implications. Given France's role in Europe and, notably, within the Normandy format, how positions evolve in Paris is of relevance way beyond the national context.

Kornely Kakachia

Georgian Narratives on Russian-Western Relations

Russia's annexation of Crimea is reshaping the geopolitical map of Europe and sending ripples of apprehension across the South Caucasus and the wider Black Sea region. In Georgia itself, the political class has largely found itself hostage to the West-Russia binary formulation. Facing strategic security challenges, many Georgians have been closely monitoring all regional foreign policy developments, particularly given the Kremlin's direct involvement in eastern Ukraine. These include the future of Georgia's relations with the West (including the processes of EU and NATO integration) and with Russia (in response to repeated attempts to re-integrate Georgia into the post-Soviet space). Moreover, the scale and dynamism of the changes in the geopolitical order in the post-Soviet region have raised further questions about their impact on Georgia's security environment and about their consequences for the entire country.

Georgia's Threat Perceptions – Russia in Focus

This chapter examines not only Georgia's security challenges, but also attempts to detect societal narratives that shape the current political debates in Georgia. As Georgia attempts to construct a collective international identity, the devotion to the idea of Euro-Atlantic integration as a "sacred destiny" amongst the country's elite has significant foreign policy implications. Based on the IRI (International Republican Institute) and NDI (National Democratic Institute) polls, as well as media reports, the author tries to identify the key causes of and motivations for Georgia's pro-Western foreign policy orientation, claiming that it stems from ideas and identity rather than from materialist and systemic factors alone. Overall, the narrative report offers a general overview of current trends in the narratives in Georgia after the Ukrainian crisis and its implication for the broader region. Arguably, the most straightforward entrée into the world of Georgian geopolitics is the West-Russia tension at the heart of its foreign policy dilemma. Over the two decades since it regained its independence, Georgia, as a weak state,[1] has faced serious domestic and international problems that have threatened its existence as a sovereign state. Beyond its domestic difficulties, Georgia's problems have been aggravated by Russian policies that have taken ad-

---

[1]   Pine Roehrs. Weak States and Implications for Regional Security: A Case Study of Georgian Instability and Caspian Regional Insecurity. Research Paper. No. 97 (2005), at: https://www.files.ethz.ch/isn/31842/rieas097.pdf (Accessed on 1 October 2016).

vantage of the conflicts in Georgia. Hence, Russia remains the main obstacle in the Georgian perception of external threats. Bilateral relations have been continuously strained as Russia's policy has been to attempt to re-establish its influence on the post-Soviet space and to pressure Georgia and other post-Soviet states to accommodate its geopolitical interests. As a result, Georgians perceive Russia as a threat. According to a recent poll,[2] 77 per cent of the respondents describe Georgia's relationship with Russia as "bad" and 67 per cent believe that Russian aggression is active and ongoing as Russian military forces still remain present in the two regions of Abkhazia and South Ossetia nearly eight years after a peace agreement was signed. This minimizes the chances of creating favourable conditions for resolving the conflict and developing sustainable security.

An identity-based account offers a comprehensive understanding of the complexities of Russia-Georgia relations. Perceiving itself as part of a greater Europe, Georgia's political class[3] – a group that sometimes acts on behalf of the state – sees Georgia's path as utterly incompatible with the Russian project[4]. First of all, Russia is defined as a successor to the Soviet Union and its self-proclaimed sphere of influence is considered a danger to Georgia's national security. Believing that Russia is a sui generis phenomenon that cannot disassociate itself from its Eurasianist ideology and imperialist ambitions, Georgia considers its northern neighbour neither European nor attractive in terms of its socioeconomic model. As Russian expert Fyodor Lukyanov (2012) observed, "Georgia has sought to create a conceptual alternative to Russia by providing an example of a complete and irreversible break of historical and cultural ties with its powerful neighbour.[5]" Georgia's political class believes that Russia offers no compelling vision of a revived Russian sphere of influence, even for its own allies, as it has already lost the battle for innovation and economic development and is gradually becoming an "industrial museum." Georgia should form partnerships with more progressive countries and should be united to the core area of global development (the West), not to peripheral areas (such as the CIS or the post-Soviet space). As this perception still prevails in the subconscious of Georgia's political elites, they believe that Georgia should continue to co-operate with the West, as other alternatives cannot satisfy Georgia's economic and security needs. On the other hand, Russia also considers Georgia as a proxy

---

2   IRI Public Opinion Survey Residents of Georgia. March – April 2016, at: http://www.iri.org/sites/default/files/wysiwyg/georgia_2016.pdf (Accessed on 10 June 2016).

3   We use Gaetano Mosca's definition of political class here, i.e. "the relatively small group of activists that is highly aware and active in politics, and from whom the national leadership is largely drawn". (Gaetano Mosca, The ruling class. McGraw-Hill Book Company, New York and London 1896; English translation 1939).

4   Georgia to move towards EU, not Eurasian union – Prime Minister. TASS. 26 March 2015, at: http://tass.ru/en/world/785068(Accessed on 1 October 2016).

5   Fyodor Lukyanov. Will Russia Lose Georgia for Good? 3 February 2012, at: http://eng.globalaffairs.ru/redcol/Will-Russia-Lose-Georgia-for-Good-15446.

for Western influence in the post-Soviet space. This resulted in the five days of war in 2008. As a result of this conflict, Russia occupied Georgian breakaway regions and Tbilisi severed diplomatic relations with Moscow.

Threat Perceptions According to Official Documents

Georgia's national security concept[6] openly describes Russia as an occupying power and states that Moscow's primary goal is to turn Georgia into a "failed state" in order to derail it from its path towards Euro-Atlantic integration and to "forcibly return Georgia to the Russian orbit.[7]" According to this document, the risk of Russian aggression exists, because the ultimate goal of the Russian Federation in August 2008 was not to occupy Georgian territory and achieve international recognition of a marionette regime, but to change Georgia's foreign policy direction and to replace a democratically elected government through violent means. According to the document, the list of other existing and potential threats includes: territorial disintegration; spill-over of conflicts from neighbouring countries; military intervention; Russian military bases stationed in Georgia; contraband and transnational organized crime; international terrorism. Thus, Georgian and Russian foreign policy visions contradict each other and leave no chance for developing a partnership in near future. Russian leaders[8] frequently argue that Georgia should abandon its aspirations for Euro-Atlantic integration, should stop calling the Russian troops in Abkhazia and South Ossetia "occupiers," and should start considering a return to the Commonwealth of Independent States (CIS). These are, according to them, the main conditions for re-establishing trust between the countries.

Public Opinion on Georgia-Russia Relations

However, according to a poll by the U.S.-based the International Republican Institute's (IRI) Center for Insights in Survey Research[9], the people of

---

6   The document reflects the changes that have taken place in the security environment of Georgia, as well as their influence on the threats and challenges to national security. See: National Security Concept. 2011, at: http://www.nsc.gov.ge/files/files/ National% 20Security%20Concept.pdf (Accessed on 13 June ,2016).

7   S. Neil MacFarlane.(2012) Georgia: National Security Concept versus National Security. Russia and Eurasia Programme Paper REP PP 2012/01, at: http://css. ge/files/ Papers/ 0812pp_macfarlane.pdf (Accessed on 1 October 2016).

8   Russia sees threat in Georgia's integration into NATO. Second Channel of Georgian Public Broadcaster, at: http://www.2tv.ge/en/news/view/ 32078.html(Accessed on 18 July 2016).

9   IRI's Center for Insights Poll: Georgians Support EU Membership; Distrust Russia but Favor Dialogue 4 April 2017, at: http://www.iri.org/resource/poll-georgians-support-eu-membership-distrust-russia-favor-dialogue(Accessed on 30 May 2017).

Georgia are overwhelmingly in favour of a pro-Western foreign policy, both as a means to stave off Russian threats and to improve their economic prospects. According to the poll, 90 per cent of those surveyed said they supported joining the European Union and 82 per cent supported joining NATO. Georgians list the European Union and the United States as important partners, while 73 per cent consider Russia to be their country's biggest threat and 57 per cent see it as an economic threat. However, following the 2012 and 2016 parliamentary elections, after accession to power of Georgian Dream government overall attitudes toward Russia in Georgia somewhat shifted. A vast majority (76%) of Georgians view the current state of Georgia's relationship with Russia as "bad," yet a combined 82 per cent "fully support" (53%) or "somewhat support" (29%) further dialogue with Russia. While in 2011, 51per cent of the population considered Russia the main enemy of the country[10], a four year later (in 2015) only 35 per cent reported the same.[11]. Moreover, the share of Georgians who named Russia as Georgia's main friend increased by five per cent in 2012 (9%) but in 2013 it dropped again and only five per cent of Georgians see Russia as a friend.[12] Analysts have explained this change by a so-called "spiral of silence".[13] According to this theory, people refrain from expressing their ideas freely if they feel that their opinions are in the minority.[14] As one expert has noted,[15] these results can be explained by some citizens' desire to make their opinions conform to those of the new ruling party, which favours a more pragmatic approach towards Moscow.

Overall, despite attempts of rapprochement[16] between Moscow and Tbilisi in economic, cultural, and humanitarian affairs, contrary to expectations, Georgia's changed tone has not overly influenced its foreign policies, and its strategic orientation toward NATO and EU remains.[17]

---

10   See Caucasus Barometer (2015). Georgia. Biggest enemy of the country, at: http://caucasusbarometer.org/en/cb2011ge/ENEMCNTR/(Accessed on 20 June 2016).
11   Ibid.
12   Ibid.
13   See http://blog.crrc.ge/2013/11/blog-post_15.html.
14   Keith Hampton, Lee Rainie, Weixu Lu, Maria Dwyer, Inyoung Shin and Kristen Purcell (2014). Social Media and the 'Spiral of Silence', at: http://www. pewinternet.org/2014/08/26/social-media-and-the-spiral-of-silence/(Accessed on 1 Oct. 2016).
15   David Sichinava (2013). The 2012 Parliamentary Elections in Georgia and Changing Attitudes Toward Russia. Caucasus analytical digest, pp. 9-12, at: http://www.isn.ethz.ch/Digital-Library/Publications/Detail/?ots591=0c54e3b3-1e9c-be1e-2c24-a6a8c7060233&lng=en&id=161014 (Accessed on 1 October 2016).
16   It is in this context that observers should understand Tbilisi's decision not to boycott the 2014 Winter Olympic Games in Sochi. The cessation of activity by Georgia's Russian-language PIK television channel, which was financed from the state budget, as well as more muted discussion on the topic of the 19th-century Circassian genocide also fits this trend. Finally, the Georgian government has appointed a Special Representative for Relations with Russia, in so doing, further displaying its readiness for dialogue.
17   Foreign Minister: "NATO membership is top priority for Georgian Gov't". Agenda.ge. October 2015, at: http://agenda.ge/news/44003/eng. (Accessed on 2 October 2016).

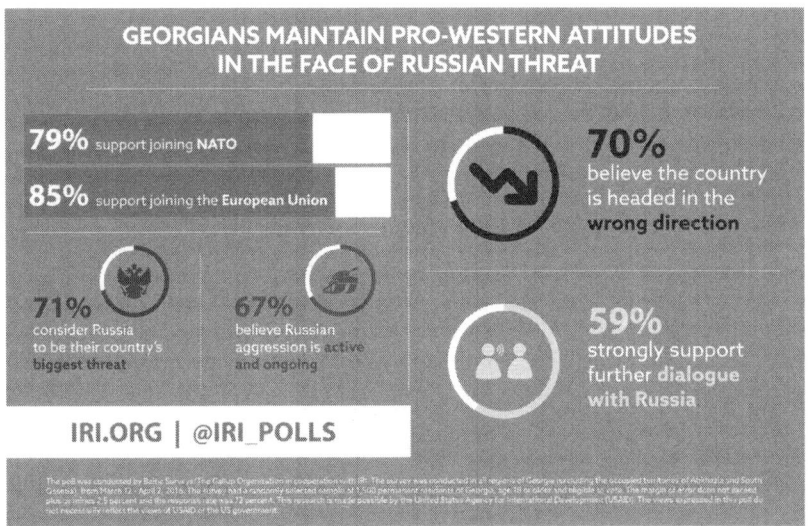

IRI's Center for Insights Poll: Georgians Maintain Pro-Western Attitudes in Face of Russian Threat. April 28, 2016, at: http://www.iri.org/resource/iri%E2%80%99s-center-insights-poll-georgians-maintain-pro-western-attitudes-face-russian-threat (accessed on 1 October, 2016).

Although there is no indication that Georgia will become a member in either NATO or the EU in the near future, Georgians still seek to enhance their security by incorporating their state into European structures and alliances. The signing of the Association Agreement (AA), including a Deep and Comprehensive Free Trade Area (DCFTA), with the EU on 27 June 2014, marked an important crossroad. The agreement not only brought Georgia closer to the EU, but also reaffirmed Georgia's position as the "centre of gravity"[18] for Western engagement in the South Caucasus, given that Georgia's neighbours, Azerbaijan and Armenia, are moving in different directions. The EU Neighbourhood Barometer for Georgia, conducted in the framework of an EU-funded opinion polling project for the neighbourhood, found that 69 per cent of Georgians feel that the EU is an important partner, with 56 per cent believing that the EU and Georgia share sufficient common values to be able to co-operate.[19] Many of those polled (56%) also believe the EU brings peace and stability in the region. The poll also revealed a high level of trust among Georgians in international institutions. The majority of those asked (61%) said they trust the EU, followed by NATO (59%) and the UN (54 %).

---

18 Richard Giragosian (2014). Regional Implications of the Georgian-EU Association Agreement. Investor.ge Issue 4. August-September, at: http://investor.ge/ article.php?art=3 (Accessed on 11 June 2016).

19 See: EU Neighborhood Barometer .Spring 2014. Citizens Mood: Current Situation vs. Expectations, at: http://euneighbourhood.eu/wp-content/uploads/2014/09/ FS-ENPI-Wave-5-GE-EN.pdf (Accessed on 22 July, 2016).

Generally, media reporting[20] on Russia-Western relations in Georgia bears a resemblance to that in other Western European countries. For Tbilisi, the crisis in Ukraine is not simply an issue of geopolitical importance, but rather a concern based on close and friendly relations between two nations, which consider each other strategic partners[21]. As Georgians feel a strong kinship with Ukrainians, they also believe that the struggle for Ukraine's sovereignty will indirectly decide their own fate as, according to popular belief, Ukraine is a more important geostrategic asset for Europe than Georgia is. In an April 2014 survey of nearly 4,000 Georgians, commissioned by US-based National Democratic Institute, half of the respondents viewed Russia as "a real and existing threat"[22], a proportion considerably higher than before the start of the Ukraine crisis in November 2013. As the crisis in Ukraine deepened, this figure increased. Similarly, more than 40 per cent of the population blamed the Russian government for initiating the conflict. As a result, Georgians have become more vocal in supporting Ukrainian independence, with some Georgians even fighting for its territorial integrity.[23]

Many Georgians believe that Russia is repeating in Ukraine what it did in Georgia in August 2008. There are many common factors – distribution of Russian passports, Moscow's reinforcement of the military infrastructure and units on the territory of another state, as well as the decision taken by the Russian Parliament to allow the Russian armed forces to protect the "interests of compatriots" living in Ukraine[24]. As such activities are considered flagrant interference in the internal affairs of a sovereign state, many Georgians believe that Russia's actions against Ukraine might have been unsuccessful if

---

20   Georgian media outlet honoured for critical journalism during the Ukraine crisis. Agenda.ge, 9 March 2015, at: http://agenda.ge/news/31074/eng (Accessed on 29 September 2016).

21   „Georgia and Ukraine are strategic partners," – David Dundua. February 16, 2015. Rustavi2, at: http://rustavi2.com/en/news/9783 (Accessed on 28 July 2016).

22   Luis Navarro. Public attitudes in Georgia: Results of a April 2014 survey carried out for NDI by CRRC-Georgia and funded by the Swedish International Development Cooperation Agency (Sida), at: https://www.ndi.org/files/Georgia_April_ 2014_Survey_ English.pdf (Accessed on 8 July 2016).

23   Giorgi Menabde. Are Georgians Participating in the Ukrainian War? Publication: Eurasia Daily Monitor 11(158) 2014, at: https://jamestown.org/program/are-georgians-participating-in-the-ukrainian-war/ (Accessed on 29 September 2016).

24   Statements were made after Russian President Vladimir Putin received approval from the upper house of parliament to use Russian troops in Ukraine, citing "threat to the lives of citizens of the Russian Federation, our compatriots, and the personnel of the armed forces" of Russia stationed in Crimea. See: Russian parliament approves troop deployment in Ukraine. BBC. 1 March 2014, at: http://www. bbc.com/ news/world-europe-26400035/(Accessed on 29 September 2016).

the international community had had a more robust response to the 2008 Russia-Georgia War[25].

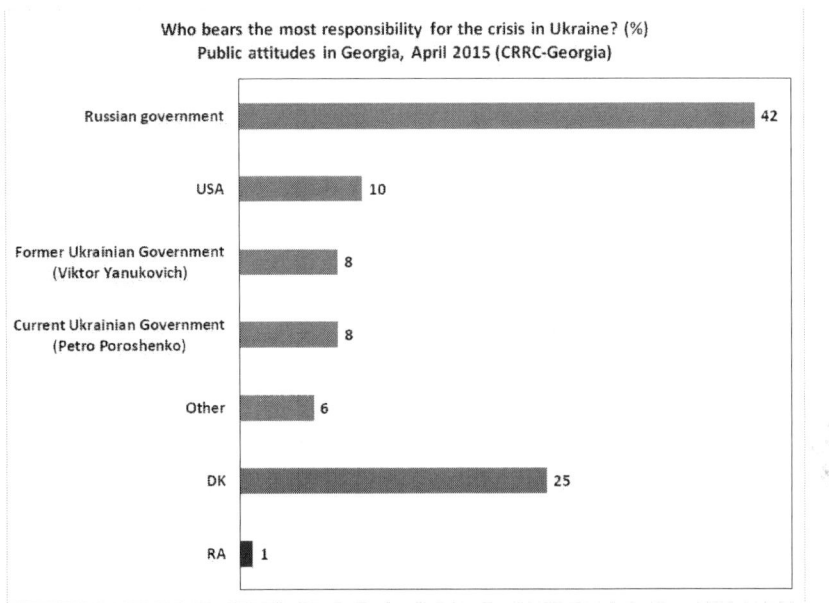

Who bears the most responsibility for the crisis in Ukraine? (%)
Public attitudes in Georgia, April 2015 (CRRC-Georgia)

The Caucasus Research Resource Center, (2015) "[Public attitudes in Georgia, April 2015]". Retrieved through ODA, at: http://caucasusbarometer.org on (accessed on 15 October, 2015). [DK: don't know and RA: refused to answer].

The weak western reaction seemed to have left Moscow believing it could get away with seizing Crimea as well. For the Georgian public, the Ukrainian crisis underlined the failure of the West to understand Russia's ambitions and objectives in the former Soviet space and how far Moscow is ready to go to achieve its objectives[26]. Moreover, as Russia's ongoing occupation of the two Georgian regions, Abkhazia and South Ossetia, poses a continuing threat to the country's national security, fears that a similar crisis could spread to other parts of Georgia have increased. Consequently, the Georgian government has felt compelled to make more aggressive calls on the NATO leadership to deliver on membership promises. This resulted in the opening of the NATO-Georgia Joint Training and Evaluation Centre (JTEC) in Georgia on 27

25   Georgia Reaction to Russian Annexation of Crimea. Civil Georgia. 19 March 2014, at: http://www.civil.ge/eng/article.php?id=27050/ (Accessed on 29 September 2016).
26   Cf. Judy Dempsey. Europe's Failure to Understand Russia's Decline. December 17, 2015, at: http://carnegieeurope.eu/strategiceurope/?fa=62304 (Accessed on 1 October 2016).

August 2015.[27] While the opening of the centre will not solve Georgia's ongoing security problems, regional experts assume that it will help the country to reform, modernize and strengthen its defence sector and enhance the inter-operability of its armed forces with NATO members and partner countries, including Ukraine.

Returning to a Realpolitik: Russia-Georgia Relations and the Role of the West

Among post-Soviet countries, Georgia clearly belongs to the containment rather than the engagement camp. With European aspirations and statements of identity[28], Georgian political leaders associate themselves with a region, which is enjoying prosperity and development (the West), rather than with peripheral areas, such as the post-Soviet space. It is because of this that many Georgians believe that the country's economic and security needs can only be achieved through co-operation with the West, which is the "most attractive political-economic model in the world"[29]. While the West-Russia dynamic has been the dominant lens through which Tbilisi has presented itself to the world (particularly under the former United National Movement regime), its actual foreign policy portfolio is – and has always been, to varying degrees – much more complicated. The ascension of the Georgian Dream to power has changed the way the Georgian government talks about Russia, adopting a milder rhetoric towards Moscow.[30] Unlike its predecessor, the new government has refused to consider possible rapprochement with Russia as a hindrance to maintaining a strong westward aspiration. According to Georgian President Margvelashvili, the combination of normalisation of Georgian-Russian relations and Georgia's uncompromised western aspirations "is a very difficult path, but this is the only way."[31]

---

27   Fact Sheet, NATO-Georgian Joint Training and Evaluation Center(JTEC), 27 August 2015, at: http://www.nato.int/nato_static_fl2014/assets/pdf/pdf_topics/20150827_ 1508 27-jtec-georgia.pdf (Accessed on 13 July 2016).

28   See: The speech of the President of Georgia at a conference in the European Parliament – "Eastern Partnership – a partnership of free choice", 5 September 2014, at: https://www.president.gov.ge/en/PressOffice/News?p=9461&i=3.

29   President Saakashvili's Inauguration Speech. Civil Georgia. January, 2014, at: http://www.civil.ge/eng/article.php?id=26694 (Accessed on 1 October 2016).

30   Mariam Naskidashvili: Georgia: Reducing Anti-Russian Rhetoric, Accelerating Co-operation with the European Union in: Unrewarding Crossroads? The Black Sea Region amidst the European Union and Russia. Edited by Anahit Shirinyan and Louisa Slavkova Sofia Platform, June 2015, pp.41-54, at: http://sofiaplatform.org/wp-content/uploads/2015/06/Georgia_Reducing_Anti-Russian_Rhetoric_Accelerating_Co-operation_with_the_European_Union.pdf (Accessed on 1 October 2016).

31   Margvelashvili (2014). Annual address. president.gov.ge, [online] (published on 21 February, 2014), at: https://www.president.gov.ge/en/PressOffice/ Documents/ Annual Reports?p=8674&i=1 (Accessed on 1 October 2016).

The Georgian government, headed by Georgian Dream coalition (GD), has also softened its rhetoric towards Russia, avoiding frequently used terms that had demonised Russia[32] and ruled out the possibility of co-operation. Interestingly, fearing a strong backlash by Moscow, the Georgian government did not join in another round of sanctions introduced by the European Union against Russia. Instead, Tbilisi decided to join only one of them, banning imports from Crimea and Sevastopol.[33] Former Prime Minister Garibashvili stated that Georgia and its Western partners "have to convince Russia that Georgia's aspiration to become a member of the European Union is not a threat to Russia."[34] The Prime Minister thus maintained that Georgia has to involve Russia in the process of Euro-Atlantic integration, at least as an informed partner, in order to avoid the complication of relations. Some Georgian analysts even think that if Western-Russian relations are restored, Germany could join the United States as a patron of Georgia's Euro-Atlantic aspirations.[35] It could also use its persuasive power to convince Moscow that a pro-European, democratic Georgia is in Russia's interest. However, for the Georgian public, it is not clear if Germany is prepared to take on such a role. Government officials have even emphasised these changes in their rhetoric.[36] This has not gone unnoticed by Moscow, which has acknowledged the shift. As the present Georgian leadership seeks to engage Russia through reinvigorating trade, cultural, and humanitarian ties, distinct challenges in diplomatic relations will remain as long as Russia occupies internationally-recognized Georgian territory. Tbilisi also has another non-negotiable red line: the freedom to choose its own alliances. Overall, as the government has reduced Georgia's level of confrontation with Russia to an extent, without sacrificing the country's overall path toward Euro-Atlantic integration, it is unlikely to produce a wholesale change in the posturing of Tbilisi and Moscow. Consequently, some Georgians think that co-operation or partnership between Russia and Georgia could be possible if Russia respects territorial integrity of its neighbours, fully restored its relations with the West and moved towards democracy.

---

32   Saakashvili: 'Help Us to Deter Russia's Mirror Propaganda'. Civil Georgia. 21 January 2010, at: http://www.civil.ge/eng/article.php?id=21909 (Accessed on 2 Oct., 2016).

33   Evidently concerned about the possible resumption of the Russian embargo on Georgian wine, agricultural produce and mineral water. See: Georgian Diplomat: Reinstating Trade Restriction by Russia Would Be 'Wrong' Civil Georgia, 5 August 2015, at: http://www.civil.ge/eng/_print.php?id=28483 (Accessed on 30 September 2016).

34   Civil Georgia, 2014b. "Georgian PM addresses Munich Security Conference". Civil Georgia, 2 February 2014, at: http://civil.ge/eng/article.php? id=26904 (Accessed on 1 October 2016).

35   "სანამ გერმანია-საქართველოს ურთიერთობები ახალ სიმაღლეზე არ ავა, ჩვენ გვექნება პრობლემები" (in Georgian) 15 June 2016, at: http://netgazeti. ge/news/123252/ (Accessed on 1 October 2016).

36   "Rhetoric towards Russia has not been relaxed" – Irakli Alasania. Georgian Journal. 1 May 2013, at: http://www.georgianjournal.ge/politics/23190-rhetoric-towards-russia-has-not-been-relaxed--irakli-alasania.html (Accessed on 30 September 2016).

Although the long-term impact of Russia's gambit remains uncertain, it has created certain disadvantages for the Georgian state. As Russian expansionism shifted westward into Ukraine, it also took Western attention with it, leaving Georgia's security challenges in the shadow of the Ukrainian crisis. However, Georgia has also been "an accidental beneficiary[37]" of events outside its control – notably Russia's preoccupation with Ukraine. Russia's ready reliance on military force encouraged Tbilisi to diversify its political, economic and cultural relations with the outside world, especially towards the European Union. Partly impelled by the crisis in Ukraine, the recent signing of far-reaching association agreements with the EU has further reinforced strategic relations between Georgia and Ukraine, as both countries have now committed themselves to EU standards and, together with Moldova, have bound themselves closer to the West. On the whole, Russia continues to represent a genuine threat to Georgia, but the Georgian government's commitment to Euro-Atlantic integration remains robust. As Georgian ties with the West are already fundamental to the country's security, economy, and long-term future, Russian and Western relations remain critical for Georgia's security.

---

37   S. Neil MacFarlane. Two Years of the Dream: Georgian Foreign Policy During the Transition - 29 May 2015. See more at: https://www.chathamhouse.org/ publication/two-years-dream-georgian-foreign-policy-during-transition#sthash.NYEOm0v3.dpuf.

Wolfgang Zellner

German Perceptions of Russian-Western Relations

This brief essay deals with the question of German perceptions of critical dimensions of Russian-Western relations after Russia's action in and around Ukraine. It aims at including three focus groups: the population as a whole, the government and the political parties and, finally, the scholarly literature. However, as the data situation is different for different questions, the approach chosen here has to remain selective.

The first paragraph deals with German threat perceptions vis-á-vis Russia harboured both by the population and the government. The second paragraph deals with the question of who is responsible for the current situation – here the focus is on the government and the political parties. The third paragraph, focusing on political actors and the scholarly literature, tries to identify the root causes that are shaping Russian-Western relations. The fourth paragraph deals with common interests and focuses on political actors and the population. The fifth paragraph follows the beginning debate on a future European order and includes positions held by political actors and from the scholarly literature. A brief summary concludes the text.

The picture given here is incomplete, provisional and subject to change. However, it gives an initial impression of how Russian-Western relations are seen in Germany. And it tells us something about the limits and the empty spots in the current debate.

Threat Perception in Germany

With respect to threats perceived from Russia, Germans rank at the lower end of the middle ground of European countries. In a major poll, conducted by the Pew Research Center in ten European countries in spring 2016, 76 per cent of the European respondents saw ISIS as a major threat and 17 per cent as a minor threat, followed by 66 per cent who perceived climate change as a major threat (27 per cent: minor threat). "Tensions with Russia" ranked only in 6th place with 30 per cent perceiving Russia as a major threat and 48 per cent as a minor threat (Pew 2016: 14). By comparison, 31 per cent of Germans saw Russia as a major threat, 52 per cent as a minor threat and 15 per cent as no threat (ibid.: 40). Thus, concerns about Russia represent for Germans and most European countries only one concern among others, or in the language of the Pew Research Center a "low-level threat" (ibid.: 18).

The German Federal Government's "White Paper 2016 on German Security Policy and the Future of the Bundeswehr" comes to a more fundamental and, at the same time, more differentiated conclusion:

"Russia is openly calling the European peace order into question with its willingness to use force to advance its own interests and to unilaterally redraw borders guaranteed under international law, as it has done in Crimea and eastern Ukraine. This has far-reaching implications for security in Europe and, thus, for the security of Germany." (White Paper 2016: 31).

The White Paper 2016 adds: "Without a fundamental change in policy, Russia will constitute a challenge to the security of our continent for the foreseeable future." (Ibid: 32). Thus, even without using the term "threat", the White Paper 2016 suggests a substantially more serious threat perception of Russia than the general population holds.

It is interesting to see in what way these perceptions of a Russian challenge or threat are framed within the entirety of threats and challenges perceived. Addressing the OSCE Permanent Council on 2 July 2015, the-then German Foreign Minister Frank-Walter Steinmeier said:

"In Ukraine, a security policy crisis is raging – undoubtedly the most serious since the end of the Cold War. At the same time, many other dangerous storms are sweeping through our neighbourhood, near and far – crises and conflicts so numerous, complex and severe as I have ever experienced in my own political biography." (Steinmeier, 2 July 2015).

This perception of 'multi-crises' or a 'poly-crisis' is echoed in the scientific literature. Volker Perthes, the Director of the German government's think tank "German Institute for International and Security Affairs" uses the term "crisis landscapes":

"Syria, the streams of refugees, terrorist threats, our relations to Russia, Turkey's domestic developments, the state of the European Union, and the capacities of individual EU states constitute partial elements of large crises landscapes flowing into one another.
Policy makers should resist the expectation of being able to resolve all crises subsequently. Frequently, the issue will rather be intelligent crisis management – or navigating through the crisis landscapes as safely as possible." (Perthes 2017: 5[1]).

Claudia K. Huber and Thomas Matussek speak about "a feeling of a loss of control" (Huber / Matussek 2015: 71) in view of the endless crises, from those in Greece to the Ukraine to the refugee crisis. With the developing crisis of the European Union and the then approaching Brexit referendum, headlines in leading German political science journals read "Chaos in the Club. Economy under Pressure, Democracy in Danger. How to Save the EU?" (Möller 2015) or "Wreck Europe" (Guérot 2016).

---

1   All translations from German to English are those of the author.

It is important to note that, although it is recognized that the different dimensions of threats perceived are interdependent in complex ways, almost no one has made an attempt to analyse these interdependencies in a more detailed way. Consequently, central elements for a broader strategic debate are lacking. Those who think about the current crises seem still to be overwhelmed by their multitude and complexity, the expert community more than the politicians and the politicians more than the broader population, which concentrates on the risks closer to their personal lives. It remains to be seen whether a more comprehensive debate will develop at all or whether it will be limited to the compartmentalized discussions we already have.

Who is Responsible for the Current Situation?

Against the background of *Ostpolitik* and the positive role the Soviet Union of Gorbachev and Shevardnadze played for German reunification, Russian policy is a salient element of German foreign policy. Traditionally, there has been both a balance and tension between so-called *Russia understanders* and *Russia critics*, not always strictly divided along party lines. As will be shown in this paragraph, both the meanings of these two categories, as well as their relationship, have substantially changed since the Ukraine crisis started in early 2014.

The historical *caesura* of 2014 was characterized by Markus Ederer, State Secretary in the German Federal Foreign Office, as follows:

> "For more than two decades, we worked within the framework of a European security order based on the rules and principles enshrined in the Charter of Paris signed in 1990. Today, however, we are confronted with a Russia that is attempting to use the unpredictability of its foreign policy actions to assert sovereignty as well as to demonstrate and project strength." (Ederer, 6 April 2016).

And Stephan Steinlein, at that time also State Secretary in the German Federal Foreign Office, added:

> "If the reliability of joint rules is replaced by a policy that understands the unpredictability of one's own action as an essential element of one's own sovereignty, but also of one's own strength, then this changes the business basis of our relations fundamentally." (Steinlein, 18 April 2016).

On the scientific side, this is echoed by Claudia Major and Jana Puglierin, who speak of "the end of a halfway co-operative security order and the beginning of a confrontational and unstable era." (Major / Puglierin 2014: 62). Rinke added: "The joint analysis of the federal government is: Russia is no longer defining its foreign policy interests with, but in dissociation from Europe." (Rinke 2015: 37). Or, as stated in the White Paper 2016: "Russia is rejecting a close partnership with the West and placing emphasis on strategic rivalry." (White Paper 2016: 32). Together, this means that the change that surfaced in 2014 is not understood as a temporary and comparatively easily reversible event, but as a deep division of unpredictable duration and significance.

From the perspective of the government (both Christian and Social Democrats), it is clearly Russia that is responsible for the current situation: "Russia's action – first on Crimea, then in Eastern Ukraine – has violated the fundamentals of our living together in Europe. The territorial integrity of Ukraine was disregarded in the same way as its state sovereignty. International law has been broken." (Merkel, 7 February 2015). And precisely in Moscow, in her joint press conference with President Vladimir Putin on the occasion of the 70th anniversary of the end of the Second World War, she even spoke of the "criminal" annexation of Crimea (Merkel, 10 May 2015). Steinmeier formulated it as follows:

> "With the annexation of Crimea and the destabilization of Eastern Ukraine, against international law, for the first time since the end of the Cold War, an OSCE participating State has turned itself openly against the sovereignty of another state and has massively questioned the principles of the CSCE Final Act" (Steinmeier, 21 April 2016).

This position is shared by the Green Party, the Liberal Party and the vast majority of the scientific literature. If it is solely Russia, which is responsible for the current tensions in Europe, then the conclusion drawn by the White Paper 2016 is convincing:

> "What is important for the common security space of our continent is, thus, not the development of a new security architecture, but rather respect for and consistent adherence to existing and proven common rules and principles." (White Paper 2016: 32).

The fact that the dividing line between Russia understanders and critics does not show up within the government, does not mean that it no longer exists. In a public appeal called "War in Europe again? Not in our names!" a group of prominent intellectuals and retired politicians took positions that, at first sight, appear equidistant between those of the two factions, but on closer look reveal more sympathy for the position of the Russian government: "Each journalist with foreign policy expertise will understand the anxiety of Russia, since NATO members in 2008 invited Georgia and Ukraine to become members in the Alliance." (Appeal, December 2014). The appeal does mention the "annexation of Crimea, against international law", but puts it on the same level with NATO's expansion. The appeal is signed by prominent Social Democrats, i.e. former Chancellor Gerhard Schröder, but also by prominent Christian Democrats, such as the former security adviser to Chancellor

Helmut Kohl, Horst Teltschik, and members of the Green Party, such as Antje Vollmer, former Vice President of the German Bundestag. Positions of this kind are shared by the Left Party and also by the new right-wing populist Alternative *for Germany* that made it into most federal parliaments and has good chances (current polls are around seven to eight per cent) of making it into the German Bundestag in the 2017 elections.

Taken together, the Russia understanders are now to be found predominantly among retired politicians of almost all persuasions as well as among active politicians of left-wing and right-wing parties. A broad centre is occupied by what would have been called Russia critics in the past. However, under the current conditions, this term has changed its meaning, because the new Russia critics are in favour of dialogue and "selective co-operation" with Russia (cf. below).

Key Factors Shaping the Development of the Russian-Western Relations

Comparable to the 2014 U.S. debate in *Foreign Affairs*, there are two largely unrelated lines of argument on what is shaping Russian behaviour: domestic factors within Russia, on the one hand, and foreign and security policy developments, substantially influenced by Western countries, on the other. Thus, for Ivan Krastev and Mark Leonard, it is

> "...much rather Russia's domestic policy than Russia's security needs, rather the fear of a regime change governed by the West than NATO expansion that stands behind Moscow's foreign policy revisionism." (Krastev / Leonard 2015: 46).

Also for Meister, the "main causes of the conflict between Russia and the West lie not only in the security perception of the Russian elites, which perceive the enlargement policies of NATO and EU as a threat, but in the internal legitimacy deficit of the system Putin." (Meister 2015: 76). This line of argument is frequently repeated in the literature: the original deal between the Russian government and the population – social progress against political abstinence – is endangered by the stagnation of a largely raw materials-based economy that started well before the Western sanctions. These sanctions, however, have provided Putin with the opportunity to blame the West for the Russian economic malaise and, thus, have resolved some of his legitimacy problems, at least for the time being.

This also means that the role of economic ties and interdependence has changed fundamentally for political relations. "The concept 'change though trade' aimed at initiating political and economic reforms in the Soviet Union and – later – Russia, which would result in a rapprochement towards the West." (Major / Puglierin 2014: 65). However, the Ukraine crisis shows that this concept no longer works and was not able to prevent the war. State Secretary Ederer adds that we are "witnessing a Russian policy of export substitution, which exacerbates some of these trends and is explicitly targeted at reducing interdependence." (Ederer, 6 April 2016). Thus, Russia tries to decouple itself to a degree from globalization processes and aims at constructing and strengthening its own integration orbit including the Euro-Asian Economic Union. Against this background, it is not by chance, that the "Ukraine crisis developed through the confrontation of two incompatible projects of multilateral integration – the Eastern Partnership of the EU and Russia's EEU." (Leonard 2016: 99). Today, it is widely recognized that economic interdependence and connectivity do, by no means, automatically translate into co-operative political relations. At best, such relations must be deliberately shaped; at worst, there is the possibility of "wars of connectivity", as the-then State Secretary Stephan Steinlein put it (Steinlein, 18 April 2016).

Whereas in the Russia understanders' camp it is common to highlight the negative consequences of NATO enlargement, this issue is rarely addressed in the new grand coalition of Russia critics. One of the few exceptions is Wolfgang Ischinger, a former state secretary in the Federal Foreign Office and Chairman of the Munich Security Conference. In a contribution in mid-2014, he described the process of NATO enlargement as

> "...a kind of two-pillar strategy. The one basic idea was: We basically give the neighbours in Central and Eastern Europe, which want to accede the Alliance, the possibility to do that. The second idea was: We must supplement this, call it NATO enlargement pillar, next to a NATO Russia pillar." (Ischinger 2014: 19).

According to Ischinger, this worked in the first round of NATO enlargement in 1997/1999, but was abandoned under George W. Bush after 2001/2002, "when NATO enlargement was progressed, but the second pillar, the NATO-Russia pact, was more and more forgotten." (Ibid.). Thus "we stumbled with seeing eyes into the conflict" (Ibid.).

Such a differentiated account of the impact of Western-driven foreign and security policy actions on the general development is extremely rare in the German debate. And what is more, the author does not know of any serious attempt to combine the domestic and the foreign policy lines of argument in a differentiated manner.

Interests Shared by Russia and the West

Among political actors, co-operative relations with Russia are no longer perceived as comprehensive and norms-based, but as case-to-case co-operation on the basis of interest. As Chancellor Merkel put it at the Munich Security Conference in 2015:

"This is true for coping with joint international challenges – from the proliferation of means of mass destruction to fighting international terrorism. The E3+3 negotiations on the resolution of the nuclear conflict with Iran and the removal of Syrian chemical weapons show that, despite all crises, co-operation with Russia on important issues can be successful." (Merkel, 7 February 2015).

This also reflects a broad consensus among the vast majority of the new Russia critics: Co-operation with Russia on selected important issues is possible and should be pursued in an active manner. In April 2016, State Secretary Ederer made up a comparatively long list, of possible co-operation fields, from

"joint work on the implementation of the Minsk Agreement", Nagorno-Karabakh, resolving the Syrian crisis, fighting the so-called Islamic State, fighting organized crime, i.e. trafficking in human beings or cybercrime, or regional co-operation in the Arctic, the Baltic sea or in Central Asia in view of China's Silk Road project" (Ederer, 6 April 2016).

Not surprisingly, these statements come very close to the EU position of "selective engagement with Russia" (see next paragraph). The opinion of the German population is less differentiated, but more fundamentally in favour of co-operation with Russia. According to a 2016 Infratest poll on behalf of the Körber Foundation 95 per cent of the Germans think that a political rapprochement between Russia and the EU is important or very important. Top candidate for EU-Russia co-operation is the resolution of the Syria conflict (49 per cent). In addition, a surprisingly large majority of Germans (69 per cent) are in favour of ending the economic sanctions against Russia (Körber Foundation 2016: 2-3).

Towards Some Kind of European Order

The starting point for the predominant discourse in Germany on a future European order is the realization, that "so-far, German and European Russia policy, based on joint rules, co-operation and integration, has failed for the time being." (Major / Puglierin 2014: 68). Despite this, Chancellor Merkel noted at the 2015 Munich Security Conference: "We want to frame security in Europe jointly with Russia, not against Russia." (Merkel, 7 February 2015). Or: "The aim is and remains: European security jointly with Russia, not against Russia." (Merkel, 18 December 2014). This objective is shared by Merkel's Social Democrat coalition partner and is supported in almost the entire scientific literature. This position is also supported by the White Book 2016:

"At the same time, however, Europe and Russia remain linked by a broad range of common interests and relations. As the EU's largest neighbour and a permanent member of the UN Security Council, Russia has a special regional and global responsibility when it comes to meeting common challenges and managing international crises. Sustainable security and prosperity in and for Europe cannot therefore be ensured without strong co-operation with Russia." (White Book 2016: 32).

The negative assessment of Russian action, combined with the desire to continue co-operation, leads to a certain dilemma: On the one hand, there is a broad consensus on 'security jointly with Russia'; on the other it

"…has become a commonplace that in this overall situation there can be 'no business as usual'. As far as I can see, this conclusion is widely accepted, not only within the European Union, but – maybe for different reasons – also in Russia. Now what does this mean in practical terms?" (Ederer, 6 April 2016).

The first element of an answer to this question is 'dialogue': "We have to talk to one another [...], if necessary also controversially, but again we must always take the way of dialogue." (Merkel, 11 June 2014). The 2016 German OSCE Chairmanship worked under the motto: "Renewing dialogue, rebuilding trust, restoring security" (Federal Foreign Office 2016). However, Foreign Minister Steinmeier specified in his speech to the Permanent Council: "What we don't need is dialogue about dialogue – we need a dialogue that cannot and does not want to hide the fact that key OSCE commitments were and are being broken – for example, in Crimea and Eastern Ukraine." (Steinmeier, 14 January 2016). Later, Steinmeier coined the term "double dialogue" (Steinmeier, 21 April 2016), a dialogue on shared positions, on the one hand, and on differences, on the other. State Secretary Ederer explained:

"A dialogue that also focuses on differences rather than on commonalities could be beneficial, indeed. Exploring openly and seriously the diverging narratives on the European order and the Russian-European relationship could help us understand the nature and the extent of our differences. They would not be removed, but they might potentially become less dangerous." (Ederer, 6 April 2016).

With respect to the form of the co-operation, both Steinmeier and Ederer speak about "compartmentalized co-operation", a kind of "co-existence of co-operation and confrontation" (Ederer, 6 April 2016). This reflects the decision of the EU Foreign Affairs Council of 14 March 2016 on guiding principles for EU co-operation with Russia that calls for, among other things, the "possibility of selective engagement with Russia on issues of interest to the EU" (Council of the European Union, 14 March 2016). From the German government's perspective, one key element of such a selective co-operation could be "talks also between the EU Commission and the Eurasian Union." (Merkel, 7 February 2015). This is supported by the Social Democrat coalition partner: "Second, for contacts between the EU and the Eurasian Economic Union, we suggest talking about technical standards, rules of trade, cross-border infrastructure" (Steinlein, 18 April 2016). And also the Minister himself underlined this point: "I have called for a dialogue between the EU and the Eurasian Economic Union, as well as with China within the framework of the EU-China platform." (Steinmeier, 18 May 2016).

'Compartmentalized co-operation' or 'selective engagement' differ from concepts such as "congagement" (Dembinski / Schmidt / Spanger 2014: II) – a combination of containment and engagement – or the sundry variants of "Harmel 2.0" (cf. Kühn 2015) insofar as their starting point is civilian co-operation and not the military dimension. To the best knowledge of the author, no representative of the government has used the latter concepts so far.

While a selective co-operation concept with respect to Russia is supported by the greater part of the scientific literature (cf. prominently Krastev / Leonard 2015: 50), it is critically discussed by a few others: "Since 2012, the Customs Union and the EEU have become protectionist instruments, in order to block or impede the EU's influence on post-Soviet countries." (Meister 2015: 79). Based on this assessment, Meister comes to the conclusion: "If the EU were to find a compromise with Russia on these countries, this would mean accepting the limited sovereignty of these states requested by Moscow and thus Russia's zone of influence." (Ibid. 78). Nevertheless, although Russia critics represent the vast majority, both in the expert and governmental camps, they pledge continued co-operation with Russia wherever this is adequate and possible.

Summary

The general attitude of German mainstream thinking on Russia has substantially changed, on the one hand, but has remained basically the same, on the other. This supposed contradiction can be more easily resolved than expected at first sight.

The element of change. Until the late 1990s or mid-2000 (depending on different perspectives), most Germans – political actors, scholars and the majority of the population alike – hoped for a fundamentally co-operative relationship with Russia, based on shared values and a common understanding of the basics of the European order. Disputes would remain, but would be resolved by discussions and compromise, and co-operation would prevail. "Strategic partnership" (EU term), "co-operative security" or even "security community" (OSCE terms) were different designations for the same notion.

This expectation of a co-operative relationship in the framework of a shared order has been – and this marks the change - fundamentally destroyed. So deep is the rupture, that almost nobody believes that such a relationship can be 're-established' in the short- or even mid-term perspective. A broad majority in all three focus groups believes that Russia is, at least predominantly, responsible for this unwelcome change. Only a smaller minority sees a shared responsibility for this return to dispute and conflict. What most people deem still possible and worth pursuing, is discussion – on shared issues as well as disputed ones – and interest-based pragmatic, 'selective' or 'compartmentalized' co-operation. This kind of limited co-operation – limited both in scope and with respect to its foundations – has now replaced the comprehensive, norm-based co-operation that is impossible to achieve under the current circumstances.

The element of continuity consists in the belief that sustainable security in Europe is impossible to achieve against Russia or without Russia. That means that strategies of military containment and disengagement (minimal co-operation) do not lead to the desired results. Thus, in this perspective there is no alternative to a "double dialogue" (Steinmeier) and pragmatic *ad hoc* co-operation where possible. Again, this position is shared by broad majorities in all three focus groups. Those, who pledged comprehensive co-operation in the past, are now in favour of selective co-operation where possible. This is nothing else than a necessary adaption to changed political circumstances or, more precisely, to a changed Russian co-operation partner.

Deficiencies of the debate. The debate on the question of how to deal with Russia is still in the beginning stages, both concerning a mid-term perspective of selective co-operation and a more long-term perspective on how a future European order might look. This is a bit surprising for a country such as Germany where policies vis-á-vis Russia have always been seen as a key issue. One explanation for this deficiency is that the scholarly expertise on Russia and Eastern Europe has been constantly declining in Germany since the end of the Cold War. Another element of explanation could be that the complex multitude of crises, highlighted by the-then Foreign Minister Steinmeier, exceeds the capability of actors to formulate realistic strategies. Perhaps one element of the 'poly-crisis' is the explicit lack of strategies on many sides, reducing political action to ad hoc improvisation.

Sources

Appeal "Again War in Europe? Not in Our Name!" in: Zeit online, 5 December 2014.
Council of the European Union, 14 March 2016, Outcome of the Council Meeting, 3457th Council meeting, Brussels, 14 March 2016.
Dembinski, Matthias, Hans Joachim Schmidt, Hans-Joachim Spanger 2014, Einhegung: Die Ukraine, Russland und die europäische Sicherheitsordnung (HSFK-Report Nr. 3/2014).
Ederer, Markus 2016, Auswärtiges Amt, Rede von Staatssekretär Markus Ederer bei der Konferenz „EU-Russia: in search of a new modus operandi", 6 April 2016.
Federal Government, Federal Foreign Office, Renewing dialogue, rebuilding trust, restoring security. The priorities of the German OSCE Chairmanship 2016, Berlin 2016.

Federal Government, Ministry of Defence, White Paper 2016 on German Security Policy and the Future of the Bundeswehr, Berlin, June 2016.

Guérot, Ulrike 2016, Trümmerhaufen Europa. Um das europäische Haus wieder aufzubauen, müssen wir uns einig sein, wie es aussehen soll, in: Internationale Politik und Gesellschaft, www.ipg-journal.de, 1 March 2016.

Huber, Claudia, Thomas Matussek 2015, Wann, wenn nicht jetzt? Eine ehrliche Debatte über die Zukunft der EU ist überfällig, in: Internationale Politik, November/Dezember 2015, pp. 70-76.

Ischinger, Wolfgang 2014, Baumängel am „gemeinsamen Haus". Warum die Anbindung Russlands an den Westen gescheitert ist, in: Internationale Politik, Mai/Juni 2014, pp. 19-21.

Körber-Stiftung 2016, Annäherung oder Abschottung?, Ergebnisse einer repräsentativen Umfrage von TNS Infratest Politikforschung in Deutschland und Russland, Hamburg 2016.

Krastev, Ivan / Mark Leonard 2015, Die neue europäische Unordnung. Die EU wird Russland nicht ändern. Aber sie sollte sich hüten, sie zu isolieren, in: Internationale Politik, Januar/Februar 2015, pp. 42-51.

Kühn, Ulrich 2015, Deter and Engage. Making the Case for Harmel 2.0 as NATO's New Strategy, in: New Perspectives, vol. 23, no. 1, pp. 127-157.

Leonard, Mark 2016, Interdependenz als Waffe. Die EU muss die Zeichen der geoökonomischen Zeit erkennen, in: Internationale Politik, März/April 2016, pp. 94-103.

Major, Claudia / Jana Puglierin 2014, Eine neue Ordnung. Der Ukraine-Konflikt stellt die Weichen für Europas Sicherheit, in: Internationale Politik, November/Dezember 2014, pp. 62-70.

Meister, Stefan 2015, Politik der Illusionen. Ein Ausgleich mit Russland auf der Grundlage einer EU-EWU-Partnerschaft ist irrig, in: Internationale Politik, März/April 2015, pp. 76-81.

Merkel, Angela 2014, Die Bundeskanzlerin, Rede von Bundeskanzlerin Merkel anlässlich des Jahresempfangs für das Diplomatische Corps am 11. Juni 2014.

Merkel, Angela 2014a, Die Bundeskanzlerin, Regierungserklärung von Bundeskanzlerin Merkel zum Europäischen Rat am 18./19. Dezember in Brüssel, 18 December 2014.

Merkel, Angela 2015, Die Bundeskanzlerin, Rede von Bundeskanzlerin Angela Merkel anlässlich der 51. Münchner Sicherheitskonferenz, 7 February 2015.

Merkel, Angela 2015a, Die Bundeskanzlerin, Pressekonferenz von Bundeskanzlerin Merkel und Staatspräsident Putin am 10 Mai 2015 in Moskau.

Möller, Almut 2015, Chaos im Club. Wirtschaft unter Druck, Demokratie in Gefahr: Wie ist die EU zu retten? in: Internationale Politik, Mai/Juni 2015, pp. 139-141.

Perthes, Volker 2017, Einleitung: Navigieren durch Krisenlandschaften, in: Volker Perthes (ed.), „Krisenlandschaften". Konfliktkonstellationen und Problemkomplexe internationaler Politik. Ausblick 2017, SWP-Studie, Berlin, January 2017.

Pew 2016, Stokes, Bruce / Richard Wike / Jacob Poushter, Europeans Face the World Divided. Many question national influence and obligations to allies, but share desire for greater EU role in global affairs, Pew Research Center 2016, http://www.pewglobal.org/2016/06/13/europeans-isis-climate-change-as-most-serious-threas/.

Rinke, Andreas 2015, Vom Partner zum Gegner zum Partner?, in: Internationale Politik, März/April 2015, pp. 36-43.

Steinlein, Stephan 2016, Auswärtiges Amt, Keynote von Staatssekretär Stephan Steinlein bei der Eröffnung des 4. east forum Berlin, 18 April 2016.

Steinmeier, Frank-Walter 2015, Address to the OSCE Permanent Council on 2 July 2015, PC.DEL/919/15, 2 July 2015 (translation, original German).

Steinmeier, Frank-Walter 2016, Renewing dialogue, rebuilding trust, restoring security, Speech to the OSCE Permanent Council, Vienna, 14 January 2016 (CiO.GAL/2/16/Corr.1).

Steinmeier, Frank-Walter 2016a, Auswärtiges Amt, Rede von Außenminister Frank-Walter Steinmeier beim Egon-Bahr-Symposium, 21 April 2016.

Steinmeier, Frank-Walter 2016b, OSCE, Deutschland 2016, Speech of Foreign Minister and OSCE Chairperson-in-Office Dr. Frank-Walter Steinmeier at the opening of the business conference organised by the German OSCE Chairmanship ‚Connectivity for Commerce and Investment, Berlin, 18 May 2016.

Serena Giusti

Italy's Special Relationship with Russia

Summary

The predominant view in Italy holds that Russia is a country that has faced a complex process of transformation and is still confronting various challenges, notably including that of modernization. The Italian political élite have been successful in building a strategic partnership with Russia. This strategic partnership is founded on interdependence and common interests. In recent years, bilateral relations have achieved a high level of excellence, deserving of "privileged relations" status. Apart from clear economic reasons, with Italy still being extensively dependent on Russian energy supplies, Rome recognizes that Moscow is a strategic partner for settling a number of conflicts in Europe and the Middle East, as well as for the fight against terrorism.

The pro-Russia policy has been shared by all recent governments in a bipartisan way: no matter what government was in power (either centre-left or centre-right) the partnership has been strengthened and broadened. Any time Russia has infringed international law – notably in the cases of Georgia and Ukraine – Italy has aligned itself with the EU's and the US' condemnation, while always promoting a stance of moderation and engagement rather than confrontation and isolation of the country.

Public opinion seems to follow the government's posture as many economic interests are involved. Although acknowledging Vladimir Putin's inclination to monopolize power and a poor record of human rights, Italians feel culturally very close to Russians. A quite new phenomenon is the sympathy expressed by some Italian populist parties for the Russian President. Those parties are the same that embrace anti-EU rhetoric. The Euroscepticism sentiment seems to intersect with empathy towards the Kremlin.

As a methodological note, it must be stressed that the Italian mass media mostly deal with domestic politics, while foreign policy and international affairs are only modestly covered. This explains the difficulty of grasping grassroots narratives intended as people perceptions on Russia. This report considers especially the narratives put forward by the political élites, either by the government or the opposition.[1] Only after the Kremlin responded to sanctions by banning Western food imports has the question of Russia been

---

1   The report considers official statements, government's reports and documents. The author, in its role of researcher at ISPI has had the possibility to discuss informally crucial topics related to Italy-Russia relationship with some Italian decision makers (politicians, diplomats, parliamentarians). Although tracing the relationship back to the Cold-War period, the contribution focuses, in particular, on the development of the relationship since the late 1990's until now.

widely raised, as it affected many economic sectors. There has been a mobilization from below, exploited in some cases by populist factions.

A Friendship Rooted in History

Good relations between Italy and Russia are rooted in history. Even during the Cold War, the two countries had many points of contact. After the end of World War II, Italian governments (led by the Christian Democrats for the best part of four decades from 1945) sided with the Western part of the Iron Curtain. Italy was, in fact, a founding member of both the North Atlantic Treaty Organisation (NATO) and the European Economic Community (EEC). Nevertheless, the Italian Communist Party (PCI), which also had strong support in the country (Italy was and is in fact polarized and divided), kept up very good relations with the Soviet *nomenklatura*. The PCI approved of the Red Army's crackdown in Hungary in 1956 and only in 1968, by condemning the Soviet invasion of Czechoslovakia, did it distance itself from Soviet orthodoxy. After the adoption of the Eurocommunism doctrine and its historic compromise, the PCI became critical of the Soviet Union's conduct, especially with respect to the satellites.[2]

Despite some tension, economic relations between Rome and Moscow continued to develop smoothly. The 1966 Fiat-Soviet agreement, for instance, fostered the entrance of the Soviet Union into the "automotive century" and engendered the first massive East-West transfer of technology and knowledge in the automobile sector of the post-World War II period. As the Italian diplomat, Sergio Romano noted, "Italy was one of the Western countries most consistent in applying the principle of peaceful coexistence between states with different social and political systems".[3]

When the Soviet Union collapsed, Italy supported the idea, shared by other European countries (notably Germany), of attracting Russia to a non-confrontational course, associating it with the West's main dialogue fora and progressively co-opting it into the Euro-Atlantic community.

The 'Economization' of the Narrative on Russia

The collapse of the Soviet Union contributed to strengthening relations between Italy and the Russian Federation and the economic recovery, under the first presidency of Vladimir Putin, tightened the two countries' economic

---

2   In 1973, the PCI's General Secretary, Enrico Berlinguer, launched a proposal in "Rinascita" (a Communist daily) for a "democratic alliance" with the Christian Democrats. The Communists wanted to enter the government to stop the crisis of the Italian political system and to achieve a socialist society.

3   S. Romano, "Ambassador Reflects", International Affairs, 34(6)1988.

relations.[4] The alternation of different political coalitions in power did not impact the relationship. The centre-left coalition government, led by Romano Prodi's and Silvio Berlusconi's (1994-1995; 2001-2006) centre right bloc, used almost identical tactics for dealing with Russia. Despite the clear personalization of the relationship under Berlusconi's second mandate, the pro-Russia orientation had clearly become a bipartisan vision.

The most lucrative contracts were achieved by Prodi's government. They ranged from co-operation on culture, education and the protection of intellectual property rights to multi-million dollar industrial contracts (the Italian defence giant, Finmeccanica, would work with Russia's Sukhoi to build a medium-range Superjet-100 civilian aircraft and co-operate with the Russian railways to develop a new track along the eastern Black Sea coast; the Russian Federal Atomic Energy Agency and the Italian fuel and energy company Enel planned to co-operate in the energy sector and over nuclear power generation; Gazprom formed a strategic partnership with Italy's ENI that allowed it access to the Italian gas market in return for letting ENI help develop Russian mineral deposits). All these contracts, among others, were meant to boost a modernization process in Russia.

Furthermore, Gazprom and ENI established a partnership for the construction of a new natural gas pipeline across the Black Sea from Russia to Europe. This South Stream pipeline was meant to give Russia a supply route straight into central and southern Europe at a time when other western countries, the US and the EU were backing projects, such as the Nabucco gas pipeline, bypassing Russia and providing Central Asia with direct access to Europe.[5] However, South Stream has had a troubled history as Russia dropped the plans for the pipeline in 2014, blaming the European Union for stalling the project. Then Russia sought to replace South Stream with Turkish Stream, a pipeline that would reach the EU at the Greek-Turkish border. However, the deteriorating relations between Russia and Turkey in the course of the Syrian crisis (in particular in November 2015, when a Russian bomber was shot down by a Turkish fighter jet) put the project on hold. Nevertheless, recent developments point to a possible renewal of the plan. Finally, Gazprom signed a memorandum of understanding with Italy's Edison and Greece's DEPA for a new gas supply route reaching Greece via the Black Sea and an unspecified third country (February 24, 2016).[6]

---

4   On the importance of the economy for relations between Italy and Russia, see N. Arbatova, 'Italy, Russia's Voice in Europe?', French Institute of International Relations, September 2011.
5   Italy is trying to diversify its suppliers as the Trans Adriatic Pipeline (TAP), transporting Caspian natural gas to Europe, proves. Connecting with the Trans Anatolian Pipeline (TANAP) at the Greek-Turkish border, TAP will cross Northern Greece, Albania and the Adriatic Sea before coming ashore in Southern Italy to connect to the Italian natural gas network, http://www.tap-ag.com/the-pipeline. The pipeline should become operative from 2018.
6   Gazprom, http://www.gazprom.com/press/news/2016/february/article267671/.

Italy's relations with Russia extended, therefore, far beyond the economic sphere and offered Rome an opportunity to bridge the political gap between Moscow and the European Union. Certainly, Italy harboured ambitions to become Russia's trading gateway to Europe. Both Berlusconi and Prodi were pragmatic in their approaches towards Moscow and human rights were seldom mentioned. Italy was also very supportive in helping to negotiate the agreement for the establishment of the NATO-Russia Council (2002), a mechanism for consultation, consensus-building, co-operation, joint decision and joint action.

The reinforcement of the partnership has been marked by a bold institutionalization (the Inter-Ministerial Summit; the Foreign-Defence Ministerial Meeting and the Economic, Industrial and Financial Cooperation Council take place annually, alternately in Italy and Russia) and by the extension of the issues of co-operation to include culture (cultural exchanges in a wide variety of topics are regulated by the Italian-Russian Cultural Agreement) and civil society. In fact, in 2004, such outreach activities also extended to grass roots organizations as the "Italian-Russian Civil Society Dialogue Forum", which fosters conferences, roundtables, concerts, and arts shows or the non-profit association Conoscere Eurasia that promotes the strengthening of economic relations. Since 2007, the Italian language has been incorporated into the educational programs of the Russian school system. Musical, artistic, and scientific co-operation have also increased.

Moreover, the friendly Italian policy towards Russia has become cross-institutional: in addition to the government, the Parliament and the Presidency have also been attuned. Only sporadically have some parliamentarians raised the question of the respect for human rights in Russia, while President Giorgio Napolitano (2006-2015), a former member of the PCI, was especially inclined to have good relations with Russia. Medvedev's proposal for a 'new European security architecture' in 2008 was well received by President Napolitano. Italy considered the integration of Russia into a revised European political-security complex a strategic goal. The Italian institutions were very keen on the EU-Russia Partnership for Modernization (2010) and many diplomats still consider it a missed opportunity (informal conversations), not only for the country, but for the whole of Europe.

This traditionally friendly path was also followed by Prime Ministers Mario Monti (November 2011 – April 2013), Enrico Letta (April 2013 – February 2014) and Matteo Renzi (February 2014 – ongoing). When Renzi came to power, Russia was Italy's sixth largest foreign trade partner, providing six per cent of all imports. The overall volume of trade between the two countries, at € 48 billion per year, remains very high to this day. Italy is generally considered to be the second largest consumer of Russian exports. The import of Russian gas covers about 42 per cent of the total Italian gas consumption.[7] But the other direction is important too: Italy is Russia's fifth-largest foreign trade partner. Russia supplies energy (15 per cent of Russian oil and 30 per cent of gas is exported to Italy), ferrous and non-ferrous metals and timber, while Italy delivers manufactured goods, machinery, chemical products, consumer wares and textile fabrics to Russia. Major Italian banks (e.g. UniCredit, Banca Intesa) are active in Russia.

Conflicts Involving Russia: the Non-confrontational Narrative

Italy has always been cautious in taking decisions which could displease Russia. When the EU's Eastern Partnership (EaP) was launched in Prague in 2009, Prime Minister Berlusconi did not attend the meeting (nor did the United Kingdom's then-Prime Minister Brown and the-then French President Sarkozy). It is not clear if this signifies that Italy was either indifferent to the EaP, viewed it as a competitor to the French-brokered Union for the Mediterranean (2008), or rather recognized it as a project strongly opposed by the Kremlin and was, therefore, not to be endorsed so as not to damage the special relationship with Russia.

Certainly, Italy opposed the US push to offer the prospect of NATO membership to Ukraine and Georgia. A clear preference for 'conciliation' or 'accommodation' informed the Italian reaction to Russia's military action in Georgia in 2008. Although Italy joined in the EU's formal condemnation of Russia's invasion of Georgia, Prime Minister Berlusconi nevertheless expressed his perplexity about the use of 'proportionality' in that complex context. The Italian government refused to discuss the possibility of imposing sanctions on Moscow and worked hard within both NATO and the EU to reactivate co-operation with the country. Berlusconi stressed the fact that Russia had to face various provocations from the West: the recognition of the independence of Kosovo by most Western countries (Italy included), as well as the US administration's plan to install parts of a US missile defence system in Poland and the Czech Republic.

During the crisis in Ukraine, Italy fully supported the EU's attempts to ease the conflict and condemned Russia's annexation of Crimea. But while Italy favours power-sharing, constitutional reform, and recognition and respect for minority rights and minority views for the resolution of the Ukrainian case, it is also more accommodating towards Russia than other EU members. The Italian Foreign Minister, Paolo Gentiloni, has remarked that we should not "close the door to Russia",[8] a recurrent formula in the Italian approach to the Ukrainian crisis. Italy has followed Europe's line on punitive measures towards Russia so far, although with some reluctance. However, no

---

7   http://luce-gas.it/faq/origine-geografica-gas-consumato-italia.
8   http://www.ecfr.eu/rome/post/italy_and_the_eastern_partnership_the_view_from_rome.

Italians were included in the list of 89 EU citizens who were banned by the Kremlin from entering Russia (May 30, 2015).[9]

After the shooting down of a Malaysia Airline civilian aircraft, the alleged direct Russian military presence in the Donbas and the non-adherence to the Minsk Protocol, Italy agreed with the EU on more stringent measures (31 July 2014). Nevertheless, apart from being concerned about the consequences on the national economy, Italy is also worried that sanctions may rather accelerate Russia's turn to the east, diluting or severing the economic and societal contacts that bind Russia to Europe.[10] Italy has repeatedly pointed out that the international community should not use informal or crossbreed methods as sanctions or other punitive measures for prompting a political change in Russia.

Italy, as other EU members, has opposed sending arms to Kyiv: at least half of the population of Germany, France and Italy would be unwilling to use military force to defend other NATO allies against Russian aggression.[11]

Soon after the annexation of Crimea, great attention was paid by the Italian mass media to the appointment of Federica Mogherini as the new EU High Representative for Foreign Affairs and Security Policy (August 2014). The political disputes at the European level over her appointment, opposed by some Central and Eastern European countries because of her supposedly lenient posture towards the Kremlin, have been widely reported.

On March 2015, Renzi visited Putin in Moscow, the first official visit by a major European leader since the Ukraine crisis erupted. On Ukraine, Renzi stressed the importance of implementing the Minsk Agreement reached by France, Germany, Russia and Ukraine. He also suggested that Trentino-Alto Adige, an autonomous Italian region which was once part of Austria-Hungary, might be a model for the Ukrainian government to consider. This meeting was met with displeasure by the US, as it came only a few days after Boris Nemtsov, the Russian opposition politician, was murdered near the Kremlin. According to the Italian narrative, the meeting was aimed at mediating with the Kremlin with the goal of re-opening a dialogue with Russia and avoiding risky isolation and frustration of the country.

Italian Eurosceptics Against Sanctions

Italy's main goal is the removal of sanctions as the country is suffering considerably because of the Russian counter-penalties. Italian exporters estimate

---

9   https://themoscowtimes.com/articles/russia-imposes-travel-ban-on-89-eu-politicians-46981.

10   See the Italian Prime Minister's Speech at the St. Petersburg International Economic Forum, June 17, 2016, http://www.governo.it/media/renzi-san-pietroburgo/5295.

11   Pew Research Institute, June 2015, http://www.pewglobal.org/2015/06/10/1-nato-public-opinion-wary-of-russia-leary-of-action-on-ukraine/.

they lost $ four billion in earnings between 2013 and 2015, a decline of 34 per cent over this period, according to the Italian small business association CGIA (26 March 2016). The Italian industrial sector is, therefore, pushing hard for lifting restrictions against the Kremlin.

Pressed by the national business community (entrepreneurs, traders, producers, chambers of commerce) the Italian government is working in that direction. Italy's Prime Minister Renzi questioned the automatic renewal of EU penalties against Moscow at the end of 2015.[12] While the EU approved the extension of sanctions against Russian and Ukrainian individuals, there is no unity on automatically prolonging economic sanctions. Italy, along with Cyprus, Hungary, Slovakia and Greece, is certainly against this possibility. The Italian Prime Minister again raised the issue of a possible removal of the food embargo at the St. Petersburg International Economic Forum (SPIEF) in June 2016, where Italy was Guest of Honour.[13]

The lenient position of Italy towards Russia is very much appreciated by the Northern League, a right-wing, anti-EU party that opposes sanctions against Russia. The Italian populist factions show an increasing dissatisfaction with the EU's 'patronising' approach towards Italy (e. g. pressing for the removal of Berlusconi from power, tight economic measures). According to Ipsos-Mori (May 2016)[14], 58 per cent of Italians would like to have a referendum on EU membership (though slightly fewer, around 48% actually want to leave). As a result, the anti-sanctions position has become part of anti-Europe rhetoric, meeting with a certain support among Italian citizens.

The rising political Five Stars Movement (Movimento 5 Stelle) also considers Russia an important strategic partner for Italy, especially for economic reasons. According to one of its prominent leaders, Alessandro Di Battista, the party intends 'to protect Italian interests, especially of the SME that suffered greatly from the sanctions regime'.[15] That is why the party is an active opponent against sanctions imposed on the Russian Federation and will promote the issue of further intensification of Russian-Italian ties, including visa-waivers for Russian citizens.[16] The Five Stars Movement is also very critical of Italy's membership in the EU and has called for exit from the common currency Euro.[17]

---

12   http://www.politico.eu/article/renzi-blocks-extension-russia-sanctions/.
13   http://www.governo.it/media/renzi-san-pietroburgo/5295.
14   https://www.ipsos-mori.com/researchpublications/researcharchive.aspx?keyword=
      Europe.
15   These words were pronounced in the occasion of Di Battista's meeting with the Chamber
      of Commerce and Industry of the Russia Federation on May 28, 2016, https://tpprf.ru/en/
      news/italian-party-5-star-movement-russia-remains-major-italian-partner-i129605/.
16   https://tpprf.ru/en/news/italian-party-5-star-movement-russia-remains-major-italian-
      partner-i129605/.
17   Immediately after the European elections of May 2014, the Movimento's leader, Grillo,
      proposed an alliance between the MEPs of M5S and those of UKIP (the UK Independence
      Party) in order to form a single parliamentary political group in the European Parliament.

Finally, the meeting between Pope Francis and the head of the Russian Orthodox Church, Patriarch Kirill, in Cuba (February 2016), the first encounter in history between a Roman Catholic Pope and a Russian Orthodox Patriarch in the nearly 1,000 years since Eastern Orthodoxy split with Rome, has had an impact on Italian public opinion[18]. The Patriarch-Pope meeting strengthened the Italian people's conviction that Russia must not be isolated since, after all, the majority of Russians are Christians. Moreover, Putin has frequently mentioned the difficult situation facing Christians in the Middle East.

Russia as a Multi-functional Actor, Useful in Various Scenarios

Recently, Renzi's policy towards Russia has been linked to other sensitive dossiers and in particular to the turbulence in the Middle East and North Africa as well as in Afghanistan, where civil wars and failing states have sent hundreds of thousands of refugees fleeing to Europe, many of them to Italy. Since 2013, the Italian government has been trying to win Russian co-operation on pacifying Syria. Italy also hopes that Russia can help to counter the spreading chaos in Libya, one of Italy's main oil suppliers. From Rome, the threat posed by IS on the other side of the Mediterranean appears more pressing than Putin's assertiveness in Ukraine.

Italy advocates forms of positive engagement with Russia by stressing that the EU's priority should be to manage its relationship with Russia so as to minimise the risk of creating new dividing lines in Europe. While Italy was quite isolated in this position last year, this has become almost the mainstream view within the EU in 2016.

Italian experts also tend to downgrade Russia as a threat for Italy and the international system.

The 2016 ISPI (Italian Institute for International Political Studies) Report Scenari Globali e l'Italia (Global Scenarios and Italy), which assesses Italy's external projection and the way the country pursues its own interests at the international level, confirms that Russia is not considered a danger to the country (The assessment is based on a scorecard developed by Italian foreign policy 130 experts – journalists, academics, think tanks, entrepreneurs). As shown in the graph below, the economic crisis and instability in Syria are at the top of the perceived menaces (25%), followed by populism (22%). Only a slim three per cent maintains that the deterioration of relations with Russia can be a threat for Italy.

---

18   Although 90 per cent of all Italians identify as Roman Catholic, only about a third of them are actively practicing Roman Catholics.

What are the major threats for Italy?

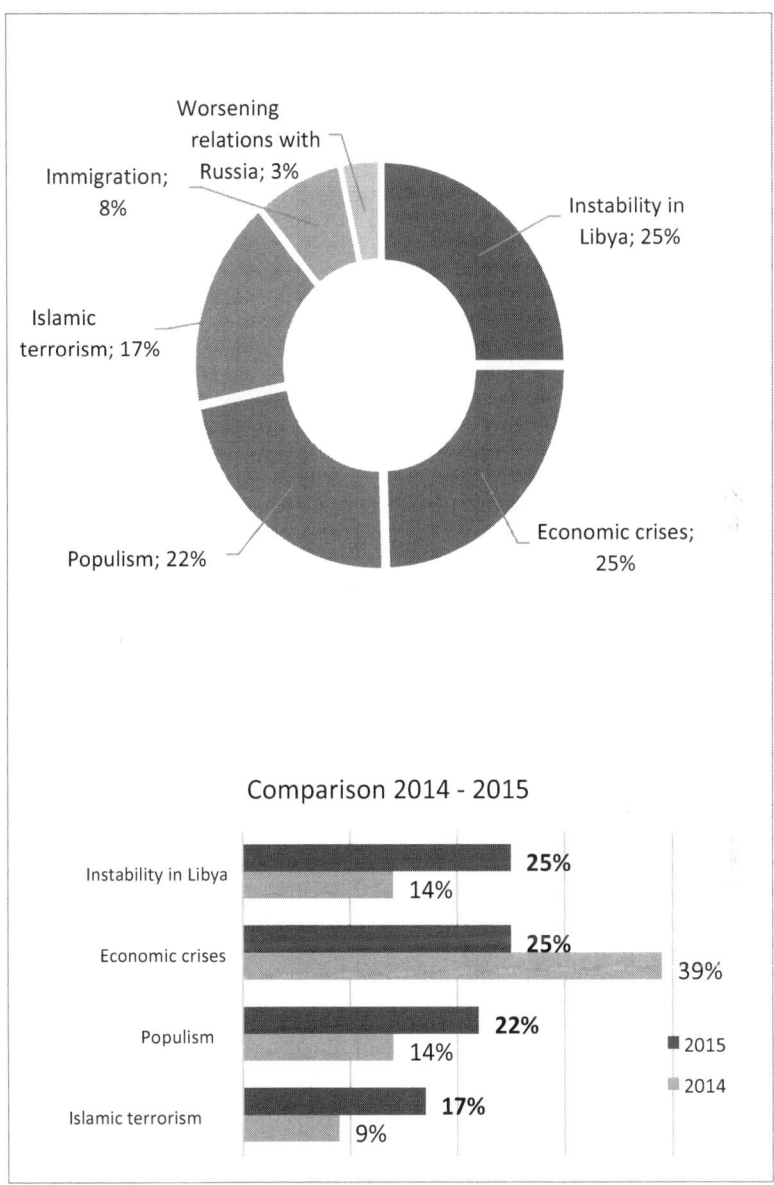

Scource: ISPI, Scenari Globali e l'Italia, 2016.

The Italian experts maintain that President Vladimir Putin is currently the most influential person in the area of international affairs (42%), followed, at some distance, by Barack Obama (28%).

Who is the most influential person?

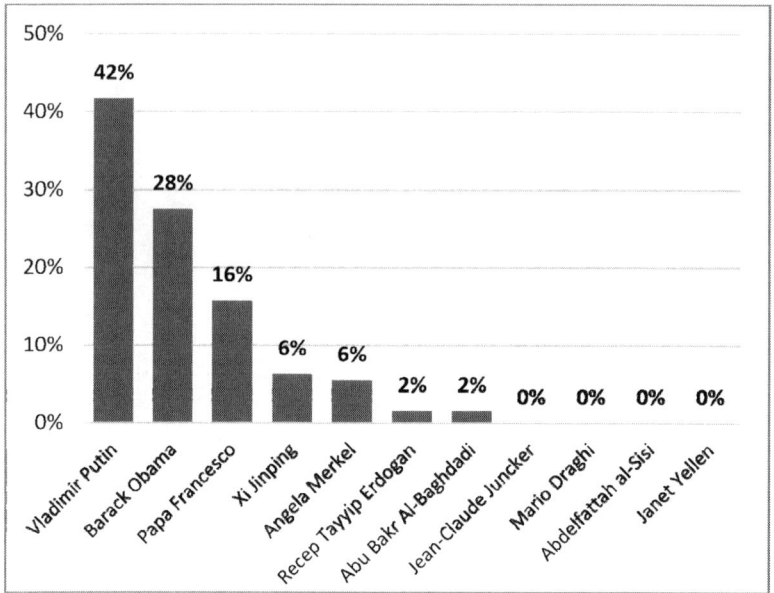

Scource: ISPI, Scenari Globali e l'Italia, 2016.

Finally, Italian experts think that Russia was a rising power in 2015, especially due to its concomitant engagement in different areas outside the traditional post-Soviet space.

In fact, while public attitudes in Italy toward both Russia and its leader have been in steady decline over the past few years, they have rebounded slightly in the past twelve months, according to a Pew Research Center poll on the public opinion of NATO. This would suggest that both at a level of elites and public opinion, Russia is not considered an enemy of Italy.

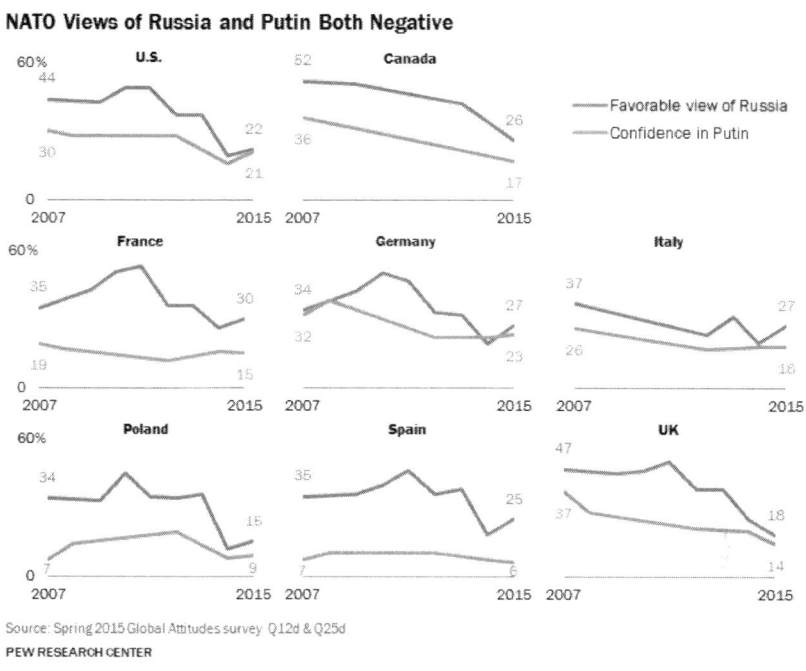

NATO Views of Russia and Putin Both Negative

Favorable view of Russia
Confidence in Putin

Source: Spring 2015 Global Attitudes survey Q12d & Q25d
PEW RESEARCH CENTER

Source: http://www.pewglobal.org/2015/06/10/1-nato-public-opinion-wary-of-russia-leary-of-action-on-ukraine/.

Conclusions

After 1989, Russian relations with all European countries improved, but links to Italy grew particularly strong, regardless of who was in power in Rome – or Moscow. As a result, Italy maintains a strategic partnership with Russia, founded on interdependence and common interests. The partnership has benefitted from growing trade and a shared view, maintained by all recent Italian governments, that Russia is a strategic partner rather than a threat.

But the Italian government also recognises that there is a risk that Russia may try to use this special *entente* against the EU to divide and rule. Rome, therefore, favours greater co-operation with Russia through EU channels and instruments. It would seem that bringing Russia closer to Europe now presents Italian foreign policy with one of its greatest challenges. Italy has prompted the idea in the European arena that Russia needs to be engaged and not isolated. Therefore, Italy is working on Russia re-engagement. For this to be possible, sanctions should not be renewed; instead, Russia should be invited to co-operate on less politicized issues, such as modernization.

Are Russia, China and the US more or less influential compared with last year?

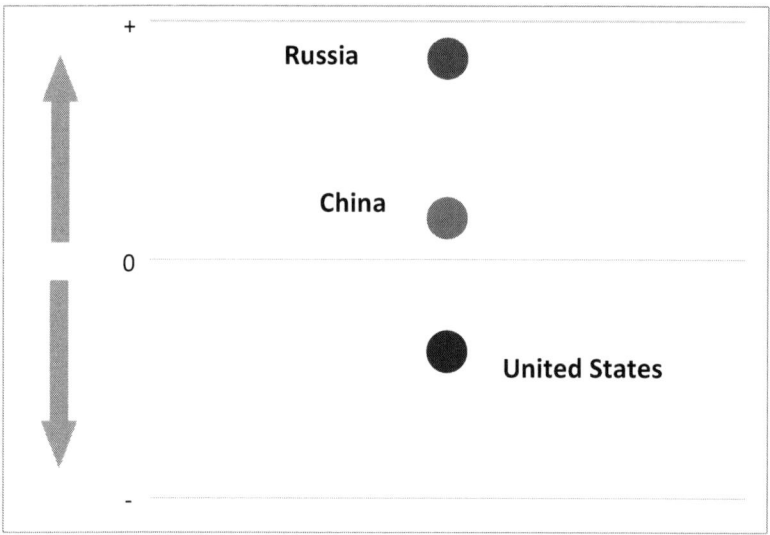

Source: http://www.pewglobal.org/2015/06/10/1-nato-public-opinion-wary-of-russia-leary-of-action-on-ukraine/.

Some Italian foreign policy-makers think that Eastern European countries and Germany are too weighed down by 20th century history to fulfil this role, while EU countries, which are anxious not to weaken NATO, tend to be cautious about close liaisons with Russia. Italy is trying to become a sort of bridge between the EU and Moscow or, at least, this is the argument used by the current Prime Minister Renzi when asked about his meetings with Putin.

Within the country, some populist parties have embraced a pro-Russian stance and criticize the EU for imposing the policy of sanctions that is causing a lot of economic damage to many sectors of the Italian economy. Sanctions have contributed to deepening Italian dissatisfaction with Brussels. It appears that Euroscepticism fits well with a pro-Russian approach.

Andris Spruds

Russia in Latvia's Security Narrative: Back to Securitization

Russia has been an important neighbour and regional actor for Latvia since regaining independence in 1991. Russia has been perceived in Latvia as both a significant trading partner and a regionally ambitious successor to the Soviet Union. Relations between the two countries have remained complicated and the narrative in Latvia on Russia has experienced transformation and adjustments, though with a strong emphasis on security. Latvia's security narrative vis-à-vis Russia has reflected both the small nation's security concerns and the necessity of pragmatism in relations with a large neighbouring country.

Evolving Perceptions and Narratives on Russia

Latvia's security narrative on Russia has undergone several phases and developments over the last 25 years. The general dynamic and particular emphasis in the narrative have been shaped by the character of the bilateral relationship and wider regional and multilateral security developments and perceptions. Latvia and Russia experienced a rather tumultuous and tense relationship back in the 1990s after the two countries began interaction as two independent entities. This has had a formative impact on societal perceptions and security narratives. The withdrawal of the Russian troops, citizenship legislation and the status of the Russian-speaking minority, as well as the Baltic quest for membership in transatlantic structures, became the contentious issues in Latvia's relations with Russia. Russia clearly became securitized in Latvia's narrative. In the meantime, Western countries, especially the United States, were perceived in the Baltics states as instrumental and indispensible partners for moderating Russia's reactions and addressing the insecurity concerns.

The integration of the Baltic countries into the European Union and NATO in 2004 contributed to expectations in Latvia about the prospective normalization of the relationship. The feeling of insecurity subsided somewhat. While Estonia experienced a "Bronze Soldier" crisis with Russia in 2007, Latvia was able to finalize the lingering border agreement in the context of "pragmatic" co-operation with Russia. The "pragmatic" narrative was both the result of a thaw in the bilateral relations and the change in Russia's foreign policy focus. It helped to partially de-securitize the narrative on Russia in Latvia. Russia's war with Georgia re-invoked the unfavourable ghosts of the past and re-invigorated the concerns over Russia's geopolitical ambitions in the post-Soviet space. The letter sent to the new Obama administration by Central and East European (including Latvian) leaders in 2009 suggested being cautious with assertive Russia. This indicated existing hesitation and ingrained mistrust in the region for the prospects of closer Russian-Western engagement.[1]

However, the economic crisis provided a new window of opportunity to reshape the security discourse in the West and Latvia. The efforts to counter the harsh economic crisis in Latvia in 2009 facilitated a de-securitization and economization of Latvia's narrative vis-à-vis Russia. This Western-Russian rapprochement, manifested in the US-Russia reset and the EU-Russia modernization agenda, was implicitly accepted and included in Latvia's security narrative. The official visit by Latvia's President Valdis Zatlers to Moscow in December 2010 was a positive culmination of bilateral and multilateral engagement. The mutual charm diplomacy and a considerable increase in economic interaction demonstrated the opening in bilateral relations and the potential for a new page in Latvia's perceptions and narrative on Russia. There were even expectations of dealing with sensitive history issues and harmonizing the respective diverging historical narratives. A visit of the Russian president to Latvia was discussed. This opening notwithstanding, it never came to pass. Russia's relations with the West were steadily cooling off after Vladimir Putin's return to the presidential office in Russia in 2012. Moreover, history and collective memory remained among the formative elements of Latvian perceptions and, consequently, of the country's foreign policy and security narratives.

The Soviet occupation is an enduring traumatic experience for the Latvian society. According to several surveys, around one third of the respondents reported that they had someone in their family deported, executed or imprisoned by the Soviet regime (by comparison, five per cent reported having suffered from Nazi regime, while six per cent reported having suffered from both).[2] This explains the annual tensions that arise around "Victory Day" on 9 May, widely celebrated by Russians in Russia and elsewhere, including in Latvia. For Latvians, the Soviet victory over the Nazis meant just a replacement of repressive occupation regimes. It caused controversy in Latvian society when President Vaira Vike-Freiberga visited Victory Day celebrations in Moscow in 2005. The president explicitly pinpointed the importance of promoting Latvia's historical perspective internationally and implicitly to strengthening ties with Western partners through a gesture of reconciliation with Russia. The divergent historical collective memory, however, continuously divides Latvia and Russia as well as Latvi-

---

1   Andris Spruds "Entrapment in the Discourse of Danger? Latvian-Russian Interaction in the Context of European Integration", in: Eiki Berg and Piret Ehin (eds.), Identity and Foreign Policy: Baltic Russian Relations and European Integration (Ashgate, 2009), pp. 101-116.

2   Nils Muižnieks, "History, Memory and Latvian Foreign Policy," in: Nils Muižnieks (ed.) The Geopolitics of History in Latvian-Russian Relations, Academic Press of the University of Latvia, 2011, p. 22.

ans and the Russian-speaking minority in Latvia. This also has a direct impact on the security narratives that are significantly strengthened in the context of deteriorating relations between Russia and the West. The annexation of Crimea was a conspicuous demonstration of this.

Crimea as a Game Changer in Latvia's Narratives

The annexation of Crimea and the war in the Eastern Ukraine have strengthened the concerns in Latvia over Russia's ambitions and its influence in the neighbouring countries. Russia's interference in Ukraine has been perceived in Latvia as a direct challenge to the regional and global security architecture and overall stability. The war in Ukraine has invoked the notions of existential threats and insecurity in Latvia. As a result, the narrative in Latvia on Russia has, once more, been thoroughly securitized. There has been strong political and societal support for sanctions imposed on Russia for the annexation of Crimea and interference in Eastern Ukraine. In Latvia's narrative, the sanctions are both a principled response to the Russian violations of international norms and a justified necessity to demonstrate a joint Western position to preclude any further assertiveness of Russia in the neighbourhood. Deterrence and the deployment of NATO troops in the Baltic countries have been perceived as a next step for addressing the justified concerns about insecurity in the context of Russia's sabre-rattling in the region.

Societal attitudes in Latvia have largely correlated with perceptions of unfavourable international developments, the country's increasing security challenges and governmental narratives.[3] In the context of the crisis in Ukraine, Latvian society has seen Russia's military threat to Latvia as feasible and probable rather than hypothetical. Apart from the war in Ukraine, Russia's massive military exercises and demonstrations of strength close to the borders of the Baltic countries further strengthened those perceptions. The critical assessment of Russia's conduct and concerns about an escalation of the military conflict to Latvia were at the top of societal concerns in Latvia in 2014 and 2015. At the early stage of the conflict in Ukraine, in early March 2014, 58 percent of respondents in an opinion poll believed that Russia had no grounds to deploy military forces to Crimea and Eastern Ukraine. However, ethnic affiliation reflected some divergences and pluralism in Latvia's societal attitudes. In the above-mentioned poll, 77 percent of Latvians agreed with condemnation of Russia's actions, while only 24 percent of other ethnicities were of the same opinion. Support or partial support of Russia's actions was expressed by only 17 percent of Latvians but 66

---

3   Arturs Bikovs, Ilvija Bruge and Andris Spruds, "Russian Presence and Influence in Latvia", Report, Latvian Institute of International Affairs, December 2016.

percent of the representatives of ethnic minorities.[4] Other research from spring of 2015 demonstrated that 60 percent of the Russian-speaking population saw Vladimir Putin in a positive light, while this opinion was shared by only 12.1 percent of ethnic Latvians.[5] These findings demonstrate that Latvia is experiencing a divergence of societal interpretations and respective narratives.

At the same time, some convergence is also observable. As the conflict in Ukraine gradually entered the stage of a "frozen conflict" and NATO demonstrated its reassurance and deterrence in the region, security concerns have lessened. A survey from June 2016 showed less insecurity and a potential for improving relations with Russia. 35 percent of the respondents indicated that Latvia should move towards more positive relations with Russia (ethnic Latvians – 24 percent; Russian speakers – 55 percent) and not engage in the Ukraine crisis, while 26 percent preferred manoeuvring between Russia and the West (Latvians – 21 percent; Russian speakers – 34 percent). A rather modest 26 percent agreed with the government position and narrative of condemning Russia's actions in Ukraine (40 percent of Latvians and only three percent of Russian speakers). The inquiry also demonstrated that 48 percent of the Latvian society sees Russia as a threat while, at the same time, 70 percent believe that Russia is crucial for the Latvian economy. Increasing scepticism about sanctions is the result of the perceived limited impact of Western sanctions on Russia and the detrimental effect of Russian counter-sanctions on some of the Latvia's businesses. In the wider context of societal perceptions, a majority of Latvia's population demonstrated a strong sense of belonging to Latvia. However, 28.3 percent of the Russian-speaking respondents expressed a sense of their belonging to Russia as opposed to only 3.6 percent of Latvian respondents, which demonstrated the limits to convergence of opinion along ethnic lines.[6] These data once more pointed to the existing challenges in forming a societally shared narrative in Latvia on Russia and Western-Russian relations.

To conclude, the Latvian government's strategic preferences and narratives largely correlate with dominant societal perceptions on security and international priorities and challenges. The strong transatlantic affiliation and close relationship with Western partners have been perceived as major security guarantees. At the same time, Russia is perceived as a major strategic challenge for Latvia due to negative historical experiences, the assertive Russian rhetoric regarding its neighbours and its military activities in prox-

---

4   "Vai saskatāt pamatu Krievijas karaspēka ievešanai un izvietošanai Ukrainas Krimā un potenciāli arī citos Austrumukrainas apgabalos?", LETA, March 2014.

5   Ģirts Vikmanis, "Latvijas krievi atbalsta Putinu. Ko nu?", Latvijas Avīze, 12 May 2015; "Putina darbību pozitīvi vērtē 60% Latvijas krievvalodīgo," Ir, 10 May 2015.

6   "Sabiedrības destabilizācijas iespējamība Latvijā: potenciālie nacionālās drošības apdraudējumi Latvijā," Latvijas Nacionālās aizsardzības akadēmijas Drošības un stratēģiskās pētniecības centrs, June 2016, at: http://www.naa.mil.lv/~/media/NAA/AZPC/Publikacijas/WP%2004-2016.ashx.

imity to Latvia's borders. Traumatic historical experiences especially create considerable emotional and political stabilizers in forming the security narrative vis-à-vis Russia. The annexation of Crimea by Russia and the war in Eastern Ukraine have clearly strengthened the security aspect in Latvia's narrative. Russia has, once more, been strongly securitized in Latvia's societal perceptions and narratives.

Barend ter Haar

Dutch narratives about Russian-Western relations

Summary

Over the centuries, relations between the Netherlands and Russia had been good (partly because Germany lay in between). After the Second World War, the Netherlands usually followed the lead of the United States in its relations with the USSR. Since the end of the Cold War it has, with some success, concentrated on developing mutually beneficial relations, mainly in the economic field, hoping that Russia would gradually develop into a stable democracy built on the rule of law.

The Netherlands does not have a tradition of independent strategic thinking. When problems, such as the Russian occupation of the Crimea, arose it usually followed the lead of its larger allies in NATO and EU. However, the downing of flight MH17 by a Russian Buk missile, which killed a large number of Dutch citizens, and the Dutch referendum that rejected the Association Agreement between the EU and Ukraine are issues that the Dutch government will have to address itself. Dutch political parties and public opinion are unused to that.

Introduction

For a proper understanding of Dutch narratives about relations between Russia and the West, it is useful to start with a short description of the characteristics of Dutch foreign policy, in particular the three main strands of thinking about Dutch foreign policy and the consequences of coalition governments for the development of a coherent foreign policy strategy.[1]

Three Dutch Views on Foreign Policy

The three main strands of thinking that define Dutch foreign policy can be characterized in short by the words *trade*, *engagement* and *withdrawal*.

The champions of international *engagement* believe that the Netherlands should contribute to a peaceful, just and prosperous world, both out of self-interest and as a moral duty. They want the Netherlands to be an active sup-

---

1   The author thanks Minke Meinders, Tony van der Togt and Dick Zandee for their critical comments. I made good use of Russia, our Distant Neighbour: The Burden of Conventional Beliefs, written by Hugo Klijn. Of course, all mistakes and simplifications remain mine.

porter of the European Union, the United Nations and other international organisations as well as of international co-operation in general.

The proponents of *trade* argue that, as international trade has made the Dutch among the most affluent people in the world, the main objective of Dutch foreign policy should be the promotion of Dutch foreign trade and investment. They usually, but not always, recognize the importance for international trade and investment of promoting international stability and rule of law

The advocates of *withdrawal* fear that international engagement comes at the expense of Dutch people themselves. They are afraid that international co-operation and immigration only serve the interests of a highly educated elite and endanger the position of the Dutch middle class.

Championing international engagement and championing withdrawal are mutually exclusive, but neither of these groups is against trade *per se*. The three strands do not neatly coincide with political parties, but it seems fair to say that most politicians of the mainstream parties feel affinity with the engagement strand, adherents of the trade strand will mainly be found within the conservative-liberal party VVD, while the proponents of a withdrawal from international engagement can be found at both ends of the political spectrum, with the populist Partij voor de Vrijheid (Party for Freedom, PVV) and with the former Maoist Socialistische Partij (SP).

Until the recent rise of the PVV and the SP, a broad consensus existed about foreign policy, at least among the foreign policy elite. Some wanted to contribute more to international co-operation than others, but they all agreed that the interests of the Netherlands were best served by a combination of trade and promotion of an international legal order, *inter alia* by active membership in the European Union and the United Nations.

However, consultative referenda that were held in 2005 and 2016 made clear that this policy was not based on a similar consensus among the Dutch people at large.

The referendum on the Association Agreement between the European Union and Ukraine, which was held in the Netherlands on 6 April 2016, seemed to be about Dutch policy with respect to Ukraine and Russia. However, appearances were deceptive: the people who took the initiative for the referendum openly admitted that they were not interested at all in Ukraine. They said that their main purpose was to destroy the EU or to withdraw the Netherlands from it, a so-called 'Nexit'.[2]

In the referendum, a substantive majority of 61% voted against the Association Agreement (although the turnout was only about 32 %). It is doubtful whether these people would also vote for a Nexit, but the outcome illus-

---

2   http://www.nrc.nl/next/2016/03/31/oekraine-kan-ons-niets-schelen-1606419: "We don't care at all about Ukraine" said Arjan van Dixhoorn, chairman of the citizens committee that took the initiative for the referendum. Its founders have only one goal: "...destroying the European Union or driving the Netherlands out of the EU, a Nexit."

trates the gap between a large segment of the Dutch people and their parliament, which had accepted the Association Agreement with about 80% of the votes.

In several respects, the referendum on the Association Agreement was a repetition of the consultative referendum that was held in 2005 about the proposed Constitution of the European Union, although in 2005 the turnout was twice as high (63,3%). About 80% of the members of parliament were in favour of the proposed Constitutional Treaty, but in the referendum 61.6% of the voters rejected it.

The Absence of a Government-wide Strategy

In 1974, in his seminal study *A faithful ally: The Netherlands and the Atlantic Alliance (1960-1971),* Van Staden characterized Dutch foreign policy as "reactive rather than active. In general [Dutch] governments were sitting on the fence and reacted only to external impulses."[3] More than forty years later, this remains a fairly accurate description of Dutch foreign policy.[4] The United States provides security to the Netherlands through NATO and, in return, the Netherlands supports American foreign policy as much as possible, e.g. by providing military forces for operations in Iraq and Afghanistan, leaving it to the US to worry about long-term strategies.

The most important difference between 1974 and 2016 is the development of a common European foreign policy from an informal consultation process between nine member states in 1974 to the current Common Foreign and Security Policy of 28 member states supported by the European External Action Service (EEAS) led by the High Representative of the Union for Foreign Affairs and Security Policy.

Nowadays, bilateral relations with countries such as Russia and positions in international organizations are usually coordinated at European level. However, when important national interests, such as energy relations with Russia, are in play, countries such as the Netherlands often give priority to their national interests. As the Dutch Advisory Council on International Affairs (AIV) stated in a recent advisory statement: „The Netherlands has a longstanding trade and investment relationship with Russia. It would not be realistic to subordinate it entirely to the imposition of sanctions in response to the Ukraine crisis."[5]

The (unofficial) explanation of the absence of government-wide strategic thinking in the Netherlands is that the space for manoeuvre of a small

---

3   Alfred van Staden: Een trouwe bondgenoot. Baarn 1974, p. 300.
4   See Barend ter Haar and Eva Maas: Threats and challenges for the Netherlands, Clingendael 2014, at https://www.clingendael.nl/publication/threats-and-challenges-netherlands.
5   The EU's dependence on Russian gas; How an integrated EU policy can reduce it, Advisory Letter No. 26, June 2014.

country is too small for strategic thinking to be of any use. In practice, so goes the argument, important decisions are taken *ad hoc* in the light of the circumstances, not on the basis of a long-term strategy. However, this argument is flawed, because decisions with a long-term impact, e.g. on membership in international organisations and investments in military capacities, do require, at the very minimum, an implicit idea about threats and challenges and how to deal with them: i.e. an implicit strategy.

A more convincing explanation for the absence of government-wide strategic thinking is that the Netherlands is always governed by coalitions of at least two, but more often three, four or even five political parties. To prevent constant wrangling among ministers from different political parties, the mandates of the ministries are clearly demarcated. This helps to prevent government crises, but impedes the development of common strategies that transcend the mandates of individual ministries. The negative consequences of a lack of a government-wide strategy are felt in the field of international co-operation in particular. In this field, for example, it is not an exception for the Dutch Ministries of Education and of Public Health, on the one hand, and the Ministry of Foreign Affairs, on the other, to work at cross purposes.[6]

Another consequence of coalition governments is the relatively weak co-ordinating role of the Dutch Prime Minister. Light co-ordination mechanisms exist but, in practice, ministries are free to follow their independent paths without giving much attention to wider geo-political and strategic considerations.[7] The unavoidable consequence is that the policies of different Dutch ministries are sometimes contradictory, e. g. on energy relations with Russia.

Dutch Concerns about Russia

The history of political, economic, cultural and strategic relations between the Netherlands and Russia is long and eventful. Since its independence, the Netherlands has been occupied twice: by France following the French revolution and by Germany in the Second World War. In both cases, Russia was invaded too: in 1812 by France and in 1941 by Germany. By repelling both invasions Russia/the Soviet Union indirectly played a major part in restoring Dutch independence. The Netherlands did not extend diplomatic recognition to the Soviet Union until 1942, after the USSR became part of the coalition against Germany. After the Second World War, political relations had their

---

6   See Barend ter Haar: Blinde vlekken van het buitenlands beleid; Clingendael Policy Brief No. 11, August 2012.
7   This explains why the Policy brief on relations with Russia pays little attention to scholarships, public health and the environment and why the Policy brief on international security, although it stresses the need for a comprehensive approach that includes infectious diseases, drugs and climate change, was not countersigned by the ministries that are competent in these areas.

ups and downs. Currently, the Netherlands is one of the largest economic partners of Russia. In 2011 the Netherlands was the largest export destination for Russia (\$ 46 billion).[8] In 2014 the Netherlands had to share first place with China because exports had gone down to \$39 billion[9], possibly as a result of sanctions.

During the Cold War, most Dutch citizens were concerned about the possibility of a Third World War between NATO and the Soviet Union, but nowadays, few Dutch people worry about Russia. Although a sizable minority (45%) is moderately to severely worried about the general international political situation, this is mostly because of the refugee problem, terrorism, the situation in the Middle East and internal EU problems and not because of Russia.[10]

The position of the Dutch government is different. It is seriously concerned about the way Russia seems to be turning away from the international legal order. As mentioned above, the Netherlands does not have an independent and government-wide geopolitical strategy. It usually follows the lead of its larger allies or leaves it to decision making within the EU and NATO. However, the downing of Malaysian Airlines flight 17 in July 2014, killing 298 people, among which were 196 Dutch citizens, has made it difficult for the government to wait and see how its larger allies will react.

Speaking more generally about relations with Russia, the parliamentary leader of the conservative-liberal party VVD, Halbe Zijlstra, said at a meeting of his party on 21 May 2016: "It's very possible that this country is going to get into a war with Russia."[11] But others in his party are less alarmist and other parties seem not to be very concerned.

The Dutch public has, so far, shown little interest in a fundamental discussion about relations with Russia. Currently, a major point of contention within Dutch society is the broader question of whether the Netherlands should actively participate in international co-operation or withdraw behind its borders.

---

8 https://en.wikipedia.org/wiki/List_of_the_largest_trading_partners_of_Russia. Nrs. two and three were China (\$35 billion) and Germany (\$31 billion). It should, however, be noted that an important part of Dutch imports from Russia was transit trade.

9 http://atlas.media.mit.edu/en/profile/country/rus/#Destinations.

10 According to polls in the first half of 2016, SCP: Kwartaalbericht van het Continu Onderzoek Burgerperspectieven; Nr.1 March 2016 and Nr. 2 June 2016, at: https://www.scp.nl/Publicaties.

11 Trouw 23/05/2016: Slijp de messen, vul de kelders, graaf de greppels. "Het is heel goed mogelijk", zei Halbe Zijlstra, fractieleider van de VVD dit weekend, "dat dit land te maken gaat krijgen met een oorlog met Rusland."

Who is Responsible for the Current Situation?

A large majority of the Dutch people believes that Russia is directly or indirectly responsible for the downing of flight MH17.[12] However, Van Dixhoorn, one of the promoters of the referendum on the Association Agreement stated: „You know the history of Crimea? There has been a coup and Russia has supported the local Russian population. That is how you can see it also. We are the cause of that annexation, because of the association agreement that has divided Ukraine".[13]

The Dutch government explained its position in two letters to parliament: a policy brief on international security on 14 November 2014[14] and a policy brief on relations with Russia on 13 May 2015.[15] In these papers, the government avoided discussing the responsibility for the downing of MH17, but stated clearly that Russia bears a heavy responsibility for the current security crisis in Europe. By showing disregard for international law, European security arrangements and human rights, Russia has caused a breach of trust that cannot be easily healed.

Key Elements of the Developments in Russian-Western Relations

The end of the Cold War was perceived in the Netherlands as a victory of Western values of freedom and democracy.[16] For a long time, it was widely expected that Russia would develop into a more or less Western type of democracy. Relations between the two countries diversified and intensified. Trade and investment grew, but also cultural, legal and scientific co-operation. As part of its Matra programme for social transformation, the Netherlands financed projects in support of a plural democracy. Typical examples were a project to support the improvement of civic education in Kaluga Region and projects to support public participation and NGO influence on environmental management.

However, with the election of President Putin, the window of opportunity for Western countries to promote the transformation of Russia started to close. In 2007, he made clear that foreign support for NGOs in fields such as

---

12   See for example: http://www.dagelijksestandaard.nl/2015/08/peiling-nederland-wijst-onomwonden-rusland-aan-als-schuldige-voor-het-neerhalen-van-de-mh17/.

13   See footnote 2.

14   Beleidsbrief internationale veiligheid DVB/VD-119/14 of 14 November 2014.

15   Beleidsbrief betrekkingen met Rusland DEU-175/2015 of 13 May 2015.

16   See: How should Europe respond to Russia? The Dutch view by Tony van der Togt, at: http://www.ecfr.eu/article/commentary_how_should_europe_respond_to_russia_the_dutch_view311233. For a short history of diplomatic relations between the Netherlands and Russia (in Dutch) see: Tony van der Togt: Wantrouwen en betrokkenheid: het verhaal van een complexe relatie, Diplomatieke betrekkingen tussen Nederland en Rusland 1942-2013, in: N. Kraft van Ermel/H. van Koningsbrugge, Nederland en Rusland, een paar apart?, Groningen, 2013.

human rights and environmental protection was no longer required. A few years later, the Netherlands government itself decided to cut back drastically on the funds available for social transformation. The initial hope that Russia would develop into a modern European country sometime soon was no longer considered a realistic perspective.

For a long time, many felt that geo-politics was something of the past, that large cuts in the defence budget were possible and that Dutch foreign policy could now concentrate on trade and investment. It is only after the interference of Russia in Ukraine that Dutch mainstream parties came to realize that the Dutch (and Western) approach to Russia had been naïve.

Factors Influencing Russian-Western Relations

Russia and the Netherlands (and other Western countries) share many interests, for example, in the economic field. Although the volume of bilateral trade between the Netherlands and Russia declined by more than ten per cent in comparison with the previous year, in 2014 it still amounted to € 24.6 billion, about 3.4 per cent of total Dutch trade.

Other fields where the interests of Russia and the Netherlands (and other Western countries) seem to coincide are the fight against terrorism, piracy, non-proliferation and transboundary crime, cyber security, climate change and arms control. It would also seem that they have a common interest in a well-functioning UN-system and in solving regional crises, such as in and around Syria. Even co-operation between the EU and the Eurasian Economic Union could be in the common interest.[17]

In its policy brief about relations with Russia, the Dutch government points out the long-standing non-governmental contacts, *inter alia* in the field of culture and emphasizes that it is important to continue people-to-people contacts, cultural and scientific exchange, particularly when the initiatives come from civil society.

The prevailing view in Dutch government circles is that because Russia and the Netherlands (and, more generally, the West) share numerous interests, the challenge is to co-operate in these areas without giving the impression that it can be "business as usual" as long Russia continues to interfere in Ukraine.[18]

---

17 See: Tony van der Togt, Francesco S. Montesano, Iaroslav Kozak: From Competition to Compatibility, Striking a Eurasian balance in EU-Russia relations, Clingendael 2015.

18 See p. 12 of the explanation of the budget of the Ministry of Foreign affairs for 2017: „Rusland ondersteunt de separatisten met onder meer militaire, financiële en politieke middelen en is zelf nog steeds direct betrokken met militaire aanwezigheid op Oekraïens grondgebied. Zolang hierin geen verandering komt, zal het noodzakelijk blijven om de druk op Rusland door middel van sancties te handhaven en tegelijkertijd in te zetten op de-escalatie door middel van dialoog."

That view might not be supported by those Dutch people who believe that the Netherlands would be better off if the government would concentrate on the problems within its own borders and let other countries look after themselves. These same people often show more understanding for the assertive behaviour of Russia than the Dutch government does.

How to Return to a Co-operative Russia – West Relationship?

Dutch views on the future of relations with Russia reflect the three strands of thinking mentioned above.

The current Dutch Minister of Foreign Affairs, the social-democrat Bert Koenders, clearly belongs to the school of engagement. His first priority is to bring Russia to the point of agreeing to a sustainable solution to the conflict in Donbass.[19] This will require a combination of pressure and dialogue. For this policy to be effective, NATO and the EU will have to continue to work in concert. Furthermore, it is essential to avoid the trap of *zero sum* thinking about exclusive zones of influence. The question is not, as some people believe, whether Ukraine will become part of a European or a Eurasian empire, but whether it will get a chance to develop fruitful relations with both the countries to its East and the countries to its West.

The basis for the Dutch Russia policy should remain that Russia and the West have many common interests and that long-term stability in Europe requires a *modus vivendi* with Russia.[20] In principle, this all fits in nicely with the five principles for EU-Russia relations, on which the EU Foreign Affairs Council decided in March 2016.[21]

A prominent representative of the interests of trade is Hans de Boer, president of the Confederation of Netherlands Business and Employers VNO-NCW. He expressed doubts about the effectiveness of sanctions and said he fears that continued sanctions will help Brazilian and Chinese firms to take over the Russian market, at the expense of Dutch interests.[22] In practice, some Dutch agricultural products boycotted by Russia have found other markets and other firms have profited from Russian import substitution for which Dutch technology is very welcome.

The supporters of withdrawal come from many different angles. It is, therefore, difficult to tell their views on future relations with Russia. On the basis of anecdotal evidence and the outcome of the referendum on the Association Agreement with Ukraine, it seems that many of them believe that by supporting Ukraine, the West has unnecessarily provoked Russia. However, the populist PVV pays little attention to relations with Russia. It is also

---

19   Beleidsbrief betrekkingen met Rusland of 13 mei 2015; DEU-175/2015.
20   Beleidsbrief betrekkingen met Rusland of 13 mei 2015; DEU-175/2015, p. 9.
21   Statement EU HR Mogherini, at: eeas.europa.eu/statements-eeas/2016/160314_02_en.htm
22   Hans de Boer in WNL Op Zondag on 7 September 2014.

unlikely that Dutch relations with Russia will receive much attention in the upcoming election campaign. After all, even the Ukraine referendum, in which some pro-Russian arguments were used by extreme left and right parties, was more about withdrawing from the EU than about anything else.

Conclusion

After the loss of its colonial empire, the Netherlands also lost the ambition to conduct an independent foreign policy. Instead it has proved itself a faithful and active member of NATO and the European Union and a staunch supporter of development co-operation. However, in 2005, a referendum made clear that a majority of the population felt uneasy about the process of ever deeper co-operation and integration. Since that time, not only the populist parties on the right and on the left, but also the main parties in the political centre have lost their interest in an active foreign policy, leading to lower budgets for diplomacy, international co-operation and defence. However, the downing of flight MH17 painfully proved that foreign policy is about more than trade promotion. It is unclear what conclusions Dutch political parties and government will draw from this for relations with Russia.

Andrei Zagorski

Russian Narratives

Preliminary remarks

A few general remarks need to be made before describing the narratives present in the Russian debates on the European security order.

The discussion of Russian and Western narratives pertaining to European security after the end of the Cold War has been on the rise since the beginning of the Ukraine crisis. Their comparative analysis has already been the subject of a number of publications (see, for example, Atlantic Council, ELN, RIAC 2015, Frear, Kulesa 2016, Panel of Eminent Persons 2015). This seems to reflect a belated realization, particularly in the West, that it does (and did) not properly understand Russia and its policies. The same concepts often reflect very different, if not diverging meanings in Moscow and the West (Liik 2015). The recent efforts to explore and better understand the differences between the mainstream narratives are meant to narrow this gap in understanding, thus making Russia and the West more predictable for each other.

It is notable that most, if not all, contemporary projects exploring relevant narratives pertaining to European security originate in the West. Little attention is paid to the issue in Moscow. This may reflect the fact that Russian political elites are confident that they appropriately understand Western and, particularly, US policies. This highlights an important deficit on the Russian side, since insufficient reflection and the lack of an open public debate on the relevant issues prevent Moscow from drawing appropriate lessons from recent developments.

At any time, in every society, there exists a variety of narratives on any specific issue. This is not only natural in pluralistic societies, but is also true for totalitarian and authoritarian political systems which seek to suppress or limit dissent. Narratives, in general, exhibit remarkable resilience and continuity over longer periods of time, although their impact may decline or rise over time. However, even if they remain dormant for a while, they may well resonate with the public mood, particularly at historic moments, but may also inform and prepare a change of public opinion in a more gradual way.

Russia is a good example of this. The different narratives of Russia-West that emerged in the Russian Empire in the second half of the 19th and early 20th century and offered distinct policy advice – the westernizers (or liberals), the Slavophiles and Eurasianists, as well as the "etatists" – were believed to have been eradicated during the Soviet period. However, they all resurfaced in the final years of the Soviet Union and, again, largely informed the public and political debates on domestic and foreign policy issues (Tsygankov 2006).

In contemporary research, scholars often deliberately imply the existence of a "single western" or a "single Russian" narrative (Frear/Kulesa 2016, p. 2) and concentrate on identified mainstream narratives. This is a legitimate reduction of research to narratives that are most relevant in the process of informing policy decisions. It is no less important, however, to explore why and how alternative narratives resonate in societies, inform change in policies and eventually become mainstream.

This is a complex process resulting from both comprehensive domestic developments as well as changes in the external environment. Although the assumption may be legitimate that the role of the external environment in this process is increasing, not least due to the globalization processes, the generation, evolution and resonation of specific narratives seem to remain primarily a product of the domestic 'fabric'. Should this assumption be true, the current debate on what went wrong in Russo-Western relations cannot be reduced to the simple question of what mistakes the West and/or Russia made in their policies towards each other.

The debate over narratives should not be confused with the search for historic truth. It is not about which narrative is right and which is wrong. It is about the tales existing in different societies and, thus, is probably most appropriately addressed by the methods of constructivism. The historic reconstruction of the developments of the last twenty five years should be left to historians, although the outcome of this reconstruction may have effects on the further life of contemporary narratives.

Threat Perceptions in Russia.

Earlier (Zagorski 2009) as well as more recent research conducted within the framework of the OSCE Network of Think Tanks and Academic Institutions (Zagorski 2014) revealed an important shift in Russian threat assessments over the past two decades away from concentrating on external military threats towards emphasizing the growing relevance of transnational non-military security threats and risks increasingly generated by non-state actors.

Threats that figured most prominently on the Russian security policy agenda before the Ukraine crisis included growing pressures from labour migration, particularly illegal migration, illegal narcotics trafficking, transnational organized crime, terrorism, armed conflicts in the proximity of Russian borders as well as trans-border environmental pollution challenges. Domestic sources of insecurity, such as economic and financial instability, vulnerability of the Russian economy to external shocks due to its dependence on volatile export markets, fears of criminalization of the economy and endemic corruption, the high probability of natural and man-made disasters, instability, or even insurgency in some regions of the Russian Federation, particularly in the North Caucasus, was increasingly emphasized as compared with external risks.

More recently, security concerns expanded to include perceived external challenges to the domestic political stability resulting from a 'regime change' policy attributed to the US. Concerns related to cyber security are also on the rise, but largely fit into a broader framework of information security, which includes concerns linked not only to possible cyber attacks or theft, but also to risks of external manipulation of public opinion as part of an external 'hybrid' attack.

During the high point of the Ukraine crisis, public opinion surveys registered a significant surge of fears of a possible war with the US. The probability of a war with other nations, including with other NATO member states, was, at the same time, ranked rather low in these surveys. Early in 2015, the regular survey, conducted by the All-Russian Center for Public Opinion Research, registered the highest level of such fears with 68 per cent of respondents admitting the existence of an external military threat to Russia. 53 per cent of them (36 per cent of the total sample) responded that this threat was presented by the US. In the fall of 2015, these fears declined, although still remained relatively high (VCIOM 2015, see also figures 1 and 2).

These findings are echoed by a recent experts' opinion survey conducted by the analytical centre of the Russian Academy of National Economy and Public Administration (RANEPA) under the President of Russia and presented in November 2016. According to the survey, experts believe that external threats and risks with which Russia is confronted prevail over those generated domestically. The major challenge for years to come is predicted to come from confrontation with the European Union and the US, not ruling out the possibility of a war with them, ranked as the second most important security threat. Other threats perceived by experts included economic challenges and terrorism (RANEPA 2016).

While public opinion obviously seems to be sensitive to tensions and confrontation between Russia and the US and while experts project years of confrontation, other research findings suggest that the recent developments have not fundamentally changed the previous more moderate threats assessments in Russia.

A recent Hamilton College Levitt Poll conducted in February and March 2016 reveals that, despite the fact that perceptions among Russian 'elites' of the US as a threat to Russia's national security are the highest since 1993, "more elites regard the inability to solve domestic problems as the 'utmost threat' to Russia's security compared to any other threat, including the growth of the US military" (Rivera 2016, p. 2, 8.). The inability to appropriately address domestic problems and terrorism were most often mentioned during the poll as the most pressing security risks to Russia. The US military threat was ranked third followed by concerns related to the eventuality of border conflicts between Russia and countries of the CIS, growth of ethnic tensions in Russia between Russians and other nationalities, an information war against Russia conducted by the West and the challenge of a possible 'colour' revolution which equates to challenges posed by alleged regime change policies of external actors (Rivera 2016, p. 9, see also figure 3).

The gap between the findings of the RANEPA and the Hamilton College Levitt Polls may be explained not only by the different sizes of their samples (the RANEPA survey sample is much smaller) but also, and probably more importantly, by the differences in the samples themselves. While the RANEPA survey was limited to experts more narrowly specializing in security issues, the Hamilton College Levitt Poll encompassed a broader range of Russian 'elites' and included face-to-face interviews with "high-ranking individuals working in Russia's federal bureaucracy, parliament, military and security agencies, private businesses, state-owned enterprises, academic research institutes, and media outlets" (Rivera 2016, p. 2).

Apparently, this difference matters. One of the interesting findings from the Hamilton College Levitt Poll is that, when Russian 'elites' are asked about potential threats, responses from the broader elite often do not reflect concerns frequently expressed by Russian officials (Rivera 2016, p. 10). On the one hand, this implies that extending the sample beyond narrow professional or politically motivated communities results in a less alarmist threat assessment. On the other hand, this would confirm the thesis of a pluralism of narratives existing in Russia parallel to each other.

Most recently adopted Russian security doctrines rather support the conclusion that domestic security concerns prevail over external military threat perceptions in Russia while, at the same time, there is an obvious shift in domestic security policy from emphasizing transnational threats generated by non-state actors towards the perceived need to protect political stability in Russia from external 'regime change' policies attributed primarily to the US. (Foreign Policy Conception 2016, Information Security Doctrine 2016, Military Doctrine 2014).

This general conclusion is also supported by the analysis of budgetary allocations. The rapid increase of the 'security' budget including law enforcement in excess of the 'national defence' expenditure has been a long-term trend in Russian policies (Zagorski 2014). This trend has not been reversed since 2014 (see figure 4). The most recent debates over the Russian federal budget for 2017 confirm this finding: confronted with the pressing need to reduce budgetary allocations, the Russian government finally decided to reduce defence allocations more radically than the security budget.

In this context, it is important to note that President Vladimir Putin has occasionally stressed that he would not think that the US would pose a military threat to Russia. He was more concerned that the US policy was often pursued at the expense of Russia's national interest (Putin 2014).

It is a widespread human habit to place the blame on someone else if things go wrong instead of asking the question about what I myself have done wrong. Russia is no exception to this general pattern (NYT 2016).

Indeed, in the Russian mainstream perception, it is the West in general and the US in particular which must be blamed for the current crisis. This thesis is boldly articulated by President Putin himself: we don't feel responsible for what happened, it was not our fault (Putin 2016c). This approach is generally supported by a majority of Russian 'elites' (Rivera 2016, p. 2). Still, even within the mainstream, while remaining critical toward the West, there is a notable flexibility with many admitting that every nation, including Russia, bears its part of the responsibility for the deterioration of Russia-West relations (Ivanov 2017, p. 149; Arbatova/Dynkin 2016, p. 71) and both sides have "committed gross assessment and strategic errors" (Entin/Entina 2016, p. 3).

The thesis that both the West and Russia share responsibility seems to be supported by large groups embracing both mainstream representatives as well as many nationalists, Eurasianists and liberals. It is rejected primarily by Russian officials, as well as right-wing nationalists who place the blame exclusively on the US, and some liberals (or super-liberals, as it was put in the discussion with the Reflection Group of the Network Project "European Security – Challenges at the Societal Level") who rather tend to place the blame on the Russian leadership under Putin alone. However, the latter view remains marginal in the Russian debate and is represented largely by Russians who have emigrated (such as Andrei Piontkovskiy, Andrei Illarionov, Yuriy Fedorov et al) and, for this reason, have little impact on the inner-Russian debate. But it is also represented by the political opposition within Russia (Yavlinskiy 2014; Zubov 2014).

There also appears to be a broad consensus across various narratives around the thesis that the Ukraine crisis did not mark the beginning of the crisis in Russia-West relations, but rather was a culmination of their deterioration that accumulated and deepened over a long period of time (Putin 2014a, Meshkov 2015; Kelin 2016). "The Ukrainian crisis has become a very explicit manifestation of the fragility of our relations. Both sides pursued their own policies toward Ukraine without any coordination or consultations with each other. [...] Through efforts on both sides we could have avoided the Ukrainian tragedy – at least in the dramatic form that it finally acquired (Atlantic Council, ELN, RIAC 2015, p. 20).

In general terms, the mainstream narrative in Russia places the blame on the arrogance of the West and particularly of the US which, for all the years after the end of the Cold War allegedly neglected and ignored Russia's articulated national interest and exploited its weakness (Frear/Kulesa 2016, p. 5).

As President Putin puts it: "We all know that, after the end of the Cold War, the world was left with one centre of dominance, and those who found themselves at the top of the pyramid were tempted to think that, since they are so powerful and exceptional, they know best what needs to be done" (Putin 2015). The current crisis "is in many respects the result of mistaken, hasty and, to some extent, over-confident choices made by some countries' elites a quarter-of-a-century ago", insists Putin. "Some countries that saw themselves as victors in the Cold War, not just saw themselves this way but said it openly, took the course of simply reshaping the global political and economic order to fit their own interests. In their euphoria, they essentially abandoned substantive and equal dialogue with other actors in international life, chose not to improve or create universal institutions, and attempted instead to bring the entire world under the spread of their own organizations, norms and rules. They chose the road of globalization and security for their own beloved selves, for the select few, and not for all. But far from everyone was ready to agree with this" (Putin 2016b).

This view is boldly presented in the Russian 'long narrative' included in the annex to the final report of the OSCE Panel of Eminent Persons: "Starting with the negotiations on German unification, the West systematically took advantage of Russia's weakness. The West never acted in the spirit of the Charter of Paris, in which the indivisibility of security was a key concept. The West never tried to address security with Russia, only without it, or against it. The United States instead seized the opportunity to dominate international affairs especially in Europe. [...] The 'common European home' failed because the West was unwilling to build new, open security architecture – and to fulfil its promises. The West talked of co-operation and expected co-operation from Moscow, but believed in Russia's perennial aggressiveness or/and weakness" (Panel of Eminent Persons 2015, p. 24).

Neglect of Russia's interests and ignorance with respect to the growing assertiveness of Moscow are, according to Arbatova and Dynkin, at the core of the recent developments: "Fifteen years ago, during the Yugoslavian crisis, Russia was experiencing a sharp transformation – and even a sovereign default – and did not have the resources to defend its interests. But in 2014, the situation had changed. This important development was disregarded by the West" (Arbatova/Dynkin 2016, p. 71).

Noting deep mutual mistrust between Russia and the West, former Foreign Minister Igor Ivanov sees its roots in "principled divergence of views pertaining to the contemporary world, dominant trends in world politics, and the desirable features of the future world order" (Ivanov 2017, p. 130).

The Russian mainstream narrative proceeds on the basis that the US policy, in particular, is not value-based, but rather represents a classic case of power politics. Not only radical proponents of conspiracy theories imply that the strategic goal of the US is to prevent any rapprochement between Russia and Europe (in particular; Germany) in order to maintain its hegemony

(Akopov 2015, Ivanov 2015). Officials in Moscow tend to interpret the Ukraine crisis in the same categories (Lavrov 2015).

Apparently, the common denominator of the mainstream narrative is that Russia did not enjoy the respect it deserved after the end of the Cold War. The West was not prepared to honour its status as a great power (Frear, Kulesa 2016, p. 5) and was pushing its own agenda without paying attention to concerns raised by Moscow and without seriously considering Russian proposals (Ivanov 2017, p. 150; Panel of Eminent Persons 2015, p. 26).

This also seems to be a personal obsession of President Putin. Commenting on the deployment of ballistic missile defence systems in Romania, he reiterated: "Nobody listens to us, nobody is willing to have talks with us, we do not hear anything but platitudes, and those platitudes mainly boil down to the fact that this is not directed against Russia and does not threaten Russia's security" (Putin 2016a).

The Russian debate certainly cannot be reduced to the mainstream thinking. Academic discussions, in particular, reveal a great variety of narratives admitting the impact of the values gap in Russia-West relations that occurred and deepened at least over the last decade (Parkhalina 2012), warning of the danger of demonizing the West (Klyamkin 2009; Liberal Mission 2013), or critically assessing possible unintended consequences of contemporary Russian foreign policy on Ukraine and Syria (Baranovskiy 2016). The civilizational divide that occurred as a result of Russia abandoning its European choice policy under Putin is often seen by opposition figures as a major source of the contemporary crisis (Yavlinskiy 2014). This debate, however, has little political effect since it does not 'resonate' with the broader public opinion.

Key Developments and Factors Shaping Russian-Western Relations

As indicated above, the mainstream view in Russia is that the West considered itself the winner in the Cold War and pursued policies that created a sort of Versailles complex in Russia.

The list of events and developments which have contributed to the deterioration of Russia-West relations is long and reaches back to the collapse of the Soviet Union. The expansion of the West eastward, not least by enlarging membership in both NATO and the European Union, is central in the Russian mainstream narrative. There is a deeply rooted belief on which this narrative is based, namely that, in 1990, the Soviet Union accepted the unification of Germany in exchange for the promise (not kept by NATO at a later point) that the Alliance would not be extended eastward (Cherkasov 2016, p. 712; Panel of Eminent Persons 2015, p. 25).

This belief is not exactly correct from a historical point of view. This account has not been confirmed by the-then President of the Soviet Union,

Mikhail Gorbachev, (Korshunov 2014), and the gradual deterioration of Russian-Western relations began not with the 1997 decision on the first wave of NATO enlargement eastward but rather, with the 1999 Kosovo War (Zagorski 2015, p. 57).

However, the enlargement of both NATO and the EU is widely considered, including by Gorbachev (Korshunov 2014), as an act that did not honour Russia's withdrawal (including its troop withdrawal) from the former Warsaw Pact member countries (Panel of Eminent Persons 2015, p. 24) and jeopardized Russia's security and economic interests (Frear/Kulesa 2016, p. 4-5.). "Under the slogan of promoting democratic values eastwards, the West continued to expand its institutions at the expense of Russian security interests. It was the main dynamic after the Cold War. Consecutive waves of NATO's expansion reduced Russia's security. The EU's expansion took over Russia's markets and, as new member states joined Schengen, the area of visa-free travel for Russian citizens was reduced. In each case, as compensation, Russia was offered a formal junior partnership" (Panel of Eminent Persons 2015, p. 24).

As a result, "the post-Cold War security order in Europe was built according to a Western design", without taking into account Russia's security interests. Furthermore, Russia was prevented, particularly by the US, from becoming an integral part of the European security order and from deeper integration with the rest of Europe. (Frear/Kulesa 2016, p. 4; Terekhov 2015, p. 74). Some authors go as far as to imply that those changes in the European order were deliberately engineered (by the US) "in order to harm Russia's interests" (Troitskiy 2016, p. 21).

Apart from direct effects pertaining to Russia's security and economic interests, the enlargement of both NATO and the EU has also had political effects due to the extension of membership to a number of East Central European states which "maintain their own grievances toward Russia" and "now influence Western decision-making towards more hostile policies on Russia" (Frear/Kulesa 2016, p. 5). As Foreign Minister Lavrov put it years ago, when discussing the consequences of the 2004 EU enlargement: "For a long time, we got used to dealing with a relatively small group of countries which pursued a pragmatic, balanced foreign policy and were ready to sacrifice something important for them for the sake of reaching a compromise, provided that the ultimate overall deal would meet the interests of all parties. This was the logic in which the EU evolved until 2004." After the enlargement, however, it turned out that, with new member states, the EU imported their legacy "of historic grievances and a new pattern of behaviour characterized by putting forward ultimatums and unpreparedness for compromises" (Lavrov 2007).

Some authors argue that, despite its critical view, Russia ultimately accepted and respected the extension of western institutions to the East Central European states (Zagorski 2013, p. 4). However, the Russian Federation increasingly experienced the continuous offers of NATO membership to a number of Soviet successor states (particularly Georgia and Ukraine in 2008) and the EU's Eastern partnership policy as pursued from 2009 as further attempts by the West to revise the new status quo. "All the elements came together in Ukraine: first the promise of NATO membership at the NATO Summit in Bucharest – a threat to Russia; then the attempt by the EU to increase its own economic space at the expense of Russia and, finally, the open Western support for the Maidan regime change movement" (Panel of Eminent Persons 2015, p. 26).

The EU's Eastern Partnership was not excluded from Moscow's criticism from the very beginning. On the contrary, the offer of political association and economic integration that it entailed was increasingly interpreted in Russia as a policy of extending the EU's 'sphere of influence' at the expense of Russia's interests thus, from Moscow's perspective, turning the EU into an important revisionist power. "The EU's neighbourhood policies and its Eastern Partnership had created a situation in which several of Russia's closest neighbours were faced with an artificial choice: either they were with the West or against it. Only in such an atmosphere of polarization and forced choices could the events that led to the coup d'état against President Yanukovych unfold" (Panel of Eminent Persons 2015, p. 26).

The list of particularly contentious issues, which have contributed over time to the progressive deterioration of Russia's relations with the West, is long. A number of them figure most prominently in the Russian mainstream narrative. These include NATO's air campaign against Serbia in 1999; the US-led intervention in Iraq in 2003; Kosovo's unilateral declaration of independence in 2008; the deployment in Europe of elements of the US global missile defence system; "poor performance in Afghanistan"; support to "flower revolutions" in Russia's neighbourhood and of the "Arab Spring"; military intervention in Libya, leading to continuing turmoil in the Middle East with catastrophic consequences, particularly for Syria (Putin 2015; Meshkov 2015; Kelin 2016; Panel of Eminent Persons 2015, p. 25).

Unilateral military interventions by the US, without the consent of the UN Security Council, with few or no protests from Europe, as well as the regime change policies are presented in the mainstream narrative as blatant violations of international and humanitarian law and breaches of the Helsinki principles, particularly those of state sovereignty and non-interference into internal affairs. They are seen as actions undermining the UN and the OSCE and irresponsibly destabilizing the international system (Panel of Eminent Persons 2015, pp. 25-26). "It is the West's actions which are threats to international peace and security" (Panel of Eminent Persons 2015, p. 26).

It is also noted that appeals and proposals submitted by Russia in order to consolidate the European order, such as the 2008 proposal for a European security treaty, were ignored and not followed up (Kelin 2016; Panel of Eminent Persons 2015, p. 25.). The key objective from this perspective is for the

US to return to common values, common interests and respect for international law (Putin 2015).

Repeated Western references to universal norms and the agreed principles and values that underpin the European security order are merely seen as an excuse for "attacking" Russia's domestic political regime and its foreign policy, undermining its sovereignty and "intervening in the affairs of others in order to instigate regime change in the West's own interests" (Frear/ Kulesa 2016, p. 4, 8).

In sum, with due differentiation in expressed opinions, the extension of the West eastwards at the expense of Russia, lack of interest in accepting Russia as equal part of the European order, not to mention Western institutions, and, increasingly, the alleged regime change policies aiming at Russia and its neighbours are seen as major developments that have deeply poisoned Russian-Western relations over the past several years and eradicated mutual trust. This general conclusion is represented in almost all Russian narratives, including the moderate mainstream, Eurasianists, and even Westerners, with the exception of those who would put the blame exclusively on Moscow itself (Arbatova/Dynkin 2016, p. 71).

Factors Influencing Russian-Western Relations

The gradual decline of Russian-Western relations during the past decade and a half is a result of an interplay of complex developments: social developments, domestic politics, changes in the external environment, structural reasons as well as personal decisions. Representatives of different narratives concentrate on different fragments of this highly complex mosaic.

Representatives of the mainstream narrative reduce the reasons for the current crisis to the assertion that Russia is returning to world politics as an independent sovereign actor exclusively following its own national interests after a period of weakness and humiliation by the West in the 1990s after the collapse of the Soviet Union. Russia is 'rising from its knees'; it is no longer prepared to follow the West and particularly the US. This is exactly what generates tension with the US since the latter's goal is to weaken Russia and prevent it from becoming a strong competitor to America. This narrative describes the assertiveness of Moscow as a logical consequence and response to the allegedly Russia-unfriendly or even hostile policy of the US after the end of the Cold War.

From this perspective, the 1990s were a temporary deviation from the traditional path of Russia's development (both domestically and in terms of its foreign policy) due to its temporary weakness. Its current assertiveness is, therefore, a logical response to Western policies of 'keeping Russia down' and, in this context, there cannot be any return to "business as usual' if the West does not accept Moscow as an equal partner and does not respect its national interests. This approach is largely common for both the mainstream and the nationalistic/Eurasianist narratives with one important difference.

The mainstream builds upon the expectation that restoring cooperation with the West, in general, and Europe, in particular, is an important goal (Foreign Policy Conception 2016), and that Russia will be able to make the West respect its interests and return to cooperative politics largely on Russian terms. The nationalist and Eurasian narrative build on the presumption that this is impossible since the US particularly pursues an incrementally Russia-hostile policy and would not tolerate any competition (Prokhanov 2016a, 2016b; Kurginyan 2012). The latter narrative would imply that Russia needs to continuously invest in increasing its strength, including military capabilities, in order to be able to resist long-term confrontation with the West led by the US.

Others would argue that Russia and the West were increasingly drifting apart starting at the beginning of the 21st century for different reasons, which included domestic developments and increasing authoritarianism in Russia (Yavlinskiy 2014), but also due to the changes in the global environment. The emergence and strengthening of the concept of a polycentric world particularly mark an important change in the Russian mainstream perception of the world and justify the development of a 'multi-vector' foreign policy pursued by Moscow ever since.

There was a remarkable shift in the Russian policy away from seeking respectful integration with the Euro-Atlantic community in the 1990s towards seeking increasing distance from it. This shift was justified by the realization of the fact that all of the new 'rising nations', such as China or India, were not Western (non-OECD) nations, as were the newcomers to the club of the ten largest economies of the world. This conclusion had several important implications for Russian policy.

First, it was a basis for the conclusion that the 'West', both the US and particularly the EU were in a relative decline and that significant shifts in the global distribution of economic power would strengthen non-OECD nations. In other words, the world is becoming increasingly non-Western. Second, this was diminishing the attractiveness of the 'Western' model of development and a perfect excuse for the increasingly authoritarian rule in Russia as it implied that a nation does not need to be a liberal democracy in order to be successful on the global scale. It is rather the contrary, as the example of China is interpreted by many. Third, the conclusion was that, in order to pretend to play a role in the concert of global powers (old and new), a nation does not need to be a liberal democracy but should lead and represent a regional group of countries (Zagorski 2010).

This, combined with concerns over the increasingly revisionist role of both NATO and the EU in the post-Soviet space, gave a boost to the idea of erecting a regional Eurasian community of states led by Russia and representing a distinct, 'non-EU' Europe, based on the Collective Security Treaty Organization (CSTO) and the Eurasian Economic Union (EAEU), as well as the Commonwealth of Independent States (CIS) as counterparts to NATO and the EU. This would lead to a bipolar configuration of the European order, which would not necessarily build upon confrontation with the West, but should imply defining the proper relationship between the institutions of the 'West' and 'Eurasia'.

This led some to describe the shift that occurred in Russian policies early in the 2000s as turning away from Europe towards a closer relationship with the rising Asian countries and particularly with China (Karaganov 2015, pp. 17-18). Although the rationale and the reality of a 'Russian pivot to Asia' is disputed, these developments increasingly made Russia and Europe, Russia and the West, in general, drift apart while being preoccupied with distinct agendas and problems and paying less attention to each other. "Both sides were distracted by other priorities and events – such as the global crisis of 2008-2009, complications in the Euro Zone, the continuous rise of China, and the explosion of the Middle East. This only shows that both the West and Russia appear to consider their relations to be of secondary importance and can, therefore, be easily shelved or sacrificed for the sake of more central and more urgent needs. It appeared unnecessary to invest time and the intellectual and political capital into thinking about new institutions, regimes, and agreements (Atlantic Council, ELN, RIAC 2015, p. 14).

Interests Shared by Russia and the West

As mentioned above, the "Westerners' narrative within the Russian debate implies the desirability of building relations with Europe and the West in general on the basis of common values (Parkhalina 2012) and prioritizes developing a strong partnership with Europe (Yavlinskiy 2014). However, the prevailing mainstream consensus proceeds on the understanding that, in current circumstances, a values-based approach would be counterproductive, and the relationship between Russia and the West should build exclusively upon common interests and be explicitly pragmatic (Ivanov 2017, pp. 130-131).

Common interests are identified in various fields as including security, economics, social development in more general terms, co-operation in managing and resolving regional issues and conflicts, and international governance (Ivanov 2017, pp. 131-132; Meshkov 2015, p. 14).

In the area of security, the emphasis is on the need for closer co-operation for the purpose of adequately responding to new transnational threats and particularly to the challenge of international terrorism. President Putin has repeatedly advocated the erection of a broad international anti-terrorist coalition that would be reminiscent of an anti-Hitler coalition which, during the World War II, brought together very different countries despite their ideological differences (Putin 2015).

Also recognized is the need to co-operatively address traditional military security issues in order to prevent further escalation of tensions between Russia and the West, restore dialogue on security issues and regular communication between the militaries (Ivanov 2017, p. 131). In economic terms, Moscow emphasizes the need to find a common denominator between different – European and Eurasian – integration processes in order to make them increasingly compatible and minimize the risks of competition between them – something that is implied in the Russian proposals pertaining to an 'integration of integrations' (Kelin 2016, p. 65). In a broader sense, while promoting the idea of a Common Economic Space to include the EU and the Eurasian space and to be built on direct co-operation between the EU and the EAEU, Moscow particularly suggests centering such co-operation around a deal that would imply an exchange of Russia's energy resources for state-of-the-art European technologies (Meshkov 2015, p. 11).

The need to restore international stability and address pressing regional issues, such as crises in the Middle East, Syria, Iraq, Libya or Yemen, as well as other security issues, such as non-proliferation of weapons and technologies of mass destruction, requires closer co-operation with – not isolation of Russia (Meshkov 2015, p. 14).

In terms of governance, and, particularly with respect to the European order, Russia certainly seeks to be accepted as a "distinct and equal partner, rather than as 'another neighbour' of the EU", and to "shield its neighbourhood from further penetration by Western institutions and domestic developments from Western influence" (Zagorski 2016, p. 13, 15). Establishing direct co-operative relations between the Euro-Atlantic and Eurasian institutions is part of that vision of a future European architecture.

This vision is very much inspired by historic examples, particularly by the Yalta order that granted the-then Soviet Union the status of a permanent member of the UN Security Council and a 'sphere of influence' in what was then considered 'Eastern Europe'. Although most often referred to in the context of global governance, the Yalta spirit is now experiencing a renaissance in Russia and has become a desirable vision for the future European order (Terekhov 2015; Yakunin 2016; Frear/Kulesa 2016, p. 5).

Another historical example that inspires Russian mainstream's thinking about a desirable European order is the Concert of European great powers which goes back to the 1815 Vienna Congress that restored the monarchic order after the Napoleonic wars (Hille/Buckley 2015).

Both concepts imply status and a geographic area of 'privileged interests' of Russia, which should be respected by the West. "For Moscow, recognizing Russia's status is more important than meeting its concrete current demands. Status is the political capital that can be used to influence multilateral decisions at any time and on any issue. Status is a universal currency; it is highly liquid, unlike agreements on a specific issue between rival players. Status is converted into profit in games with both high and low levels of antagonism. Russian leaders insist on recognition of the country's status when they demand "equal partnership" with other actors, regardless of the specific nature of the problem being negotiated" (Troitskiy 2016, p. 21).

At the same time, virtually all narratives imply that isolating Russia does not serve the interests of either side (Atlantic Council, ELN, RIAC 2015, p. 15). In more practical terms, Moscow suggests that, while reconfirming the Helsinki principles, Russia and the West should agree on their more uniform interpretation in order to minimize sources for tensions in the future. This goes particularly for the recognized need to further clarify the relationship between the principles of territorial integrity and self-determination, to further specify the principle of non-intervention into internal affairs in order to rule out any possible subversive actions and external support for any unconstitutional change of power in any country. Moscow also suggests agreeing on the right of states to maintain special ties with compatriots living abroad, and to protect their interests (Meshkov 2015, p. 14; Kelin 2016, p. 65–65).

Figures

Figure 1

VTSIOM surveys 1990-2015: responses to the question "Is there any country that poses a military threat to Russia today?" (Yes, there is)

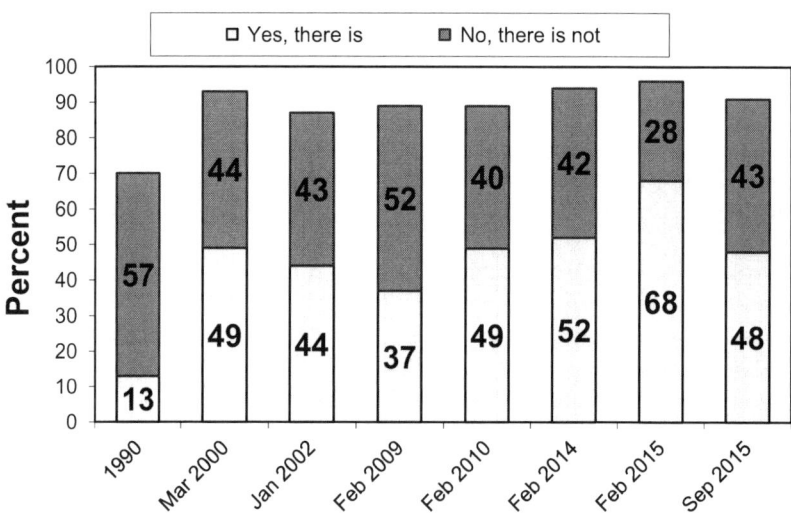

Source: VTSIOM 2015.

Figure 2

2016 Hamilton College Levitt Poll: responses to the question "Do you think
that the USA represents a threat to Russia's national security?"

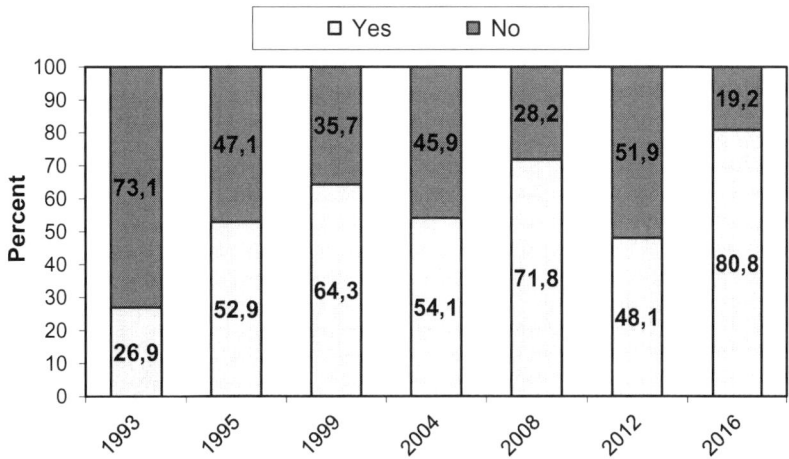

Source: Rivera 2016, p. 7.

Figure 3

2016 Hamilton College Levitt Poll: 'utmost threat' to Russia's security
Ethnic tensions

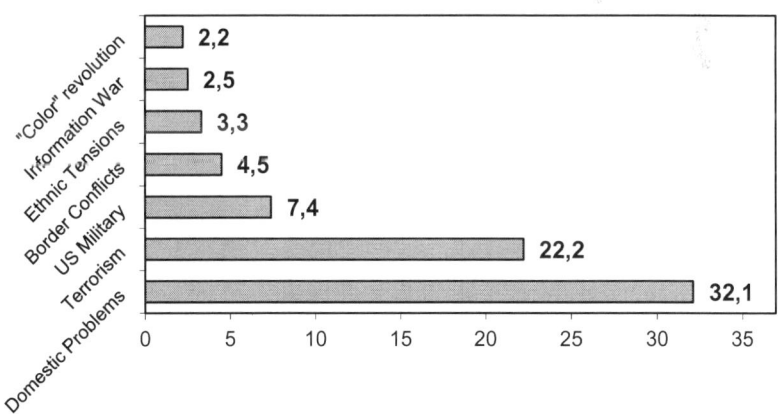

Source: Rivera 2016, p. 10.

Figure 4

Russian national defence and security budgets, 1997-2016

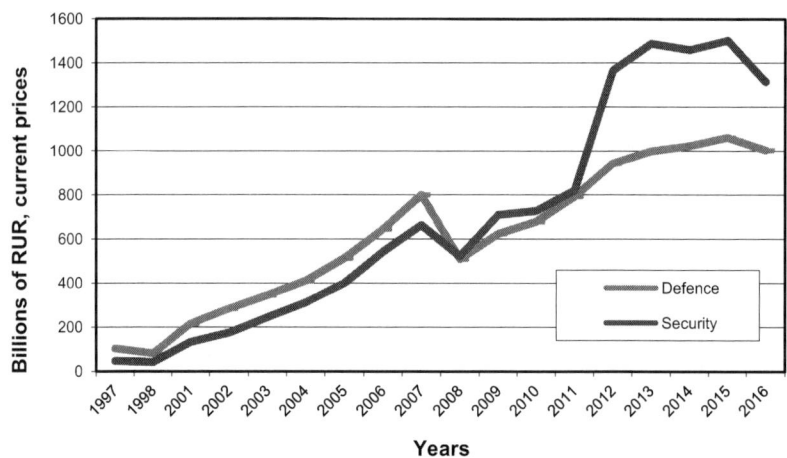

Source: calculated from Federal budget statistics, www.minfin.ru Defence

Sources

Akopov P. (2015). „Rossiya nazvala nedopushchenie soyuza Moskvy i Berlina strate-
gichesloy tselyu SShA" [Russia says the prevention of an alliance between Moscow and Berlin is the strategic goal of the U.S."], *Vzglyad*, 23 April,
http://vz.ru/politics/2015/4/23/741621.html (accessed 13.11.2015).

Arbatova N.K., Dynkin A.A. (2016). "World Order after Ukraine", *Survival*, Vol. 58,
no 1, pp. 71-90.

Atlantic Council, ELN, RIAC (2015). *Managing Differences on European Security in
2015. US, Russian and European Perspectives*. Washington; London; Moscow:
Atlantic Council; European Leadership Network; Russian International Affairs
Council.

Baranovskiy V. (2016). "Novaya vneshnyaya politika Rossii: vliyanie na mezhduna-
rodnuyu sistemu" ["Russia's new foreign policy: Implication for the international
system"], *Mirovaya ekonomika i mezhdunarodnye otnosheniya* 60, no 7: 5-15.

Bertelsmann, ISP (2016). *Frayed Partnership. German public opinion on Russia*.
Gütersloh; Warsaw: Bertelsmann Stiftung; Instytut Spraw Publicznych.

Cherkasov P. (2016). *IMEMO. Ocherk intorii [Essay on IMEMO History]* (Moscow:
Ves' mir).

Entin M., Entina E. (2016). *New agenda for Russia-EU relations*, RIAC Policy Brief
No 4.

Foreign Policy Conception (2016). *Foreign Policy Concept of the Russian Federation*
(approved by the President of the Russian Federation Vladimir Putin on November 30, 2016), Ministry of Foreign Affairs of Russia, 1.12.2016, http://www.

mid.ru/ru/foreign_policy/official_documents/-/asset_publisher/CptICk B6BZ29/ cotent/id/2542248?p_p_id=101_INSTANCE_CptICkB6BZ29&_101_INSTAN-CE_CptICkB6BZ29_languageId=en_GB (accessed 10.12.2016).

Frear T., Kulesa L. (2016). *Competing Western and Russian narratives on the European order: Is there common ground?* Conference Report. London; Moscow: European Leadership Network; Russian International Affairs Council.

Hille K., Buckley N. (2015). "Powers in the balance", *Financial Times*, 6 July, p. 5.

Information Security Doctrine (2016). *Doktrina informatsionnoy bezopasnosti Rissiyskoy Federatsii [Information Security Doctrine of the Russian Federation]*, (approved by the President of the Russian Federation Vladimir Putin on December 5, 2016), Ministry of Foreign Affairs of Russia, 1.12.2016, http://www. mid.ru/documents/10180/2563110/Ukaz_Prezidenta_Rossiiskoi_Federatsii_ot_05 122016.pdf/b579d736-cb99-46ac-b4f7-a0b6bc102ed1 (accessed 10.12.2016).

Ivanov A. (2015). "Novaya bitva za Grmaniyu" ["New Battle for Germany"], *Svobodnaya pressa*, 24 April, http://svpressa.ru/all/article/119860/ (accessed 13.11.2016).

Ivanov I.S. (2017). *Evropeyskiy vektor vneshney politiki sovremennoy Rossii [The European Vector of the foreign policy of the contemporary Russia]* (Moscow: NP RSMD, 2017).

Karaganov S. (2015). "Net prostykh resheniy. O perspektivakh rossiysko-evropeyslikh otnocheniy" ("There are no simple solutions. On the prospects for Russo-European relations", *Mezhdunarodnaya Zhisn'*, no 9, pp. 16-25.

Kelin A. (2016). "Vzglyad v proshloe i bezopasnost' miroustroystva segodnya" ["Looking back and the security of the world order now"], *Mezhdunarodnaya Zhisn'*, no 1, pp. 60-65.

Klyamkin I.M. (2009). *Rossiya I Zapad. Vneshnyaya politika Kremlya glazami liberalov [Russia and the West. Kremlin's foreign policy in the perspective of liberals]*, ed. by I.M. Klyamkin (Moscow: Liberal Mission Foundation).

Korshunov M. (2014). "Mikhail Gorbachev: I am against all walls", Russia beyond the Headlines, October 16, http://rbth.com/international/2014/10/16/mikhail_ gorbachev_i_am_against_all_walls_40673.html (accessed 09.06.2016).

Kurginyan S. (2012). *Sut' vremeni [The Essence of the time]*, in 4 volumes (Moscow: MOF ETW).

Lavrov S. (2007). "Statement of Foreign Minister Lavrov at a meeting with the extended Board of the Russian Union of Industrialists and Entrepreneurs devoted to relations between Russia and the European Union", 6 July, *author's archive*.

Lavrov S. (2015). "Interview. V gostyach: Sergey Lavrov, ministr inostrannykh de RF" ["Interview. The Guest: Sergei Lavrov, Minister of Foreign Relations of the Russian Federation"], *Ekho Moskvy*, 22 April, http://echo.msk.ru/programs/ beseda/1534726-echo/ (accessed 13.11.2015).

Liberal Mission (2013). "Rossiya v global'nom mire i kak etot mir vliyaet na Rossiyu" ["Russia in the global world and how this world affects Russia"], *Liberal Mission Foundation*, 16 May, http://www.liberal.ru/articles/6145 (accessed 15.10.2016).

Liik K. (2015). *The Minsk Agreement – How to Talk with Russia?* ECFR's EU-Russia Strategy Group November 2015.

Meshkov A. (2015). "Rossiya-Evropa: chto dal'she?" ["Russia and Europe" what next?"], *Mezhdunarodnaya Zhisn'*, no 9, pp. 6-15.

Military Doctrine (2014). *Voennaya doktrina Rossiyskoy Federatsii (Military Doctrine of the Russian Federation)* (approved by the President of the Russian Federation on December 25, 2014), The Security Council of the Russian Federation, http://www.scrf.gov.ru/documents/18/129.html (accessed 10.12.2016).

Panel of Eminent Persons (2015). *Back to Diplomacy Final Report and Recommendations of the Panel of Eminent Persons on European Security as a Common Project.*

Parkhalina T. (2012). "Zasedanie Ekspertnogo soveta Komiteta Soveta Federatsii po mezhdunarodnym delam 11.04.2012 g." ["Meeting of the Advisory Council of the Committee on Foreign Relations of the Council of Federation, 11.04.2012"], Council of Federation, 11 April, http://international.council.gov.ru/ activity/activities/expert_activities/48363/ (accessed 7.10.2016).

Prokhanov A. (2016a). "Antidot protiv zapadnyks vliyaniy" ["The antidote against western influences"], *Zavtra*, http://zavtra.ru/ (accessed 03.12.2016).

Prokhanov A. (2016b). "Pyataya imperiya – put' Rossii" ["The fifth Empire – the way of Russia"], *Evraziyskiy vector*, http://евразийство.рф/public/item/61-aleksandr-prokhanov-pyataya-imperiya-put-rossii.html (accessed 03.12.2016).

Putin V. (2014a). "Soveshchanie poslov i postoyannykh predstaviteley Rossii' ("Conference of ambassadors and permanent representatives of Russia") *President of Russia*, July 1, http://www.kremlin.ru/transcripts/46131 (accessed 17.06.2016).

Putin V. (2014b). "Meeting of the Valdai International Discussion Club", *President of Russia*, October 24, http://en.kremlin.ru/events/president/news/46860 (accessed 29.10.2016).

Putin V. (2015). "70th session of the UN General Assembly. Vladimir Putin took part in the plenary meeting of the 70th session of the UN General Assembly in New York". *President of Russia*, September 28, http://en.kremlin.ru/events/president/ news/50385 (accessed 17.06.2016).

Putin V. (2016a). "Joint press conference with Prime Minister of Greece Alexis Tsipras", *President of Russia*, May 27, http://en.kremlin.ru/catalog/persons/433/ events/52024 (accessed 17.06.2016).

Putin V. (2016b). "Meeting of the Valdai International Discussion Club", *President of Russia*, October 27, http://en.kremlin.ru/events/president/news/53151 (accessed 29.10.2016).

Putin V. (2016c). "Vladimir Putin's annual news conference", *President of Russia*, December 23, http://en.kremlin.ru/events/president/news/53573 (accessed 24.12. 2016).

RANEPA (2016). *Nikolay Kalmykov podelilsya rezul'tatami oprosa expertov otnosityel'no ikh vospriyatiya ugroz i riskov bezopasnosti Rossii* [*Nikolay Kalmykov shared the findings of an experts' poll on their perception of security threats and risks for Russia*], The Russian Presidential Academy of National Economy and Public Administration (RANEPA), 16 November, http://expert. ranepa.ru/nikolay-kalmyikov-podelilsya-rezultatami-oprosa-ekspertov-otnositelno-ih-vospriyatiya-ugroz-i-riskov-nashey-bezopasnosti/ (accessed 17.11.2016).

Rivera Sh. W. (2016). *The Russian Elite 2016. Perspectives on Foreign and Domestic Policy*. 2016 Hamilton College Levitt Poll. Supported by The Arthur Levitt Public Affairs Center, Hamilton College, Clinton, NY. May 11, 2016, Version 2.0.

NYT (2016). "Russia Puts the Blame on Everyone Else", *The New York Times*, August 29, p. 16.

Terekhov V. (2015). "K 60-letiuy ustanovleniya diplo,aticheskikh otnosheniy s FRG" ["Towards the 60th anniversary of establishing diplomatic relations with the FRG"], *Mezhdunarodnaya Zhisn'*, no 9, pp. 64-78.

Troitskiy M. (2016). "The Procedural Foundations of the European Security Order: Russian and 'Western' Perspectives", Frear T., Kulesa L. (eds.), *Competing Western and Russian narratives on the European order: Is there common ground?* Conference Report. London; Moscow: European Leadership Network; Russian International Affairs Council.

Tsygankov A. (2006). *Russia's Foreign Policy: Change and Continuity in National Identity.* (Lanham, MD: Rawman & Littlefield Publishers).

VCIOM (2015). *Russian Army-2015 in Brief.* Press release №1783. The Russian Public Opinion Research Centre (VCIOM), 10.16.2015. URL: http://wciom.com/index.php?id=61&uid=1191 (accessed 07.21.2016).

Yakunin V. (2016). "Yalta – Potsdam – Helsinki – istoricheskiye uroki v aktual'noy politicheskoy povestke" (Yalta – Potsdam – Helsinki – lessons of history on the current political agenda", *Mezhdunarodnaya Zhisn'*, no 1, pp. 66-72.

Yavlinskiy G. (2014). "Grogoriy Yavlinskiy: Rossiya sozdaet vokrug sebya poyas nestabil'nisti" ["Grigoriy Yavlinskiy: Russia creates a belt of instability around itself"], *Vedomosti*, 27 February, http://www.vedomosti.ru/opinion/articles/2014/02/27/grigorij-yavlinskij-otkazom-ot-evropejskogo-vektora (accessed 1.3.2014).

Zagorski A. (2009). "The limits of a global consensus on security: the case of Russia", Luis Peral (ed.), *Global security in a multipolar world*, Chaillot Paper n° 118 (Paris: EUISS, 2009), p. 67-84.

Zagorski A. (2010). "Russian Approaches to Global Governance in the 21st Century", *The International Spectator* 45 (December), no 4: 27-42.

Zagorski A. (2013). A. Zagorski (ed.) et al), *Russia and East Central Europe: A Fresh Start* (Berlin: Friedrich-Ebert-Stiftung).

Zagorski A. (2014). *Russia: External Threat Perceptions*, unpublished manuscript submitted for the project of the OSCE Network of Think Tanks and Academic Institutions on *Threat Perceptions in the OSCE Area*, (Hamburg et al., OSCE Network, 2014).

Zagorski A. (2015). "The Transformation of Russia–ECE Relations", A. Zagorski (ed.), *Russia and East Central Europe after the Cold War: A Fundamentally Transformed Relationship* (Prague: Human Rights Publishers), 23-58.

Zagorski A. (2016). *Russia—EU Relations at a Crossroads. Common and Divergent Interests* (Moscow: NPMP RIAC).

Zubov A. (2014). "Andrey Zubov: Eto uzhe bylo" ["Andrey Zubov: this was already"], *Vedomosti*, 1 March, http://www.vedomosti.ru/opinion/articles/2014/03/01/andrej-zubov-eto-uzhe-bylo (accessed 5.03.2014).

Christian Nünlist and Benno Zogg

Swiss Narratives on the Evolution of European Security, 1990 – 2016

Introduction

For Switzerland, the core principles of the European Security system as established in the Helsinki Final Act (1975) and the Paris Charter (1990) are fundamentally important. Rule of law rather than power politics is crucial for the survival of a small neutral state. Switzerland still remains bound to permanent neutrality and outside of the EU, unlike other former European neutrals who joined the EU in the 1990s. Nevertheless, Swiss foreign and security policy since 1990 has changed from the traditional one of strict neutrality to a less absolute version, which reduced neutrality to its military core and allowed for more European solidarity within Swiss foreign policy. Traditionally, Switzerland rarely picks sides in a conflict or blames one party, not least in order to keep open its option to mediate between parties to the conflict. Even so, Switzerland is deeply anchored in the Western camp: culturally, historically, economically and, of course, geographically. Switzerland shares the liberal values of the West, such as rule of law, gender equality etc. and overwhelmingly conducts trade with its immediate neighbours, all of them members of the EU.

Since the end of the Cold War, the former contradiction between neutrality and international co-operation has all but disappeared. Switzerland has joined NATO's Partnership for Peace (PfP), contributed to military stabilization in the Western Balkans, and twice chaired the OSCE (1996 and 2014). It established a strategic partnership with Russia in 2007. During the 2014 Ukraine crisis, Switzerland as OSCE chair contributed to the de-escalation of the crisis and successfully walked the delicate line between keeping the dialogue with Russia open yet clearly siding with the West in condemning Russia's breach of OSCE principles and international law. Thus, Switzerland's foreign policy today provides useful services to mediate and de-escalate international conflicts and, as well-placed "brokers of peace-building ideas"[1], Swiss diplomats contribute to finding multilateral solutions to current global challenges. In so doing, Swiss foreign policy is deeply anchored in traditional Swiss principles and values. Also, Swiss citizens enjoy strong direct-democratic participation rights. By threatening to use or actually using instruments, such as popular initiatives or referenda, they can shape Swiss foreign policy. Swiss Members of Parliament, particularly members of the

---

1   Laurent Goetschel, "Neutrals as brokers of peacebuilding ideas?" in: Cooperation and Conflict 46(3)2011, pp. 312-333.

Security Policy or Foreign Policy Commission, also influence Swiss foreign policy by preparing, in consultation with the Federal Council, foreign policy dossiers which are aimed at passing the parliamentary vote in the plenary.

The following article will first outline the evolution of threat perception in Switzerland and Swiss policies addressing these challenges. It will then examine Switzerland's relationship with Russia since the end of the Cold War. Said relationship was remarkably close, with Switzerland balancing a condemnation of Russian action in Crimea without taking action in form of sanctions. In a last section, varying Swiss narratives on European security, and on Russia and Ukraine in particular, will be broken down across the political spectrum.

Switzerland's Most Acute (Perceived) Threats

In early 2014, Russia's military invasion of Ukraine came as a strategic surprise and shock to Swiss security policy practitioners. However, similarly to the Russo-Georgian War in 2008, Russia's revisionist security policy did not dramatically shift Swiss security policy. Russia did not become Switzerland's most acute perceived threat. According to the Swiss intelligence service (NDB), Switzerland's most acute threats are, in descending order (as of May 2016): 1) returning European jihadist foreign fighters, 2) terrorism (Islamic State and lone wolves), 3) foreign espionage, and 4) Russia (East-West conflict).[2] Generally speaking, fundamental changes in Switzerland's threat perceptions are mostly event-driven and are reflected in related media coverage. 9/11 and the rise of Islamic State pushed jihadist terrorism up on Switzerland's agenda; Fukushima in 2011 led to increased fears among the population about environmental harm.

The terrorist threat from jihadists, both from foreign terrorist fighters returning to Europe from Syria and Iraq and from home-grown, self-radicalized terrorists, remains the most acute concern[3] – even if jihadist radicalization is less of a problem in Switzerland than in other comparable small European states, such as Belgium or Sweden. According to a recent study, Swiss Muslims are socially, economically, and culturally relatively well integrated into society, and some 80-90 percent originate from Turkey or the Balkans. The vast majority of Muslims from these two regions traditionally espouse forms of Islam that are apolitical and tolerant.[4] There is popular concern that the current migration crisis might bring more radical Islamists to Switzerland, or

---

2   Nachrichtendienst des Bundes (NDB), Sicherheit Schweiz 2016, 2 May 2015, p. 11.

3   Bundesrat, Bericht über die Sicherheitspolitik der Schweiz (SIPOL-B 2016), 24 August 2016.

4   Lorenzo Vidino, Jihadist radicalization in Switzerland (Zürich: ETH, 2013), pp. 37f; Miryam Eser Davolio et al., Hintergründe jihadistischer Radikalisierung in der Schweiz (Winterthur: ZHAW, 2015), p. 7.

would at least change the demographics of Switzerland's Muslim community in favour of a more activist, politicized Islam.[5] The August 2016 government report on security policy states that migration is not of immediate concern for security though.[6] The terrorist threat in general has become more prominent since 2015, at least in the perception of the government and the public, despite no actual attacks occurring.[7] In the popular perception, despite the fact that objective security threat levels are low overall, the uncertainty about the continuation and implications of the so-called 'refugee crisis' still needs to be mentioned as a perceived threat that goes beyond terrorism. Particularly politically right-wing circles linked the recent high numbers of immigrants as well as open borders in the EU over the course of 2015 to "high crime rates compared to the rest of Europe" and Switzerland being seen as "the main target for burglary in Europe".[8]

Cyber threats have moved up on the agenda of top concerns of both the government and the Swiss public, in particular after the 'Snowden affair' in June 2013. In May 2016, a cyber-attack against the Swiss Ministry of Defence and the state-owned armament firm RUAG, apparently orchestrated from Russia, made headlines and will keep the topic on the government's agenda in the years to come.[9]

The implications for Swiss security of Russia's military aggression against Ukraine in 2014 are less direct and less clear. Even after 2014, the Swiss Federal Council believes that a direct military threat to Switzerland is improbable.[10] In May 2016, the NDB re-emphasized that an armed attack on Switzerland remains unlikely.[11] Thus, Switzerland's military threat level remained largely unaffected by the Ukraine crisis.

---

5   Bundesrat, Bericht über die Situation der Muslime in der Schweiz, 8 May 2013, p. 63. In 2015, the Liberals (FDP) requested in a parliamentary motion to provide Swiss intelligence services with the necessary resources to carry out investigations on the terrorist risk potential of asylum seekers and refugees. FDP, Motion 15 3900, "Sicherheit ist eine Kernaufgabe des Staates", Bern, 23 September 2015. See also „Geheimdienst überprüft Asylsuchende", in: Neue Zürcher Zeitung (NZZ), 18 January 2015; "Jeder Zweite fürchtet sich vor IS-Schläfern", in: 20 Minuten, 29 December 2015; „Umfrage belegt Terrorangst: Die Furcht der Europäer vor den Flüchtlingen", in: NZZ, 12 July 2016; „Die potenziellen Terroristen", in: NZZ, 3 September 2016.
6   Bundesrat, SIPOL-B 2016, p. 20.
7   See Tibor Szvircsev Tresch et al., Sicherheit 2015: Aussen-, sicherheits- und verteidigungspolitische Meinungsbildung im Trend (Zürich: ETH, 2015), p. 85; Bundesrat, SIPOL-B 2016, p. 20.
8   "Sicherheit", in: SVP: Die Partei für die Schweiz: Parteiprogramm 2015-2019 der SVP, www.svp.ch, 28 February 2015.
9   „Cyberangriffe aus Moskau", in: Der Tages-Anzeiger, 4 May 2016.
10 Bundesrat, SIPOL-B 2016, p. 24f. See also Christian Nünlist, "Swiss Security Policy after 2014", in: European Security & Defense (3-4)2015, pp. 18-21.
11 NDB, Sicherheit Schweiz 2016, p. 17.

In general, Swiss narratives perceived the 1990s as a 'golden era' and the end of the Cold War as a win-win situation. The Swiss government strongly supported democratization in Central and Eastern Europe. NATO's transformation from a military pact into a political instrument for stability in Europe was a key reason for the Swiss decision to participate in NATO's PfP initiative in 1996.[12]

The 1999 Kosovo War was one of the key episodes in Russia's estrangement from the Paris Charter vision. Switzerland's policy was ambivalent and torn between a traditional, strict neutrality policy demanding isolation and Switzerland's new foreign policy course established in 1993. This latter, new strand of foreign policy advocated co-operative security and multilateral diplomacy in a Euro-Atlantic framework.[13] During NATO's war against Serbia, Switzerland decided to put its new foreign policy into effect and maintained its arms embargo against Serbia. Thus, by still exporting military equipment to NATO states but not Serbia, Switzerland chose sides rather than sticking legally to neutrality. Switzerland prohibited NATO military flights over Swiss territory though, only allowing transits for humanitarian reasons.[14]

Switzerland returned to credible impartiality both vis-à-vis the West and Russia when East-West relations returned to a more strained phase after 1999. In 2005, the Swiss government launched selected strategic partnerships with non-European countries, including Russia in 2007. From 2007 to 2014, Switzerland and Russia continuously strengthened their relations, including military interactions. Politically, both Switzerland and Russia were non-members of NATO and the EU, thus forming a 'special relationship' in Europe. Switzerland's early recognition of Kosovo in 2008 did not negatively affect bilateral relations with Russia.[15] Even after the 2008 Russia-Georgia war, Switzerland kept intensifying its strategic partnership with Russia, where it figured among the top ten foreign investors. Russia was also important for Switzerland as an energy supplier. Switzerland successfully mediated between the conflicting parties Russia and Georgia, thus paving the way for Russia's WTO entry in 2011. Several Swiss diplomats have successfully

---

12 Andreas Wenger et al., "Die Partnerschaft für den Frieden: Eine Chance für die Schweiz", in: Bulletin zur schweizerischen Sicherheitspolitik (1997/98), pp. 66-88.
13 Bundesrat, Bericht über die Aussenpolitik der Schweiz in den 90er Jahren, 29 October 1993. For a first emphasis on ‚security through co-operation‘, see also Bundesrat, Schweizerische Sicherheitspolitik im Wandel: Bericht 90 über die Sicherheitspolitik des Bundes, 1 October 1990.
14 Jürg Martin Gabriel, „Verpasste Chancen: Inkohärente Schweizer Politik im Kosovo-Krieg", in: Jürg Martin Gabriel (ed.), Schweizerische Aussenpolitik im Kosovo-Krieg (Zürich: Orell Füssli, 2000), pp. 9-39.
15 Eidgenössisches Departement für auswärtige Angelegenheiten (EDA), Aussenpolitischer Bericht 2009, 2 September 2009, pp. 6350f.

mediated in the Chechen Wars and in the Southern Caucasus, thereby earning the Kremlin's trust.[16]

During the 2014 Ukraine crisis, the Swiss government strongly condemned Russia's illegal annexation of Crimea and put several Swiss-Russian projects (including the training of Russian soldiers in the Swiss mountains) on hold.[17] However, the celebrations of 200 years of diplomatic relations between Switzerland and Russia took place as planned.[18] In the current geostrategic conflict between Russia and the West, the Swiss government has repeatedly emphasized the importance of the principles for a peaceful and stable European security system, which had been commonly agreed upon among CSCE/OSCE participating States (including Russia and Switzerland) between 1975 and 2010.[19] To emphasize its independent foreign policy, however, Switzerland did not join Western sanctions against Russia after the shooting down of the MH17. Yet, it put measures in place to avoid Switzerland being used by Russia to circumvent Western sanctions.[20]

Security Narratives within Swiss Society

It was the Swiss OSCE chairmanship in particular which shaped the balanced Swiss approach in the Ukraine crisis, both in narrative and in Realpolitik: In an important public speech in 2015, Swiss Foreign Minister Didier Burkhalter explained the crisis in European Security in retrospect as a basic disagreement between Russia and the West. While Moscow had been seeking a veto right in a pan-European security system, the West had only offered consultation and co-operation.[21] In the 2016 Security White Book, the Swiss government briefly summarized the origins of the current confrontation between Russia and the West and, again, carefully avoided blaming one side for this development. However, Russia's readiness to change internationally recognized borders in Europe by military force and to illegally annex territory was noted with great concern. Also, the White Book argued that "Russia's domestic discord and Russia's more offensive behaviour triggered the

---

16   See Jonas Grätz, „Partnerschaft mit Russland: Bestandsaufnahme einer aussenpolitischen Akzentsetzung", in: Bulletin zur schweizerischen Sicherheitspolitik 2013, pp. 43-70.

17   „Maurer stoppt Russen-Ausbildung in Andermatt", in: Tages-Anzeiger, 5 March 2014; „Bildete Schweizer Armee in Andermatt russische Geheimagenten aus?", in: Aargauer Zeitung, 5 March 2014.

18   „Der Schweizer Mittelweg in der Krim-Krise", in: NZZ, 27 March 2014; „ Schweiz-Russland: 200-Jahr-Jubiläum wird trotzdem gefeiert", in: Swissinfo, 15 July 2014.

19   See e.g. Didier Burkhalter, Empowering the OSCE to Reconsolidate European Security as a Common Project, Vienna, 24 June 2014; Didier Burkhalter, Implications of the Crisis in and around Ukraine for European Security at Large, Newport, 5 September 2014.

20   „Sanktionen gegen Russland: Bundesrat zieht die Zügel an", in: NZZ, 27 August 2014.

21   Didier Burkhalter, Ungeteiltes und freies Europa? Betrachtungen zur europäischen Friedensordnung zwischen Krise und Erneuerung aus Sicht der Schweizer Aussenpolitik, Bern, 17 June 2015.

Ukraine Crisis".[22] According to the Swiss intelligence service (NDB), which is generally more critical towards Russia, Moscow is responsible for the current "new phase of the East-West conflict".[23]

Among the Swiss population at large, perceptions of Russian-Western relations have varied since the end of the Cold War. Blame for the current situation is shared between Russia and the West. Knowledge about Russia is relatively sparse among the Swiss public and ostensible support for Putin among the political Right is actually often the result of a mix of Anti-Americanism, Anti-Europeanism, some admiration for authoritarianism, and a very strict and narrow view that neutrality should be the dominant guiding principle of Swiss foreign policy.[24] A large part of the right-wing national conservatives (who total at about 30% of Swiss voters) have generally not supported Switzerland's more international and multilateral foreign policy course of the last 25 years, which is represented by the 1990s slogan "security through co-operation".[25] On the contrary, they have strongly emphasized the need for independence and neutrality in the spirit of the 19th century, and have often blamed the US and the EU for their perceived "power politics" since 1990. They embrace any opposition or counterweight to the EU, including China, because they consider the EU too intrusive with respect to their ideal of nation states.[26] In the Ukraine crisis, the EU (in addition to the US) became Putin's main adversary, and Swiss national conservatives therefore sided, to some degree, with Putin.[27] Similarly, Swiss right-wing politicians have requested in parliamentary bills that Switzerland does not join Western sanctions against Russia (in September 2014)[28] and that Switzerland takes up

---

22 Bundesrat, SIPOL-B 2016, pp. 5, 29f.
23 NDB, Sicherheit Schweiz 2015, 4 May 2015, p. 11 (transl. from German by the authors): „Main reason for this development is Russia's overcoming after 25 years of a phase of weakness considered a national catastrophe as well as Russia's self-perception as an entity outside of a Western European frame of reference and its denial of the predominant balance of power in Europe. ... In turn, the West is increasingly pushing back Russian attempts to increase its influence." See also, NDB, Sicherheit Schweiz 2014, 5 May 2014, p. 11 (transl. from German by the authors): „In so doing, the Russian leadership triggered the most severe conflict in Europe between East and West since the end of the Cold War."
24 Bundesversammlung, Interpellation: Massnahmen für eine glaubwürdige Neutralitätspolitik der Schweiz, 18 December 2015. See also „Europa muss unabhängiger von den USA werden", in: SRF News, 27 July 2015; „Heikle Geste in Moskau", in: Blick, 9 May 2016.
25 Karl W. Haltiner, „Vom schmerzlichen Verlieren alter Feindbilder: Bedrohungs- und Risikoanalysen in der Schweiz", in: Thomas Jäger and Ralph Thiele (eds.), Transformation der Sicherheitspolitik: Deutschland, Österreich, Schweiz im Vergleich (Wiesbaden: Springer, 2011), pp. 39-58, at pp. 48ff.; Andreas Wenger, „Sicherheitspolitik", in: Peter Knoepfel et al. (eds.), Handbuch der Schweizer Politik, 5th ed. (Zürich: NZZ, 2014), pp. 645-669, at pp. 649 and 660.
26 „Die EU hat sich eindeutig zum Lakaien der USA degradieren lassen", in: Zeit-Fragen Nr. 20/21 (2014).
27 See e.g. Junge SVP, „Medienmitteilung: Neutralität wahren – keine Sanktionen gegen Russland", at: www.svp.ch, 5 August 2014.
28 Bundesversammlung, Interpellation: Keine Sanktionen gegen Russland, 8 September 2014.

negotiations for a free trade agreement with Russia again (in February and December 2015).[29]

On the political left, there was consensus about the need to condemn Russian breaches of international law and the importance of an arms embargo. Nationalist policies of the provisional Ukrainian government for its treatment of ethnical and linguistic minorities were criticized as well. However, the Left, even within the Social Democratic Party, could not agree on whether sanctions by the EU and the US should be implemented as well. Some like the party's president argued that sanctions should not be supported in order not to harm Switzerland's neutral stance as a mediator, emphasizing in the same breath that economic considerations should not influence a decision on sanctions.[30]

Strong anti-Americanism and a strong anti-EU attitude actually contribute to a pro-Russian worldview at both political poles. In this respect, left-wing pacifists and right-wing isolationists have unexpectedly found common ground. For the right-wing SVP, the Americans were responsible for the Kosovo War and the party held the view that Switzerland should uphold its strict neutrality. During the Kosovo War, the left, with its predictable aversion towards NATO, shared with the right a critical posture towards the US, even if for different reasons. Proponents of the leftist factions of Social Democrats and Greens found at least part of the blame for recent developments in Ukraine in the EU and US's expansionism and support of revolutions in Russia's vicinity and Russia's need for security and reassurance.[31] The left generally advocates an internationalist and humanistic peace order for the 21st century. On the political right, anti-Americanism is a rather new phenomenon, which originated in the Holocaust assets controversy[32] and George Bush's Iraq war. Before, America used to be Switzerland's 'sister republic'.[33] This new perception of the US as a hegemonic power was fuelled by recent US interventions against sacred Swiss institutions, including banking secrecy, which drew a lot of right-wing criticism.[34]

Other secondary reasons are to be found within the "clash of orientations" between the liberal, secular West and Russia's orthodox anti-Western

---

29 Bundesversammlung, Motion: Freihandelsabkommen mit Russland, 18 June 2015; Bundesversammlung, Interpellation: glaubwürdige Neutralitätspolitik, 18 December 2015.

30 „SP-Chef Christian Levrat spricht sich gegen Russland-Sanktionen aus – und zitiert Maurer vor die Aussenpoltische Kommission", in: Watson, 23 March 2014; Martin Naef, „Ukraine: Politische Überzeugungen vor wirtschaftliche Interessen", in: eSPress, 5 May 2014.

31 „Vischer und Gross: Das grosse Gespräch zum Schluss", an: http://cedricwermuth.ch, 24 October 2015.

32 Jacques Rossier, „Switzerland, Gold and the Banks: Analysis of a Crisis", in: American Swiss Foundation, n.d.

33 James H. Hutson, The Sister Republics: Die Schweiz und die Vereinigten Staaten von 1776 bis heute (Bern: Stämpfli, 1992).

34 "Wie die USA vom Freund zum Feind wurden", in: Schweiz am Sonntag, 9 June 2013.

course.[35] Putin's worldview has found supporters in a circle of Swiss right-wing conservatives, who are impressed with Putin's self-image as a defender of conservative traditional values against Western liberalism, decadence, and tolerance. Like Putin, they favour traditional family values over gender equality and LGBTQ rights and prefer nation-based states rather than multicultural melting pots.[36] Some politicians have gone so far as calling Yanukovich's ouster a staged coup with active Western support, and describing pro-Russian separatists in Eastern Ukraine as legitimate fighters for freedom and independence against an oppressive regime.[37]

Switzerland's leading quality newspaper, the Neue Zürcher Zeitung (NZZ), debated Switzerland's position during the Ukraine crisis. While the Swiss OSCE chairmanship was praised for contributing to mediation and de-escalation of the conflict, several key articles emphasized that Switzerland should position itself on the side of the West and as part of the Western values community.[38] The NZZ thus recommended a Western-oriented neutrality rather than a neutrality of absolute impartiality and equidistance. At times, NZZ editorials pursued a clear pro-Western campaign, comparing Putin's Russia with Hitler's Germany, asking the West to remember ill-fated Western appeasement in 1938 and to vehemently stand up against Russia's revisionist foreign policy.[39]

Overall, the Swiss public has been split among defenders of Western values and 'Putin understanders' ('Putin-Versteher') since the Ukraine crisis of 2014.[40] While there is no evidence yet that Russia is supporting right-wing parties or groups in Switzerland financially (as it allegedly does in other European countries[41]), Russia's message as a leader of global conservatism has resonated in Switzerland, as evidenced in letters to the editor and online comments in the Swiss media, including the Neue Zürcher Zeitung and

---

35   See Jonas Grätz, "Russia as a Challenger of the West", in: Strategic Trends (2014), pp. 11-30, pp. 16f, 27.
36   Oliver Kessler, „Die Schweiz im Neuen Kalten Krieg", in: Schriften für die Freiheit, 10 July 2015.
37   Yvette Estermann, „Unangebrachte Sanktionen gegen Russland", in: SVP Blog, 17 September 2014.
38   Simon Gemperli, "Bitte keine Gesinnungsneutralität", in: NZZ, 20 March 2014. For more NZZ examples as well as a broad analysis, see Olivia S. Wernli, „Instrumentalisierte Neutralität? Eine Analyse der aktuellen Neutralitätsdebatte in der Schweiz", MA thesis (Centre international de formation européenne, Nice, May 2014).
39   Jürg Dedial, „Putins braune Lehrmeister", in: NZZ, 22 April 2014, p. 9.
40   On 22 July 2014, an online poll of „20 Minuten" revealed that 77% wanted Switzerland not to join Western sanctions against Russia. On 30 July 2014, another poll conducted by the "Berner Zeitung" informed that 64.7% rejected Swiss sanctions against Putin's Russia. See also Andreas Umland, "Die Putin-Versteher und ihre Irrtümer", in: NZZ, 11 January 2016.
41   Andrew Rettman, "Reports multiply of Kremlin links to anti-EU parties", in: EU Observer, 26 November 2014.

Tages-Anzeiger.[42] Right-wing commentaries supporting Putin's Russia are complemented by suspected Kremlin-hired trolls, as well as leftists and conspiracy theory believers who support Putin because of their anti-Americanism.[43] This Putin factor weighs less heavily with a broader audience. For Markus Seiler, director of the Swiss intelligence services, Russia's foreign and security policy would not fundamentally change if Putin were unexpectedly no longer the dominant leader in Russia. Seiler also disclosed that the NDB is not expecting mass street protests against Putin (as in 2011-12).[44]

Outlook: Back to Co-operative Security

From the Swiss perspective, both shared norms and shared interests are important for sustainable Russian-Western co-operation. In the 1990s, Switzerland shared the Western perspective that Russia was drifting towards Western norms and values and strongly supported Russia's democratization. For the Swiss elite, Russia was part of Europe and Switzerland shared the Russian preference for strengthening the OSCE rather than strengthening an eastward expanded NATO (against Russia, which would be left outside of NATO).[45]

In its recently updated foreign policy strategy for the next four years (2016-2019), the Federal Council emphasizes the necessity of political coordination and co-operation between great powers to find solutions to global problems.[46] Swiss diplomacy aims at combining independence and engagement, thus building bridges as a Western country, despite not being a member of EU or NATO.

There is consensus that security in Europe can only be achieved by including Russia. Switzerland is willing to engage with Russia. During the 2014 Swiss OSCE Chairmanship, Swiss diplomacy innovatively promoted "economic connectivity" (within the OSCE's traditionally neglected 2nd dimension) to transform the spheres-of-interest thinking into a win-win-situa-

---

42 „Putin und die sechste Gewalt", in: NZZ, 4 March 2014; „Rebellion unter den Lesern", in: NZZ, 2 May 2014; „Putins Internetpiraten", in: NZZ, 18 June 2014.

43 Reinhard Meier, „Putins Trolle sind nicht nachhaltig", in: Journal21, 20 June 2014; Jürg Vollmer, „So arbeitet das geheime Netzwerk der Russland-Propaganda", at: www.juerg-vollmer.ch, 26 June 2014; „Twittern für den Kreml: Pro-russische Propaganda aus der Schweiz", in: NZZ am Sonntag, 29 June 2014.

44 „Wir haben den USA durchaus etwas zu bieten: Interview mit Markus Seiler", in: Bulletin zur schweizerischen Sicherheitspolitik 2015, pp. 89-104, here: pp. 99f.

45 Edouard Brunner, Bericht der Studienkommission für strategische Fragen, February 1990. See also Laurent Goetschel and Franz-Josef Meiers, „Die doppelte europäische Herausforderung an der schweizerischen Sicherheitspolitik", in: SVPW Jahrbuch (32)1992, pp. 39-52, here: pp. 44ff.; Jürg Martin Gabriel, Die Überwindung der Schweizer Neutralität, Beiträge Forschungsstelle für Internationale Beziehungen no. 5 (Zurich: ETH, 1996), p. 8.

46 EDA, Aussenpolitische Strategie 2016-2019, 17 February 2016, pp. 3-5.

tion.[47] In the fields of transnational threats and crisis prevention, Russian and Western security interests often overlap.

Both the Swiss government's 2016 Security White Paper and the most recent NDB reports note their pessimistic expectation that a confrontational Russia-West relationship will continue for the next few years. Yet, Swiss diplomacy aims at rebuilding trust, particularly within the OSCE with its co-operative and comprehensive security model. To strengthen the OSCE (and thus, also European Security), Switzerland would like to 1) include more robust elements and related planning capabilities in the OSCE's field missions; 2) strengthen economic connectivity; and 3) revitalize conventional arms control and confidence-building measures in Europe. In addition, finding solutions to transnational challenges, including jihadist terrorism by returning foreign fighters, or the refugee crisis might also improve Russia-Western relations step by step.[48] Even if a major armed conflict involving Switzerland remains unlikely, the Swiss Army needs to update its military doctrine to reflect new trends such as hybrid warfare.

While strongly supporting the right of each OSCE participating State to join an alliance, Foreign Minister Burkhalter suggested in June 2015 that the countries between Russia and the West claim a neutrality status for the moment rather than rushing to EU and NATO memberships, with security guarantees offered by both the West and Russia.[49] However, threatened by Russia, Ukraine and other 'In-Between-Countries' would currently prefer NATO membership over neutrality and are less confident about legal promises and guarantees since Russia broke the 1994 Budapest memorandum.

As a first step, the West and Russia should continue an informal, confidential high-level dialogue on European Security. Positive examples include side events at the OSCE Ministerial Councils in Basel and Belgrade in 2014 and 2015. In addition, Switzerland encourages Track II diplomacy including brainstorming among Russian and Western academics about how to return to co-operative security in Europe – thus continuing the 'Ischinger exercise' of 2015.[50] While new rules for a pan-European security order are not required, the existing CSCE/OSCE rules need to be followed – most notably by Russia. Dialogue may enable a better understanding of these rules.[51] Official Swiss foreign policy emphasizes that all parties have to adhere to the Minsk

---

47 See Didier Burkhalter, More Economic and Environmental Cooperation for More Security in Europe, Prague, 10 September 2014.

48 Didier Burkhalter, Statement at the 22nd OSCE Ministerial Council, Belgrade, 3 December 2015. See Petri Hakkarainen and Christian Nünlist, "Trust and Realpolitik: The OSCE in 2016", in: Policy Perspectives 4(1)2016.

49 Didier Burkhalter, Addressing the crisis of European security resolutely and comprehensively: Some reflections on the way forward, Vienna, 17 June 2015.

50 See Hakkarainen/Nünlist, Trust and Realpolitik.

51 Burkhalter, Ungeteiltes und freies Europa?, p. 13.

Agreement, but that both sides should try to co-operate with pragmatism to reach progress despite disagreement over the question of status.[52]

Status-neutral solutions might contribute to pragmatic Russian-Western co-operation without legitimizing Russia's land grab of Crimea. Such initiatives will critically depend on the agreement and co-operation of states involved. Given their willingness to engage, status-neutral arms control could be an interesting concept for re-launching a security-policy dialog, building on the success of a status-neutral mission statement for the OSCE Special Monitoring Mission (SMM) adopted in March 2014 or the Swiss-mediated compromise trade deal between Russia and Georgia in 2011 establishing a neutral company that conducted checks on all trade between the two nations.[53]

52   Ibid., p. 10.
53   Hakkarainen/Nünlist, Trust and Realpolitik.

Hüseyin Bagci and Ali Serdar Erdurmaz

Turkey-Russia Relations in the Era of the Justice and Development Party (AK Party). From Honeymoon to Separation and Reconciliation Again

Introduction

Turkey and Russia, two leading countries from the beginning of history, are on the stage of the international system. Rapid and important improvements in the political arena have been observed between the two countries since the beginning of the 2000s. In recent years, a peaceful and constructive atmosphere in Turkey and Russia relations has been dominant, even though they were suspended, due to a crisis which emerged after Turkey downed a Russian fighter plane in November 2015.

During the AK Party era, Moscow and Ankara have shared the same attitudes towards international problems. For years, both countries have indicated their wish that bilateral relations not remain only economic, but also include regional and global interests. In the light of this confidence and respect, they have become a "multi-dimensional partnership" (Celikpala 2007).

For all that, it cannot be denied that there are some problems between the two countries. Ultimately, they are competing in the same geographical area. Even though Russia is no longer a direct neighbour of Turkey since the collapse of the Soviet Union in 1991, it is, nevertheless, the most important great power in its vicinity. From the end of the Cold War up until 2000, despite a great deal of bilateral effort put into improving mutual relations in political, economic and other areas, these efforts were not fruitful, since there was competition between the two countries in the fields of energy, ethnicity and regional dominance (Ozbay 2010). First of all, Turkey does not share Russia's views on the post-Soviet republics because it sees itself as a decision-maker in ongoing conflicts in the post-Soviet republics in the Caucasus region, especially with respect to the Chechen problem (Ozdal et al. 2013). Second, the Russian Federation's support of the PKK was a challenging problem for the two countries which made it difficult to create mutual confidence in each other (Ozdal et al. 2013). Third, Turkey is in favour of the territorial integrity of Azerbaijan and against the Armenian occupation and possession of one-fifth of Azerbaijani territory, including Karabakh, while Russia asserts that it has a right in this region. Today, Turkey's ally, Azerbaijan, does not have effective control over its territory. Turkey has been the leading country in supporting Azerbaijan in the international arena (Republic of Turkey Ministry of Foreign Affairs 2012), especially in its struggle to regain control over the territory occupied by Armenia (Anon 2016f). Nevertheless, toward the end of the 1990s, it was announced by Prime Minister Bulent Ecevit that one Chechen militant would be extradited to Russia, which contributed to improving relations. Moreover and similarly, Russia closed the PKK's Moscow office (Ozdal et al. 2013). These efforts can be considered the initiation of the initiatives taken to improve relations between the rivals at the turn of the century.

Relations from 2000 up until 2011 (Syrian Crisis)

Political and Diplomatic Relations

In the first decade of the new millennium, relations between these two important states in the Eurasian region and Black Sea Basin showed rapid advancement in political-diplomatic, economic, trade, cultural, scientific and educational fields. As a result, the strong co-operation, particularly between the top-level politicians, Recep Tayyip Erdoğan and Vladimir Putin, and rapidly improving and expanding political, diplomatic and economic relations created a substantial element of peace, security and welfare in both countries within the understanding of "win-win" (Özbay 2011).

During the presidencies of Putin and Erdoğan bilateral relations between Turkey and the Russian Federation have witnessed gradual improvement in the economic and political fields. In December 2002 Recep Tayyip Erdoğan, the winner of the general election of 3 November, visited Moscow as the leader of the AK party (AKP) and was received by President Vladimir Putin and Prime Minister Kasyonov respectively (Hurriyet 2002). This initiative heralded a new approach in the foreign policy of the new Turkish government. In this respect, the Turkish Grand National Assembly's (TBMM) rejection of the request by the United States to base its troops in Turkey (1 March 2003) was gladly welcomed by Russia (Aras 2009; Anon 2003). This decision paved the way for Russia to realize that Ankara would follow a foreign policy independent from Washington.

As a matter of fact, the "AK Party Program, Section VI. Foreign Policy" described the new approach to foreign policy as cited below (AK Parti 2002). In this program, the AKP adopted a new, independent and flexible foreign policy with its neighbours in order to maintain good relations through dialogue and co-operation. Relations with the Russian Federation were considered to be based on mutual co-operation. Later on, this approach was formulated as "zero problem with neighbours" by Ahmet Davutoğlu, author of the book "Strategic Depths" (Davutoglu 2010); (Aras 2009). When Davutoğlu, the Foreign Policy Advisor, was appointed as Minister of Foreign Affairs later on, a pro-active foreign policy toward Turkey's neighbours was introduced, which lasted up to the first months of the Arab Spring. Davutoğlu stated that Turkey's position was built on four main principles and listed these as "general security for the whole region, dialogue for crisis resolution, economic interdependence, and pluralism and common cultural existence" (Minister of Foreign Affairs 2011). He thought that Turkey could be a "soft power actor" with its democracy (Bagci 2009), as is outlined in the following paragraphs:

> "The particularity of military alliances and blocks to become the determinant elements of international relations has been greatly reduced, and cooperation projects have become a common tool of relations between States. In this new environment, Turkey must also rearrange and create its relations with centers of power with alternatives, flexibly and with many axes....
> Our party is of the opinion that the regional security environment makes an important contribution to economic development. For this reason, Turkey shall make more efforts to provide security and stability in its near surroundings, shall increase its attempts to maintain good relations with its neighbors based on dialogue and, thus, it shall contribute more to the development of regional cooperation....
> Friendly relations with the Russian Federation shall be maintained based on cooperation rather than competition in Middle-East and the Caucuses. ..."(AK Parti 2002)

While Russia has given support to Turkey's EU membership, Ankara supported the Russian observer status in the Organization of Islamic Cooperation (Nureddin 2009; Shlykov n.d.) and tried to take the initiative in establishing the Russia-Islamic World Strategic Vision Group (Shlykov n.d.). These efforts led to Russian Foreign Minister Sergey Lavrov and then-OIC Secretary General, Ekmeleddin Ihsanoglu, signing the Framework Agreement on Cooperation between Russia's Ministry of Foreign Affairs and the Permanent Secretariat in early October 2013 (Kosach 2015).

The high level political dialogue between Turkey and Russia gained further momentum with the official visit of Vladimir Putin to Turkey on 5-6 December 2004 (Anon 2016d). This was the first presidential visit in 32 years. During the visit, the 'Joint Declaration on the Intensification of Friendship and Multidimensional Partnership' was signed by the presidents of both countries. Shortly after this visit, the Turkish Prime Minister Erdoğan also paid a visit to the Russian Federation on 10-12 January 2005 in order to participate in the inauguration ceremony of the Turkish Trade Center in Moscow (Anon 2016d), and again on 8-9 May 2005 on the occasion of the 60th Anniversary of the World War II Victory Day. Further mutual visits – Mr. Erdoğan and Mr. Putin met ten times in five years – added new momentum to the development of bilateral relations and strengthened mutual confidence between the two countries. Turkey also enhanced those visits with official visits by President Ahmet Necdet Sezer in June 2006 (Anon 2006) and President Abdullah Gul in 2009 respectively (Engdahl 2009). President Sezer's visit was the first presidential level visit to Russia since the founding of the RF and was highly significant in terms of showing the importance of bilateral relations for both countries (Özbay 2011). President Gul paid another significant visit, including Moscow and Kazan, the capital of Tatarstan. The Tatarstan visit, in particular, reflected that confidence and trust were being established by Moscow and Ankara. In previous decades, requests by Turkey to visit Turk communities in Russia had created great political disturbance (Anon 2009b). This time, the Russian Izvestia, an official newspaper, responded to the Kazan visit with a very moderate approach (Anon 2009c).

In 2009, 20 cooperation protocols were signed, including, on the one hand, "co-operation in natural gas issue" and "co-operation in the petroleum field" or, on the other hand, economic, technological and cultural co-operation (Anon 2009a).

Full speed, high level diplomatic relations continued in 2010. A visit by Prime Minister Erdoğan was followed by President Dmitry Medvedev's visit to Ankara. In the same year, the first meeting of the High-Level Cooperation Council (HLCC) was held in Ankara with President Medvedev (Nesterenko 2010). According to a 15 January 2010 briefing by Russian MFA Spokesman Andrei Nesterenko the main outcome of the visit was as follows;

> "Discussions centered on the full range of bilateral co-operation issues, the current state of economic and trade ties, and pressing international and regional issues; the prospects for the formation of a new European security architecture, the state of affairs in Transcaucasia as Turkish-Armenian relations are getting normalized, the condition of the Middle East peace process, as well as interaction within the BSEC and other international entities" (Nesterenko 2010).

Particular attention was paid to ways of carrying out joint Russian-Turkish energy projects, such as constructing the South Stream and Blue Stream-2 gas pipelines, the Samsun-Ceyhan oil pipeline and a nuclear power plant in Turkey. The two sides exchanged views on the progress in implementing the agreements reached during Vladimir Putin's working visit to Ankara in August 2009 and legally enshrined them in a number of intergovernmental and interdepartmental documents.

It can be said that the principal outcome of the visit was the reaffirmation of the high level of mutual understanding and awareness of the commonality of interests of the two countries (Nesterenko 2010). This shows that trust, understanding and co-operation had reached a very high level between the two former rivals.

Table 1: Turkey-Russia, Mutual High Level Visits (2000-2012)

(Ozdal et al. 2013)	City	Date
Prime Minister (PM) Mikhail Khazyanov & PM Bülent Ecevit	Ankara	September 2000
Foreign Minister (FM) Igor Ivanov & President Ahmet Necdet Sezer, PM Bülent Ecevit and FM İsmail Cem	Ankara	June 2001
President Vladimir Putin & President Ahmet Necdet Sezer, PM Recep Tayyip Erdoğan	Ankara	December 2004
PM RecepTayyipErdoğan & President Vladimir Putin	Moscow	January 2005
PM RecepTayyip Erdoğan & President Vladimir Putin	Sochi	July 2005
President Vladimir Putin & President Ahmet NecdetSezer	Moscow	June 2006
President Abdullah Gul & President Dmitri Medvedev	Moscow	February 2009
PM Recep Tayyip Erdoğan & PM Vladimir Putin	Ankara	August 2009
PM Recep Tayyip Erdoğan& President Dmitri Medvedev	Moscow	January 2010
President Dmitri Medvedev & PM Recep Tayyip Erdoğan	Ankara	May 2010
PM Recep Tayyip Erdoğan & PM Vladimir Putin	Istanbul	June 2011
PM Recep Tayyip Erdoğan & President Vladimir Putin	Moscow	March 2011
PM Recep Tayyip Erdoğan & President Vladimir Putin	Moscow	June 2012
President Vladimir Putin & PM Recep Tayyip Erdoğan	Ankara	December 2012

Source: Russian Embassy in Ankara, at: http://www.turkey.mid.ru/tur/.

Economic and Trade Relations

Geographical proximity provides a significant advantage to both countries with respect to improving economic and trade relations. In 1998, an economic crisis experienced by Russia caused a decrease in the Turkish-Russian foreign trade volume, which continued in 1999 (Table 2) (Anon 2016g). The most important reason for these deficits was that Turkey was not able to export enough goods in return for the natural gas imported in accordance with the Agreement on Natural Gases signed with the USSR on September 18, 1984 (Anon 2010).

In 2008, the trade volume between the two countries reached an all-time high of 37.85 billion US dollars. But it showed a 40.1 per cent decline in 2009 (16.23 billion US dollars, Anon 2010; Özbay 2011). After 2010, the foreign trade volume radically increased again up until the end of 2015, from

135

26.2 billion dollars in 2010 to 31.2 billion dollars at the end of 2014 (1.73 per cent increase, Figure 1). The Russian share was 5.9 billion dollars, 3.8 per cent of Turkey's total export of 1576 billion dollars in 2014 and 3 billion dollars (2.5 per cent) of 107.3 billion dollars total export to Russia in the period from January to September 2015 (Gart and Taggart 2015).

Figure 1: Turkey-Russia Foreign Trade Values (thousand $) ("Turkiye ile Ticaret" 2016)

Years	Export	Import	Volume	Balance
2002	1,172,039	3,891,722	5,063,761	-2,719,683
2003	1,367,591	5,451,316	6,818,907	- 4,083,725
2004	1,859,187	9,033,138	10,892,325	-7,173,951
2005	2,377,050	12,905,620	15,282,670	-10,528,570
2006	3,237,611	17,806,239	21,043,850	-14,568,628
2007	4,726,853	23,508,494	28,235,347	-18,781,641
2008	6,483,004	31,364,477	37,847,481	-24,881,473
2009	3,202,398	19,450,085	22,652,483	-16,247,687
2010	4,628,153	21,600,641	26,228,794	-16,972,488
2011	5,992,633	23,952,914	29,945,548	-17,960,281
2012	6,680,586	26,625,286	33,305,872	-19,944,700
2013	6,964,209	25,064,214	32,028,423	-18,100,004
2014	5,945,713	25,293,392	31,239,105	-19,347,679
2014 (January-November)	5,016,438	21,105,711	26,122,149	-16,089,272
2015 (January- November)	3,065,230	17,338,445	20,403,675	-14,273,215

Source: TUIK

Another important economic factor for Turkish-Russian relations is tourism. According to the 2014 Turkish Central Bank data, 35.9 million tourists visited Turkey in 2013, of which 13 per cent were Russians. (Sezgin 2015). This number decreased radically in 2014 (Sezgin 2015): Turkey lost one third of its Russian tourists in 2014/15 (Wheatley 2015). Both the fact that Turkey shot down a Russian war plane at the end of 2015 and the economic embargo placed on the RF by the USA and the EU contributed to the number of Russian tourists decreasing by 79 per cent in the first three months of 2016 compared to the same period of 2015 (Anon 2016a).

In the energy sector, Turkey decided in the 2000s to fulfil a significant amount of its energy needs through the RF. Turkey purchased 23.8 billion m^3 and 19.9 billion m^3 natural gas from Russia in 2008 and 2009 respectively, thus constituting one of the main factors of Ankara's economic and trade relationships with Moscow (Anon 2016g). The Russian share of Turkey's natural gas imports was 55 per cent (27 billion m^3 of the total of 49.2 billion m^3). According to a long term agreement between the two countries, this level must be maintained by Ankara for another ten years (Kazokoğlu 2015). The most sensitive issue here is that Turkey not only depends on natural gas imports from Russia, but also on the infrastructure of the main pipelines which carry it.

Relations from 2011 Onwards

With the beginning of the Arab Spring, significant changes occurred in the politics of both Turkey and Russia. Their approaches to Syria, in particular, became a dilemma. While Turkey's position is near that of the West, Russia supports the Assad regime in Syria.

Turkey has been one of the most consistent supporters of revolutionary changes in the Middle East. Ever since November 2011, Ankara has been actively supporting regime changes in Tunisia, Egypt, Libya and Yemen, while in Syria it has almost taken the leading role in supporting rebels against the government of President Bashar al-Assad (Sotnichenko 2015). Turkey's policy in Syria aims to overthrow the Assad regime and establish a democratic government instead (Falk 2014). Contrary to this, in Russian political discourse, no regime change operation is acceptable under any circumstances (Valdai 2014). Turkish policy thus runs directly counter to Russian policy in the Syrian case, resulting in ongoing disputes over violations of Turkish airspace etc. On 24 November 2015, a Russian Su-24m bomber aircraft was shot down by a Turkish F-16 fighter jet while it was allegedly performing a routine combat task in northern Syria against terrorist targets. Following the incident, divergent explanations were reported by the two sides, each accusing the other (Erdurmaz 2015). While Turkey claimed that the Russian jet had violated its airspace for 17 seconds, during which they had warned the jet's crew of the violation no fewer than 50 times, Russian officials denied having violated the Turkish airspace and claimed not to have received any warning messages from the Turkish military. Relations between Moscow and Ankara have deteriorated dramatically since then (Anon 2015d). In fact, Russian support for Assad's regime and its recent activities in Syria had been heavily criticized by President Recep Tayyip Erdoğan for a while before this incident.

As an immediate reply to the situation, Russia cut off all military communication with Turkey, launched a significant military build-up in Syria and announced that it would deploy an S-400 air defence system to its airbase near the city of Lattakia in the eastern Mediterranean. Meanwhile, Turkey turned to NATO to get a strong statement justifying Turkish reaction to the violation. Indeed, NATO Secretary General Jens Stoltenberg announced that NATO endorsed Turkey's action (Lantier 2015).

According to most international relations experts, the deterioration of relations between Turkey and Russia does not benefit either side. However, Russia announced that it would review political, economic, social and military relations with Turkey immediately. It imposed sanctions on Turkish goods, such as fruit, vegetables, textiles and auto spare parts, and stopped granting entry visas to Turkish trucks en route to Central Asia, thereby causing an estimated $ two billion worth of damage to Turkish exports (Zhanaltay 2016). Moreover, Russia advised its citizens not to vacation in Turkey, seen as the most popular holiday destination by Russian tourists.

These policies seem to have been backed by Russian public policy-makers and some academic officials. Vladimir Avatkov, a Turkey scholar and professor at the Moscow State Institute of International Relations, for example, severely criticised Turkey stating that it should be held responsible for its actions: "Turkish leadership crossed the line and should pay for its act of aggression" (Borik 2015). He also said that Ankara's rash decisions not only jeopardized Russian-Turkish relations, but also undermined efforts on the creation of a global anti-terrorist coalition.

In order to justify his policies, Vladimir Putin has publicly claimed that Turkey was villainously stabbing Russia in the back, while he was waging a heroic battle against terrorist organizations, such as ISIS (Islamic State in Iraq and Syria) in Syria (Shaheen & Shaun 2016). He openly blamed Turkey for supporting ISIS (Anon 2015f) by smuggling and selling Syrian oil on international markets, even though there is no hard evidence for this (Chulov 2015).

Still another issue, through which Russia has striven to minimize Turkish influence, has been the presence of Turkish troops at the base camp of Basheeqa in Northern Iraq. Turkish officials claim that their troops have been deployed since 2014 to the military base in the northern Iraqi city of Mosul, which was seized by ISIS militants in June of that year, at the request of Iraqi Prime Minister Haider al-Abadi, to train Iraqi forces to launch an operation against the terrorist group to retake the ISIS-controlled city. However, Iraqi authorities suddenly perceived the situation as a problem. They issued an ultimatum for Turkey to withdraw its soldiers within 48 hours. Otherwise, they threatened to take the case to the UN Security Council. The deadline passed and Russia took the case to UNSC, but the Council refused it. Baghdad is believed to have taken this stance against Turkey at Moscow's instigation, as Russia vowed to punish Turkey using means other than military retaliation (Anon 2015a; Anon 2015b).

By contrast to this, the Turkish government has been trying to stay calm, maintaining that no country would accept its territorial sovereignty being violated by another country. Several attempts by President Erdoğan to improve strained relations remained unsuccessful (Druzhini 2016; Anon

2016e). Turkish leaders have repeatedly called for a bilateral meeting with Russia and offered to solve the problem through diplomatic channels. According to R. Tayyip Erdoğan, Russia's response to the downing of its war plane in Turkish airspace is too emotional. He also stated that Turkey would not respond in kind to Russia's sanctions (Anon 2015k). However, Turkey has already started to seek new suppliers of natural gas and is negotiating bilaterally with some other gas suppliers, such as Qatar, Northern Iraq, even Israel and Azerbaijan, in order to become independent from Russian resources. Meanwhile, Russia has allowed the PYD to open an office in Moscow and has shown its open support for PYD, which is seen by Turkey as a terrorist organization (Sharkov 2016). Moscow, for its part, has claimed that Turkey was co-operating with and purchasing oil from the IS (Luhn 2015).

In fact, Turkey is afraid that Russia's intervention in the regime in Damascus will worsen the existing fraught situation, continue the war, and make the refugee crisis along Turkey's border worse (Anon 2015j; Anon 2015l).

From Confrontation to Reconciliation

The first reconciliation signal came from President Vladimir Putin during a two day visit to Greece on 28 May 2016, during which he announced that "we want to mend our relations with Turkey" (Anon 2016c). At the end of June, the Kremlin declared that Turkish President Recep Tayyip Erdoğan had sent a letter of apology in which he had pledged to repair diplomatic relations. This letter reportedly said that Erdoğan promised to do "everything possible" to restore relations with Russia (Anon 2016b, Anon 2016h).

As a matter of fact, both sides have suffered economic and political loss in the aftermath of this incident. According to Vice Prime Minister, Mehmet Simsek, the economic loss reached approximately nine billion US dollars, thus 0.3-0.4 per cent of the Turkish GNP (Anon 2015g). On the Russian side, it seems that the deterioration of relations between the two countries has also placed a heavy load on the Russian leader's shoulders, which he could not carry for a long time (Alexei 2016; Bilgrami 2016). In consequence, both sides have made the utmost effort to re-establish relations as they were before the downing of jet.

At the end of the recent referendum victory on 16 April 2017, the Russian president was one of the first leaders to congratulate President Recep Tayyip Erdoğan . President Erdoğan made his first visit after this victory to Russia on 3 May. In this meeting, Ankara probably implied that "whoever is interested in the Middle East cannot pursue this without Turkey's co-operation, regardless of who is leading the country" as Huseyin Bagci told Al-Monitor. This underlines the fact that Turkey "has colossal geopolitical and economic importance" (Idiz 2017). In this meeting, Russian President Putin said: "It is good that we have a chance to meet in due course and discuss key issues of bilateral co-operation and major issues on the international agenda, including such pressing issues as the Syrian crisis." Also, President Erdoğan stressed that he is sure that those steps that we are taking together will change the fate of the whole region (Anon 2107). In this vein, normalising trade relations seems a much easier task than political compromising on the Syrian issue, on which the two countries have their own strategies and military operation ideas, in accordance with their own national interests. However, it seems that either Turkey or Russia (or both) will try to improve their bilateral relations and will make the utmost efforts not to harm mutual relations any more. "The mere fact of this regime of our joint work shows that Russian-Turkish relations are becoming of a special character and are being restored in a full format," he said.

Conclusion

There was a notable change in the dynamics of socio-economic relations and those in the field of security co-operation between Turkey and Russia in the period of 2002-2015. Until 2015, relations in the field of security mainly evolved on the basis of profound economic and trade co-operation, significant mutual investments in the construction and tourism fields, as well as high-level diplomatic dialogue. Ultimately, this increase in diplomatic and economic relations brought about increased human and cultural interaction as applied in the fields of trade and tourism. With the 24 November 2015 shooting down of a Russian aircraft by the Turkish army, the prior Turkish-Russian relations were wiped out. Russia's political stance on Syria played a crucial role in this event. As a result of that shooting, a new era started between Turkey and Russia.

It is clear that there have been several power conflicts between Russia and Turkey. The lack of confidence is also observed in mutual relations. At the same time, a dominance issue over the Middle East has always been one of the major topics or conflicts between the two countries. Russia, from the earlier times of history, has always desired to be the one and only hegemon in the region. In fact, the desire to be the super power in Central Asia and the Middle East is the main reason for this long-term dispute.

Nevertheless, despite Russia and Turkey having some conflicting interests in the region, the two countries also have mutual economic and diplomatic relations, which could not be undermined by the two sides without taking into consideration severe economic and political losses. In this respect, both countries, especially Turkey, have tried to preserve relations. As a result, Russian President Vladimir Putin's initiative paved the way to reestablish and repair mutual relations after the fighter jet incident. And, the recent meeting in Sochi on 3 May 2017 clinched the reconciliation of the two countries despite the military disparities in Syria. This was the most significant change between the two countries "from confrontation to reconciliation" in the hope of no crises anymore!

References

AK Parti, 2002. AK Party Program. AK Parti Program. Available at: https://www. ak-parti.org.tr/english/akparti/parti-programme#bolum_ [Accessed October 9, 2016].

Alexei, L., 2016. 5 economic reasons for reconciliation between Russia and Turkey. Russia Beyon the Headlines. Available at: rbth.com,business,2016/06/29 [Accessed August 4, 2016].

Anon, 2016a. Antalya'da Rus pazarı yüzde 79 daraldı. Hurriyet newpaper. Available at: http://www.hurriyet.com.tr/antalyada-rus-pazari-yuzde-79-daraldi-40096555.

Anon, 2012. Davutoğlu Esad'a ömür biçti. NTV. Available at: http://www.ntv.com.tr/turkiye/davutoglu-esada-omur-bicti,Nsez_e7zmEO7uz5O9Pv6hw.

Anon, 2016b. Erdoğan "sorry" for downing of Russian Jet. Al Jazeera. Available at: www.aljazeera.com.

Anon, 2015a. Getting Tough on Turkey: Kremlin Vows to Punish Ankara for Downed Jet. sputniknews, p. 1. Available at: https://sputniknews.com/world/2015 1125/1030721781/russia-turkey-relations-jet.html [Accessed October 9, 2016].

Anon, 2015b. Iraq appeals to UN and demands Turkey withdraw troops from its north. The Guardian. Available at: https://www.theguardian.com/world/ 2015/dec/12/iraq-appeals-to-un-and-demands-turkey-withdraw-troops-from-its-north.

Anon, 2003. Putin: Meclis kararı haftanın olayı. Radikal newspaper. Available at: http://www.radikal.com.tr/haber.php?haberno=68041.

Anon, 2015c. Putin: Turkey's downing of jet a "stab in the back." Al Jazeera. Available at: http://www.aljazeera.com/news/2015/11/russia-turkey-jet-syria-shot-151124140238943.html.

Anon, 2016c. Putin'den İlişkilerde Yumuşama Sinyali. Milliyet Newspaper. Available at: http://www.milliyet.com.tr/putin-den-iliskilerde-yumusama/dunya/detay/2253 355/default.htm.

Anon, 2009a. Putin'in Ankara Ziyareti ve Gelişen Türkiye-Rusya İlişkileri. USAK. Available at: http://www.usak.org.tr/tr/yayinlar/usak-haberleri/putin-in-ankara-ziyareti-ve-gelisen-turkiye-rusya-iliskileri [Accessed May 16, 2016].

Anon, 2015d. Putin declines Erdoğan to meet in Paris over downed Russian jet. Hurriyet daily news. Available at: http://www.hurriyetdailynews.com/putin-declines-Erdoğan -to-meet-in-paris-over-downed-russian-jet.aspx?pageID=238&n ID=91871&NewsCatID=352.

Anon, 2015e. Russia halts Turkish Stream project over downed jet. RT News. Available at: https://www.rt.com/business/324230-gazprom-turkish-stream-can-cellation/ [Accessed June 10, 2016].

Anon, 2015f. Russia has "more proof" ISIS oil routed through Turkey, Erdoğan says he'll resign if it's true. RT News, p.1. Available at: https://www.rt.com/news/324045-putin-erdogan-su-downing/ [Accessed October 9, 2016].

Anon, 2010. Rusya ülke raporu, Istanbul. Available at: http://www.aia-istanbul.org/files/bilgibankasi/pazarlar/ulkeler/russia_ulkeraporu.pdf.

Anon, 2006. Sezer's visit to cap growing cooperation with Russia. Hurriyet daily news. Available at: http://www.hurriyetdailynews.com/sezers-visit-to-cap-growing-cooperation-with-russia.aspx?pageID=438&n=sezers-visit-to-cap-growing-cooperation-with-russia-2006-06-25.

Anon, 2015g. Simsek: Kayıp 9 milyar doları bulabilir. Deutsche Welle Türkçe. Available at: www.dw.comşisek-kayıp-9-milyar-doları-bulabilir [Accessed August 3, 2016].

Anon, 2015h. Syria crisis: Where key countries stand. BBC News. Available at: http://www.bbc.com/news/world-middle-east-23849587.

Anon, 2009b. Tataristan'a tarihi ziyaret. Radikal newspaper. Available at: http://www.radikal.com.tr/yorum/tataristana-tarihi-ziyaret-921786/.

Anon, 2016d. Turkey′s Political Relations With Russian Federation. Available at: http://www.mfa.gov.tr/turkey_s-political-relations-with-russian-federation.en.mfa.

Anon, 2015i. Turkey's downing of Russian warplane - what we know. BBC News. Available at: http://www.bbc.com/news/world-middle-east-34912581.

Anon, 2015j. Turkey condemns attack on Syrian Turkmen village, summons Russian envoy. Hurriyet daily news, p.1. Available at: http://www.hurriyetdailynews. com/turkey-condemns-attack-on-syrian-turkmen-village-summons-russian-envoy-.aspx?pageID=238&nID=91459&NewsCatID=352.

Anon, 2016e. Turkey warns Russia after "airspace breach." The Associated Press, Ankara, p.1. Available at: http://english.alarabiya.net/en/2016/01/30/Turkey-accuses-Russia-of-airspace-breach.html [Accessed October 9, 2016].

Anon, 2015k. Turkish, Russian FMs to discuss downed Russian jet. Yeni Şafak. Available at: http://www.yenisafak.com/en/world/turkish-russian-fms-to-discuss-downed-russian-jet-2350450.

Anon, 2015l. Türkiye'den Rusya'ya "Bayırbucak" uyarısı. Hurriyet newspaperpaper. Available at: http://www.hurriyet.com.tr/turkiyeden-rusyaya-bayirbucak-uyarisi-40016598.

Anon, 2016f. Türkiye - Azerbaycan Siyasi İlişkileri. Minister of Foreign Affairs. Available at: http://www.mfa.gov.tr/turkiye-azerbaycan-siyasi-iliskileri.tr.mfa [Accessed April 15, 2016].

Anon, 2016g. Turkiye ile Ticaret, Ankara. Available at: https://www.ekonomi.gov. tr/portal/faces/home/disIliskiler/ulkeler/ulke-detay/Rusya Federasyonu/html-viewer-ulkeler?contentId=UCM#dDocName:EK-160814&contentTitle=TürkiyeileTicaret &_afrLoop=1641181087377618&_afrWindowMode=0&_afrWindowId=3atxnkq ng.

Anon, 2009c. Türkiye-Rusya; Tarihin İki Yüzü. TASAM. Available at: http://www. tasam.org/tr-TR/Icerik/1020/turkiye-rusya_tarihin_iki_yuzu [Accessed May 16, 2016].

Anon, 2015m. Turkey summons Russian envoy over bombing of Turkmens in Syria: PM. Reuters. Available at: http://www.reuters.com/article/us-mideast-crisis-syria-turkey-russia-idUSKCN0T91MO20151120.

Anon, 2016h. Vladimir Putin received a letter from President of Turkey Recep Tayyip Erdoğan . President of Russia. Available at: http://en.kremlin.ru/events/president/news/52282 [Accessed July 30, 2016].

Anon, 2017. Putin: Russia and Turkey restoring full-format relations. Russia Beyond the Headlines. Available at: https://www.rbth.com/news/2017/05/03/putin-russia-and-turkey-restoring-full-format-relations_755461[Accessed May 20, 2017].

Aras, B., 2009. Türkiye ve rusya federasyonu: çok boyutlu ortaklik 1, Ankara. Available at: http://arsiv.setav.org/Ups/dosya/6743.pdf.

Bagci, H., 2009. Changing Geopolitics and Turkish Foreign Policy. Internationales Institut dur Liberale Politik Wien, XVI, p.10. Available at: http://edoc.bibliothek.uni-halle.de/servlets/MCRFileNodeServlet/HALCoRe_derivate_00004940/IILP_06_09_Bagci_Changing_Geopolitics_and_Turkish_Forei.pdf.

Bagci, H., 2015. Strategic Depth in Syria-from the begining to Russian Intervention. Valdai Papers, 37(December), pp.1-19.

Bilgrami, M.P., 2016. Putin's myopia creates upheaval in Russian-Turkish relations. Daily Sabah. Available at: https://www.google.com.tr/url?sa=t&rct=j&q=&esrc=s&source=web&cd=1&ved=0ahUKEwik9vqs6KXOAhWnAJoKHa7TDzgQFggaMAA&url=http://www.dailysabah.com/op-ed/2016/04/02/putins-myopia-creates-upheaval-in-russian-turkish-relations&usg=AFQjCNGxIYQ32HJo.

Borik, A., 2015. Russian-Turkish tensions and the global fight against ISIS. Russia Direct, p.1. Available at: http://www.russia-direct.org/analysis/russian-turkish-tensions-and-global-fight-against-isis-seen-think-tanks [Accessed October 9, 2016].

Burgleigh, M., 2016. The Sultan and the Tsar: Will the imperial ambitions of Russia's Putin and Turkey's Erdoğan spark a new World War, asks historian MICHAEL BURLEIGH. Dailymail. Available at: http://www.dailymail.co.uk/news/article-3446089/The-Sultan-Tsar-imperial-ambitions-Russia-s-Putin-Turkey-s-Erdogan-spark-new-World-War-asks-historian-MICHAEL-BURLEIGH.html.

Celikpala, M. (TOBB U., 2007. 990'LARDAN GÜNÜMÜZE TÜRK-RUS İLİŞKİLERİ. Avrasya Dosyası, 13(1), pp.267–298. Available at: https://www.academia.edu/586701/%C4%B0K%C4%B0L%C4%B0_%C4%B0%C5%9EB%C4%B0RL%C4%B0%C4%9E%C4%B0NDEN_%C3%87OK_BOYUTLU_ORTAKLI%C4%9EA_1990DAN_G%C3%9CN%C3%9CM%C3%9CZE_T%C3%9CRK-RUS_%C4%B0L%C4%B0%C5%9EK%C4%B0LER%C4%B0.

Cetinkaya, O. & Dianova, Y., 2016. Business implications of Russian sanctions against Turkey. British Chamber of Commerce Turkey. Available at: http://www.bcct.org.tr/news/business-implications-of-russian-sanctions-against-turkey/16340.

Chulov, M., 2015. Is Vladimir Putin right to label Turkey "accomplices of terrorists"? The Guard, p.1. Available at: https://www.theguardian.com/world/2015/nov/24/vladimir-putin-turkey-isis-terrorists-warplane-analysis.

Davutoglu, A., 2010. Turkey's zero problem foreign policy. Foreign Policy. Available at: http://foreignpolicy.com/2010/05/20/turkeys-zero-problems-foreign-policy/.

Demirtas, S., 2015. Erdoğan, Putin discuss Syria, Assad's future in tête-à-tête. Hurriyet daily news. Available at: http://www.hurriyetdailynews.com/erdogan-putin-discuss-syria-assads-future-in-tte--tte.aspx?pageID-238&nID-91224& NewsCatID=510.

Druzhini, A., 2016. Is Putin giving Turkey the cold shoulder? , p.1. Available at: http://www.cbsnews.com/news/turkish-president-erdogan-putin-not-responding-latest-russia-jet-incident/.

Engdahl, W., 2009. The Geopolitical Great Game: Turkey and Russia Moving Closer. Voltairenet.org. Available at: http://www.voltairenet.org/article159189.html [Accessed May 14, 2016].

Erdurmaz, A.S., 2015. Uçağın Düşürülmesinin Ardından Rusya'nın Tutumu. turksam.org. Available at: http://www.turksam.org/tr/makale-detay/1267-ucagin-dusurulmesinin-ardindan-rusya-nin-tutumu [Accessed June 12, 2016].

Falk, R., 2014. Can the U.S. Government Accept an Independent Turkish Foreign Policy in the Middle East? Insight Turkey, 16(1), pp.7–18.

Galt and Taggart, 2015. Turkey-Russia Standoff Much Ado about "Something". Available at: file:///C:/Users/user/Downloads/Turkey%20Russia%20Standoff%20-%20Much% 20Ado%20about%20'Something'%20.pdf [Accessed May 20,2017].

Gismatullin, E., 2016. Putin's Decade-Old Dream Realized as Russia to Price Its Own Oil. Bloomberg, p.1. Available at: http://www.bloomberg.com/ news/articles/ 2016-04-28/putin-s-decade-old-dream-realized-as-russia-to-price-its-own-oil [Accessed October 9, 2016].

Gotev, G., 2015. Russia shelves Turkish Stream pipeline project. EurActiv.com. Available at: http://www.euractiv.com/section/europe-s-east/news/russia-shelves-turkish-stream-pipeline-project/ [Accessed June 10, 2016].

Idiz, S., 2017, Can Erdoğan juggle Trump and Putin at the same time?. Al-Monitor. Available at: http://www.al-monitor.com/pulse/originals/2017/04/turkey-united-states-erdogan-expectations-high-from-trump.html [Accessed May 20, 2017].

Hurriyet, 2002. Putin: Mavi Akım ile ilişkiler kuvvetlenecek. Hurriyet newpaper. Available at: http://www.hurriyet.com.tr/putin-mavi-akim-ile-iliskiler-kuvvetle-necek-117717.

Kazokoğlu, C., 2015. Türkiye doğalgazda Rusya'ya ne kadar bağımlı? BBC Türkçe. Available at: http://www.bbc.com/turkce/ekonomi/2015/12/151204_rusya_tur-kiye_dogalgaz_cuneyt_kazokoglu.

Korybko, A., 2015. "The New Middle East": Russian Style (IIA). Oriental Review. Available at: http://orientalreview.org/2015/10/08/the-new-middle-east-russian-style-iia/ [Accessed June 11, 2016].

Kosach, G., 2015. Organization of Islamic Cooperation: Priorities and Policies. Russian International Affairs Council, p.1. Available at: http://russiancouncil. ru/ en/inner/?id_4=5100&active_id_11=37#top-content [Accessed October 9, 2016].

Luhn, A., 2015. Russia steps up hostility against Turkey with war room briefing. The Guardian. Available at: http://www.theguardian.com/world/2015/dec/02/russia-steps-up-hostility-against-turkey-with-war-room-briefing-in-kremlin.

Minister of Foreign Affairs, 2011. policy-of-zero-problems-with-our-neighbors @ www.mfa.gov.tr. Available at: http://www.mfa.gov.tr/policy-of-zero-problems-with-our-neighbors.en.mfa.

Nesterenko, A., 2010. Briefing by Russian MFA Spokesman Andrei Nesterenko, January 15, 2010. Russian MFA. Available at: http://archive.mid.ru//brp_4. nsf/0/7551B45A1E61D1CFC32576B1002C8056 [Accessed May 16, 2016].

Nureddin, M., 2009. BÜYÜYEN TÜRK-RUS ORTAKLIĞI: 60 MİLYAR DOLAR-LIK ANLAŞMALAR.... Available at: http://www.byegm.gov.tr/turkce/ haber/byyen-trk-rus-ortaklii-60-mlyar-dolarlik-anla350malar/12602.

Özbay, F., 2011. The Relations between Turkey and Russia in the 2000s. Perceptions, XVI(3), pp. 69-92. Available at: http://sam.gov.tr/wp-content/uploads/ 2012/02/ FatihOzbay.pdf.

Ozbay, F. (Bilgesam), 2010. Türkiye-Rusya İlişkilerinde Üçüncü Dönem. Bilgesam. Available at: http://www.bilgesam.org/incele/108/-turkiye-rusya-iliskilerinde-ucuncu-donem/#.VzbLoPmLTRY [Accessed May 14, 2016].

Ozdal, H. et al., 2013. Türkiye-Rusya İlişkileri: Rekabetten Çok Yönlü İşbirliğine, Available at: http://www.usak.org.tr/_files/2942016115209-RKQMBZTTXK.pdf.

Republic of Turkey Ministry of Foreign Affairs, 2012. Relations between Turkey and Bulgaria. Republic of Turkey Ministry of Foreign Affairs, (July 2001), p.2012.

144

Available at: http://www.mfa.gov.tr/relations-between-turkey-and-azerbaijan.en. mfa [Accessed October 9, 2016].

Sezgin, A.S., 2015. Rusya ' daki Ekonomik Gelişmelerin Türkiye ' deki Sektörlere Olası Etkileri, Istanbul. Available at: https://ekonomi.isbank.com.tr/UserFiles/pdf/ar_02_2015.pdf.

Shaheen, K. & Shaun, W., 2016. Putin condemns Turkey after Russian warplane downed near Syria border. The Guardian. Available at: https://www.theguardian.com/world/2015/nov/24/turkey-shoots-down-jet-near-border-with-syria.

Sharkov, D., 2016. SYRIAN KURDS OPEN OFFICE IN MOSCOW, AS RUSSIA-TURKEY ROW CONTINUES. Newsweek. Available at: http://europe.newsweek.com/syrian-kurds-open-office-moscow-russia-turkey-row-continues-425177?rm=eu.

Shevtsova, L., 2005. Putin's Russia 1st ed., Washington: A Carnegia Endowment Book.

Shlykov, P., Chapter 3 Russian Foreign Policy in Eastern Mediterranean Since 1991. In A. Litsas, Spyridon, Tziampiris, ed. The Eastern Mediterranean in Transition: Multipolarity, Politics and Power. London: Routledge, p. 5.

State, F., Service, S. & Pocketbook, S., 2015. Rosstat, Moscow: RF. Available at: http://www.gks.ru/free_doc/doc_2015/rus15_eng.pdf.

Valdai, C., 2014. GLOBAL PROBLEMS FOR GLOBAL GOVERNANCE, Moscow. Available at: http://valdaiclub.com/publications/reports/global_problems_for_global_governance/.

Wheatley, M., 2015. Tourism: Outbound Travellers Declined by 40 Percent. Russia Insider. Available at: http://russia-insider.com/en/business/tourism-outbound-travellers-declined-40-percent/ri7848 [Accessed June 10, 2016].

Zhanaltay, Z., 2016. How Tension between Russia and Turkey Could Affect Trade Relations between Turkey and Kazakhstan? Akhmet Yassawi University, EURASIAN RESEARCH INSTITUTE. Available at: http://eurasian-research.org/en/research/comments/economy/how-tension-between-russia-and-turkey-could-affect-trade-relations-between.

Oleksiy Semeniy

Ukrainian Narratives

After the start of the Ukraine crisis, relations between Russia and the West continually and substantially deteriorated, reaching their lowest point since the end of Cold War in autumn 2016. There were many reasons and events that accounted for this negative development, some of which are of a fundamental nature and, therefore, are not easy to reverse or repair. The issue of narratives, namely serious differences between them in different countries, is one of the crucial reasons in this respect. Narratives themselves are quite complicated and complex because they include many views and beliefs referring to different spheres of our life. But, in this study, we will address the narratives mainly with respect to the issues of security, politics, history, economy and partly on societal level. The Ukrainian narrative represents quite an interesting case study if we analyze its development since 1991 and, especially, the substantial changes since 2014.

In general, there was and there is no absolute dominant narrative in Ukraine, due to long-term, significant internal differences over its relations both to the West and to Russia. In line with these differences, there used to be three major macro-regions (matrix) and two minor ones, with quite distinctive differences over a set of important issues[1], namely politics, history, societal and economic structures. Now, after more than three years of war experience, a more or less obvious mainstream narrative has been formed in Ukraine, but its exact frame will largely depend on midterm developments in and around the country, namely the direction chosen at a few important crossroads – for example, issues of territorial integrity and successful sociopolitical reforms, possible ways of and a time frame for settling the Ukraine crisis, the development of relations with major foreign partners and neighbours, and the general architecture of Euro-Atlantic security.

Furthermore, the official narrative quite often has not and does not fully coincide with the mainstream perceptions in the society and vice versa. Nevertheless, ruling elites and institutions are 'coerced' by the reality at the end of the day, i.e. they have to take the mainstream into account. Such disconnects are largely explained by the high level of mistrust in Ukraine towards almost all power structures (president, government, parliament, law enforce-

---

1   The matrix definition is the author's innovative idea for better explaining the Ukrainian landscape, taking leave of the simplified and destructive East-West approach. For example, in the following representative and very indicative survey, conducted by the Kyiv International Sociology Institute and published in April 2014 in "Mirror Weekly", you can find this division and differences exactly according to the mentioned macro-regions used by reputable sociology institutions for last few decades. Available at: http://gazeta. zn.ua/internal/yugo-vostok-vetv-dreva-nashego-_.html.

ment institutions)[2] which try to impose their narratives onto society. Although issues of socio-economic development are at the top of the polls[3], issues of relations to the West and Russia (especially NATO or EU membership options)[4] and their relations to each other have attracted quite a lot of attention recently, for obvious reasons. Before this, they also played an important role, but were mainly emphasized and utilized politically on the eve of elections to attract or mobilize their 'own voters'.

From 1991, the de-facto mainstream view in Ukraine was a 'balancing approach', sometimes even enshrined in official documents (such as the non-bloc policy in 2010). It was supported by both the majority of the Ukrainian society and the political ruling class and had its origin in the 'Central Ukrainian matrix' (covering, territorially, the central, northern and some parts of the eastern regions). Nevertheless, it was never politically consolidated or structured. Therefore two other matrixes – 'Donbass' (including south-eastern regions) and 'Western' (all western regions) were much more active and dominant, especially during the last decade. This imbalance finally caused a number of serious problems and negative consequences which needed to be tackled comprehensively In addition to the three matrixes mentioned, the 'Southern matrix' and the 'Crimean matrix' tended to join other dominant matrixes (either Donbass or sometimes Central). Since 2004, representatives of the Donbass and Western matrixes have played a destructive role, trying to impose their views and matrixes onto the whole of Ukraine and thus (because of resistance from other matrixes) ultimately pushing the whole system out of balance, which was inefficient in general, but well-balanced in form.

This development, coupled with the Russian Federation's aggression, contributed, in turn, to substantial changes in the general narratives, starting in 2014 and is still going on today. This will have a crucial impact on the Ukrainian view of the European security system as a whole and relations to Russia as its major part. Future political campaigns and elections can slightly change the form, but the general trend for the midterm future seems to be

---

2   See Kiev International Institute of Sociology. Study "Trust in social institutions and groups". 15 January 2016, at: http://kiis.com.ua/?lang=eng&cat=reports &id= 579& page=7.

3   See Kiev International Institute of Sociology. (2016a). Well-being of the Residents of Ukraine in May 2016: Economic Issues and Happiness Despite Difficulties, at: http://kiis.com.ua/?lang=eng&cat=reports&id=636&page=2, as well as Kiev International Institute of Sociology. (2016b). Issues the Ukrainians are Concerned About, at: http://kiis.com.ua/?lang=eng&cat=reports&id=640&page=2.

4   Democratic Initiatives Foundation. Opinion poll on attitude to NATO (November 2015 – dynamics since 2008), at: http://www.dif.org.ua/en/polls/2015a/chi-hochut-ukrainci-vstupu-do-nato-zagalnonacionalne-opituvannja-.htm. Opinion poll on Foreign Policy issues (July 2015), at http://www.dif.org.ua/ua/ polls/2015a/zovnishnja-politiennja-.htm. Razumkov Centre (2016). Results of the poll "Foreign policy preferences of Ukrainian citizens" (27.September 2016). Available at: http://razumkov.org.ua/ ukr/news.php?news_id=781.

almost set.[5] It is based on rejection of the current Russian regime as unacceptable for Ukraine and its statehood project, with the related necessity of a confrontational stance to Russia by Ukraine, unless Russia changes itself or is forced (coerced) to make such a change. This view mainly supports Western policy (especially that of the US) and imposes the major responsibility for the confrontation on Russia or its current regime. In addition to that, some crucial moments in Ukrainian history are now definitely separated from their Soviet (Russian) explanation[6] which, in turn, automatically makes them opposed to current basic elements in the Russian narrative. In general, this Ukrainian mainstream narrative is focused both on interests (security and prosperity) and some essentialist positions (mostly related to Russia),[7] such as a future modus of bilateral relations, full restoration of Ukraine's territorial integrity, internal dynamics in Russia and the Ukrainian reaction to this, as well as the outcomes of Ukrainian-Russian confrontation.

Nevertheless, two other narratives – currently non-mainstream – one of which could potentially become a mainstream narrative, should be mentioned, The first one is 'moderate pragmatic'[8] (mainly originating from the Central Ukrainian matrix in peaceful times) and is aimed first of all at strengthening Ukraine's statehood capacity, the development of its economy and successful transformations inside society, focusing on a strategic approach (having strategic aims in view, such as strengthening the whole state and establishing good governance, Ukraine's future security status, European security architecture and Ukraine's position in it – without too much of a fixation on tactical issues), which, in turn, is hoped to bring about positive results. The narrative supposes that, until some kind of agreement between the West and Russia is reached, there is almost no chance for stable and sustainable development in Ukraine. Therefore, Ukraine should undertake efforts to change the current confrontational modus in Europe – initially by itself – provided some crucial conditions for Ukraine are met. Due to the currently prevailing confrontational modus in West-Russia relations, the narrative has little chance of becoming influential. The second narrative (with almost no chance of becoming mainstream in the foreseeable future) is 'pro Soviet-Russia', based mainly on the rest of the previous Donbass (and Crimean) matrix and people of the older generation in those regions. Here, we can find quite a lot of similarity with a current Russian narrative: for exam-

---

5   See the respective analysis of bilateral relations and their perspectives in "National Security and Defense" 2015, Issue 8-9, at: http://www.razumkov.org. ua/ eng/ files/category_journal/UA_Rosiya_8_9-2015-ENG.compressed.pdf or in "National Security and Defense" 2014, Issue 5-6, at http://www.razumkov. org.ua/ eng/files/category_journal/5_6_Ukr_Ros_2014_Eng_site_rdc.pdf.

6   The process started in 1991, but was not so obvious until recently.

7   Democratic Initiatives Foundation. Ukraine turns 25: achievements and defeats (public opinion), at: http://www.dif.org.ua/en/publications/press-relizy/ukraine25.htm and http://www.dif.org.ua/ua/publications/press-relizy/ukraine25.htm.

8   One of its elements was the idea of a neutrality status for Ukraine as a strategic solution.

ple, blaming the West for its general approach and perceived aggressive actions as well as praising the leadership in the Kremlin for opposing such policies and justifying all actions undertaken in this respect. The narrative is closely connected with a nostalgia phenomenon, especially shared by the groups which feel they have been disadvantaged or hurt by many developments since 1991 (such as, miners or workers at industrial plants or military industry), i.e. looking mainly to the past as the best option that should be repeated.

Threats, Challenges and Concerns Perceived

The latest National Security Strategy[9], approved in May 2015, defines Russian aggression and the consequences of that as threat #1 on a list of nine actual threats to Ukraine's security (regaining territorial integrity is aim no.1 of 14 major directions of the national security policy). The change in security perceptions is evident when we compare the current National Security Strategy with the previous one, adopted in 2012.[10] The basic document indicates the focus for all other security sphere-related normative documents already adopted or being drafted. Within the society, the perception of Russia as threat no.1 for Ukraine is also becoming predominant, although here, we can find differences, more or less connected to previously mentioned divisions (even though regions of occupied Donbass and Crimea are no longer covered by such polls). In all the regions throughout the country, there was never a dominant view on any threats coming from the West, although the attitudes towards specific countries (the USA, Germany, Poland, etc.) differed and still differ with quite interesting preferences for the country's models and particular security options.[11] Among other external threats (raised mainly by the government or media), we can point to international terrorism, uncontrolled migration flows, and disruptions in the international financial system.

In the 1990s, threat perceptions mainly related to domestic challenges and some indefinite *force majeures* outside. In the 2000s, there was no definite perception of threats identified from outside, other than international terrorism or an imbalance of the international system in general, though in the Western part of Ukraine, Russia was always perceived by large number of people as a threat. Being a part of Europe and claiming to move success-

---

9   The National Security Strategy of Ukraine, approved by the Decree of the President of Ukraine as of 26t May 2015. Available at: http://zakon5.rada.gov.ua/laws/show/ 287/ 2015.

10 The National Security Strategy of Ukraine, approved by the Decree of the President of Ukraine as of 8 June 2012, at: http://www.niss.gov.ua/content/articles/files/ project-Litvinenko-dcd38.pdf.

11 What do Ukrainians think about their country's Foreign Policy? Results from a sociological survey, conducted by the TNS at the request of the Institute of World Policy. September 2016, at: http://iwp.org.ua/eng/public/2115.html.

fully along the path of integration into the EU meant some kind of automatic acceptance that aggression or threat from the outside could no longer be any kind of challenge for it. The people of Ukraine perceived conflicts in the aftermath of the dissolution of Yugoslavia and USSR as unhappy accidents related to concrete persons and circumstances. Definite success by settling the Crimean issue with Russia in the 1990s was seen as good evidence for such stance.

Nevertheless, we can document the process of more and more differences from the Soviet-Russian narrative since 1991.[12] At the same time, some crucial turning points (except those since 2014) influencing the establishment of a Ukrainian narrative, different both from the Western and the Russian one, should be mentioned. They include:

-   The dissolution of Yugoslavia – perceived as a very negative example for settling such processes, which greatly influenced Ukrainian policy towards Crimea and Russia;
-   The solution of the Crimean problem in 1990s – experience of quite emotional negotiations on the brink of open political and military confrontation with the Russians;
-   The wars of Russia in Chechnya – a very negative example for Ukraine of trying to regain territorial integrity through massive military actions inside the country, violating many international human rights norms and standards;
-   The operation in Kosovo in 1999 – an example of ambiguous Western policy which may have violated some international norms, on the one hand, and a negative role of one person (Milosevic) in the nation becoming his hostage, on the other hand;
-   The war in Iraq since 2003 – one more example of ambiguous Western policy in non-European regions and not very good justification for the start of the military actions, coupled, once again, with the negative role of one person (Saddam Hussein) for his own nation;
-   The conflict around Tuzla (tiny island between Crimean and Taman peninsula, which controls the Kerch straits) in 2003 – a striking example that, even with a co-operative approach by Ukraine, some forces in Russia, backed *de facto* by highest officials, perceive all post-Soviet neighbours as their vassals and are even ready to coerce them, if need be, despite all the declarations on brotherly relations;
-   The Orange Revolution – first example of massive involvement from outside (both from Russia and the West) in domestic Ukrainian events, trying to support their "own parties", together with the sharp reaction of

---

12   The first systematic indicator of that process was a book, written in the 2000s by the President of Ukraine (1994-2004), Leonid Kuchma, who can be considered quite moderate and sophisticated in his policy towards Russia, with a symbolic title "Ukraine is not Russia", where he quite clearly presented these differences in many important issues.

Russian policy afterwards to the "alien regime", which resulted in the start of systematic destabilization of the whole Ukrainian statehood;

- The war in Georgia in 2008 – an example of Russia's readiness to go far beyond red lines, openly violating the territorial integrity of a neighbour state, and non-ability (readiness) of the West to effectively address such development.

- The gas wars in 2006-2009 and the trade war in summer 2013 – clear indications that Russia is prepared to harm itself and its partners for the sake of some of its ultimate political interests (real – or perceived as such – by the rulers).

Until 2014, all of these turning points formed a narrative which was distinctively different from the Russian and Western ones, namely providing different explanations for the events, indicating different actors to blame, and pointing out other reasons for the developments. Since 2014, however, the mainstream, as mentioned above, is moving closer to the Western narrative, while nevertheless retaining some distinctive features. The narrative is largely dependent on domestic development dynamics, especially on the capability of ruling groups to deliver positive results in the economic and social spheres.

Who is Responsible for the Current Situation?

If until 2014 there was some kind of mixed explanation – criticizing both Russia and the West for the confrontation as a result – then the picture changed dramatically after the Russian aggression. Russia has since been viewed as the definite troublemaker no.1 for everybody in Europe. But the criticism of the West has not fully disappeared, although it has changed its emphasis – claims of insufficient assistance to Ukraine, ambiguity with Russia (not taking a firm enough stance against the aggressor), and suspicions over a possible deal on Ukraine, over our heads. At the same time, the Ukrainian narrative more and more subdivides the West into some parts – USA and EU first of all, but also the EU itself to Western Europe, Central Europe, Southern Europe, Scandinavians with their own preferences and policies, be they towards Ukraine and Russia or on general issues.[13]

Ukrainians see two major reasons for the current crisis: Mr. Putin and his regime, first of all, and second, fundamental differences between the Russian statehood model. All other models in Europe (perceiving them to be incompatible from the beginning). The difference in interests is not seen as a real reason for the conflict, because these differences existed before and not

---

13   See IRI [what is this?] poll "Dynamics of social and political views in Ukraine 25.05-14.06.2016", conducted by Rating Group, at: http://ratinggroup.ua/en/ research/ukraine/ opros_iri_demonstriruet_skepticizm_ukraincev_s_probleskami_nadezhdy.html.

only with Russia, but between many states, including Ukraine but, nevertheless they did not cause military conflicts or violations of international law.

Key Elements in the Developments in Russian-Western Relations

The Cold War is mainly perceived as a confrontation between two systems in
which Ukraine was definitely a part of the one that actually 'lost the game'.
But, at the same time, Ukrainians do not see themselves as losers in this respect, insofar as the direct consequence of the failure was the dissolution of
the USSR and Ukraine's regaining its independence. Therefore, the stand-
point is not black-and-white, but more complex. The following are seen as
key points in Western-Russian relations: the presidencies of Yeltsin and
Putin, the dissolution of Yugoslavia and the war in Kosovo in 1999, the war
in Iraq in 2003, the Orange Revolution in 2004, the NATO summit in Bucharest and the war in Georgia in 2008 and, of course, the Ukraine crisis. With
respect to Russia itself, it's not so much about misunderstanding the West as
about the lack of real will to behave according to its rules. The Ukrainian
narrative perceives that, from the beginning, the West did not succeed in
understanding that Russia was not going to be its partner no matter under
what conditions and that Russia would always claim some special rights
regarding its 'near neighbourhood'. And Ukrainians are claiming that they
are now paying the price for the misunderstanding of Russia by the West.
The issue of red lines is very complicated because the perception has changed
dramatically since 2014. Now Ukrainians suppose that Russia, in general, has
no red lines. As for the West, Ukrainians perceive the following red lines:
further NATO enlargement, direct military confrontation with Russia (the
West is perceived as not being able 'to die' or sacrifice something in a confrontation against Russia), use of weapons of mass destruction (WMD), the
territorial integrity of both NATO and EU members in case of an emergency,
Ukraine's statehood if really challenged by Russia.

Factors Influencing Russian-Western Relations

Both Russia and the West are seen to be influenced by domestic and external
factors, but to a different degree, the West more by external and Russia more
by domestic factors. By comparison to the West, Russia is seen as much
more dependent on the personality factor in its relations with counterparts
than is the West. Insofar as Ukraine turned out to be at the centre of 'integration competition', it is mainly seen as such between Russia and the West,
whereas Russia is trying to establish some kind of modified USSR and regain
its sphere of influence and the West is just offering something for respective
countries and slowly moving eastwards, promoted by its attractiveness.

The West has been losing its attractiveness for Ukraine, compared to the degree of attractiveness it had ten years ago and especially in the 1990s. Some countries in the EU are definitely seen to be in decline due to their economic and social problems, but there are still good examples for Ukraine, such as Germany or the Scandinavian countries. Therefore, the EU is perceived as definitely less attractive and successful than before, but still quite a good enough benchmark for Ukraine in the current world crisis times. As a result, no Eurasian or Chinese perspectives are seen as any kind of alternatives to adjusting themselves to the success story of the EU, although there is huge interest in economic co-operation with China (mainly its market and investments) and not losing, where possible, its own shares and co-operation links in Eurasian markets.

Factors Conducive for Russian-Western Co-operation

Most Ukrainians think that there are not many factors conducive for Russian-Western co-operation. Mainly, such factors relate to economic co-operation (trade, investments, markets, source of natural resources, etc) and crucial global issues where the West needs some involvement from Russia. There is a high degree of scepticism about whether some valuable shared norms between two parties could now be identified. The mainstream narrative in Ukraine tends more and more, to reject the option that Russia is a European country and state. Nevertheless, it is seen that the West will continue to co-operate with Russia, especially if the Ukraine crisis is somehow settled, the tensions therefore minimized and the confrontation stance reversed.

Interests Shared by Russia and the West

The first substantial interest perceived by Ukrainians is economic co-operation because of its ability to bring profits to each side, while simultaneously largely avoiding the political factor. For the West, it includes exports to Russia and full-scale access both to its markets and natural resources; for Russia, sources of new technologies are crucial as investments and payments for the resources it exports. Global threats and challenges are only partly seen as possible shared interests between the West and Russia, because the mainstream perception in Ukraine considers Russia to be a declining ambiguous state, which will have less influence globally in the future. Threats and challenges refer mainly to hard-security topics, such as proliferation of WMD, terrorism and organized crime. There is substantial scepticism about the possibility of solving crises jointly due to growing political tensions between the West and Russia. Nevertheless, this does not rule out some agreements to avert possible negative impacts for both parties, if needed.

In the near-term, a growing or stable level of confrontation is seen as a basic scenario for the relations. As for the mid-term future, there is a difference in expectations and no evident mainstream in Ukraine: one segment supposes that the containment policy from the West and permanent provocations or escalations from Russia are also fixed for the mid-term; another segment sees a transition to co-existence modus where some red lines are fixed and adhered to, while both the West and Russia will be waiting for a weakening (decline) of the other. As for the pre-conditions[14] for resuming co-operation, the resolution of the Ukraine crisis (removal of Russia from Donbas and readiness to constructively discuss the "Crimean problem" are essential parts) is anticipated as the first one and the centrepiece. The second one refers to the changes inside Russia and stopping its intimidating actions against its neighbours. Currently, almost no viable option for a win-win policy is anticipated, unless some substantial changes (mainly inside Russia or its foreign policy) happen. The ideal strategy for Ukrainians would look like a return to international norms and standards (mostly referring to UN and OSCE catalogues), restoration of Ukraine's territorial integrity, compensation from Russia to other parties for the losses incurred (caused by Russia) and a general, a legally binding agreement on cohesive security architecture in Europe.

Final Remarks

As indicated before, the mainstream narrative has changed (and is still changing) quite substantially in Ukraine due to the dramatic events since 2013-2014. Despite some high degree of emotions in Ukraine, the main changes in this respect are unlikely now to be reversed in the mid-term future. This means that until Russia makes real steps forward in its relations towards Ukraine (as it is seen in Kyiv), the confrontation modus or negative attitude from Kyiv towards Moscow will prevail, thus negatively influencing the whole set of relations between the West and Russia. The most crucial and painful issues to be settled in the nearest future somehow are the following: Donbass, economic losses and devastation due to direct Russia or its proxies' actions, and levels of militarization in societies on both sides. The process of leaving the Soviet (nowadays mostly Russian) narrative by Ukraine started in 1991, but until the middle of the 2000s was quite gradual, then it accelerated substantially due to external and internal shocks.

Nevertheless, the narrative is not going to be equal to Western narratives in the mid-term future, even after such shocks. Moreover, growing disillusionment and dissatisfaction with Western policy as well as its development in the most recent period make more and more Ukrainians quite scepti-

---

14   The option with no pre-conditions currently has no substantial support in Ukraine.

cal about it, thus putting emphasis on its own efforts to be undertaken for general success. A direct consequence of such a turn is the start of seeking a solution of its own for Ukraine's security (insofar as international agreements and commitments have failed, in the perception of the Ukrainians), dramatically increasing its own military capabilities and being much more flexible and not so dogmatic as before (not hoping that joining some military alliances would solve security problems or, in general, is possible in the near future) in its security arrangements.

Ideally, some agreement on the general security architecture in Europe would be welcomed by Ukrainians[15], but is seen as an unrealistic option for a mid-term future. Major external responsibility for the crisis is attributed to Russia and its regime, although some critical points are addressed to the West, especially with respect to its assistance and commitments towards Ukraine. Therefore, only under the condition of changes in Russia and its policy is some sustainable agreement and respective resolution anticipated, although not expected in nearest future. Current international organizations are quite critically evaluated by Ukrainians because of their perceived inability to deliver feasible results on the ground, when urgently needed. Based on this assumption, the lesson drawn by Ukraine is to rely on real power instruments, such as its own backbone, rather than on international agreements and commitments. Taken together, in all of these elements of the general Ukrainian narrative, we can expect more emphasis on the country's own efforts and independent policy requested by citizens from the authorities, accompanied by minor expectations for a favourable international environment, be it Russia's policy or Western attitudes.

---

15 Centre of sociological studies "Sofia". Poll "War and peace: issues of national security in public views", at: http://www.sofia.com.ua/page174.html.

James Gow

UK Strategic Defence and Russia: A Brief History of Unrequited Wooing

The 2015 UK National Security Strategy explicitly judged Russia to be a threat. This was a marked change from the 2010 equivalent, which did not even mention Russia, and the preceding quarter of a century, in which, despite frustrations and clear problems, the post-Cold War emphasis had been on seeking co-operation with Moscow. Of course, those 25 years were not without continuing and, indeed, increasing confrontation, occasionally in the open, but mainly out of public view. Crucially, however, London continued to seek to find the best in its relationship with Moscow. But, Russian behaviour after 2010 was so rude that it could not be glossed over. This brought an end, effectively, to Britain's wooing of its former Cold War adversary. How did this story transpire? In the present contribution, I shall, first, briefly outline the public discourse of the period to 2015, including Russia's intrusions in Ukraine, then sketch perspectives on Russia, in late 2016, before reviewing how disappointment over attempts to work with Russia over Syria and the emergence of Theresa May as UK Prime Minister focused a far more acute and firm position regarding Russia, including Foreign Secretary Boris Johnson's suggesting that a 'more kinetic' approach might be needed.[1]

Courting Russia: From the Failed Putsch to Failure in Ukraine

Britain's wooing of Russia had begun with very strong support for Boris Yeltsin, as he spearheaded resistance to the attempted coup against Mikhail Gorbachev, in August 1991, led the break-up of the Soviet Union to make the Russian Federation independent (against the initial UK position), and then led Russia through a period of major transformation in the early 1990s. In this period, the political and diplomatic relationship was highly positive and a source of great optimism – although, in the background, members of the old Soviet security apparatus continued in opposition to the UK and the West, and privately warned that 'this was 1939, half-time, we will be back.'[2] The initial welcome in the relationship went into a phase of misunderstandings between 1993, when the high mark of Russian diplomatic co-operation over

---

1   The Daily Telegraph, 13 October 2016.
2   This formulation was put to the author by a former member of the GRU, the Soviet Military Security organization in 1993, but represented a general sense of continuing hostility in traditional security sectors, as well as some parts of the political spectrum, it seemed.

the Vance-Owen Plan for the Bosnian War was, essentially, spurned, and 1999, when the UK led a Western and NATO approach to Kosovo that ran counter to Russian positions, culminating in a near confrontation at Pristina airport. None the less, diplomatic co-operation continued. Throughout these years, London constantly sought to engage Moscow in military and defence co-operation, only for letters, memos and faxes to go unanswered for months and years, if ever, or planned events not going ahead, with British (and other) representatives never certain if the Russians would even turn-up.[3]

This pattern continued through the 2000s, with London's futile wooing continuing against the background of Russia, under Putin, returning, in some respects, to the ways of the Soviet era. However, despite the clear hardening of the Moscow approach under Putin, the willingness to try continued, even after the 2006 murder of Aleksandar Litvinenko in London by Russian operatives and Russia's disrupting the plans of London, Washington and Brussels regarding Kosovo's status and a new UN Security Council Resolution about it, in 2008 (although the latter was understandable, given that Russia had discerned an element of deceit in the Western approach that prompted its breaking ranks). All of this, plus Russian action in Georgia in 2008, could – and probably should – have been more than enough material to make some mention of problems with Russia, at least, in the 2010 UK National Security Strategy.

Following Russia's annexation of Crimea, in 2014, and subsequent operations in Eastern Ukraine, it was clear that the British welcome of the early 1990s, via a period of good will mixed with the possibility of misunderstandings had given way to a sense of disappointment. The UK quickly moved to bolster defence in Central and Eastern Europe, sending troops to the Baltic states, quietly deploying logistics and engineering capability to Poland, both as reassurance to Warsaw and a building block for potential future use, should the situation arise in the wider Eastern European region, which could include Ukraine. London also funded consultants to work in parallel to Kiev's own national security structures – although it took some time for this to be properly supported as Prime Minister David Cameron was seen as being slow fully to appreciate the situation. These steps also came with a strong commitment to an EU sanctions regime imposed in the wake of events in Ukraine. However, the UK position continued to lack sharpness and focus in addressing Russia directly, until late 2016.

---

3   Although records probably do not exist, or will be inaccessible, senior figures involved in engagement with Russia, who made some progress, were good humored and phlegmatic about their nervousness that Russian participants would actually appear, or, alternatively, be ready to meet them when visiting Moscow. I had a small personal experience of this (albeit not in an official capacity) around 2001, when a Russian official who had been positively engaged in discussion and with whom I had met several times, did not fulfill an engagement, nor then respond to faxes and, when finally we spoke by telephone, made clear that the particular activity (preparation of a document) was done.

In October 2016, Russian military ships passed through the English Channel, shadowed by vessels from the Royal Navy. The Russian ships were on the way to Syria, which had been transformed within a year from the prospective focus of greater co-operation between London and the West, on one side, and Moscow, on the other, to the centrepiece of growing confrontation. The proximity of the ships to the British Isles was partly a provocative action, in line with incursions into airspace in recent years by Russian military planes and attempts to intimidate and provoke more broadly. While the ships themselves were harmless, they were a strong and visible symbol of the tension between Russia and Western countries, with echoes of the Cold War – although, clearly, nothing like a return to the Cold War itself. The Russian passage, however, provoked renewed discussion about the UK and Russia, which reflected the different perspectives that had been present and evolving in British opinion since the end of the Cold War itself.

One immensely popular BBC radio discussion of the issue opened by asking if the transit of the Russian ships via European Waters was part of a new 'Cold War' and by reporting how East European states had become so nervous about Russia that the UK had sent further troops to Estonia to bolster the NATO commitment to that country.[4] Vitaly Shevchenko, from the BBC Monitoring Service, presented an account of Russia as found in Russian news media, which, he said was dominated by international issues. He reinforced the sense that Russia saw the West as a threat, showing threatening signs that required Russia to be prepared for war – and that St. Petersburg had already been advised about approved rations (for example, amounts of bread allowed) for wartime. He underlined that the Russian press were describing the confrontation over Syria as the worst crisis since the missile crisis of 1962, although he also emphasised scepticism that ordinary Russians believed the bellicose rhetoric they heard from Russian officials accusing the West of hostile action.

The former UK Ambassador to Moscow, Sir Tony Brenton, damped any suggestion of a new Cold War, noting that Russia was vastly inferior to the West, in his view, on all measures and suggested that many of its actions, such as provocative exercises and abrogating agreements with the US were, in practice, confirmation of this. However, he continued to present a view of Russia as fearful of Western influence, especially in Ukraine and Syria, and fearful of the prospect of the United States with Hilary Clinton as president. Russia was a threatened animal 'whistling' and the UK and the West needed to be careful, as anything else could make the threatened animal a great deal more dangerous. He underscored this by arguing against further strong meas-

---

4   The Jeremy Vine Show (hosted by Vanessa Feltz) BBC Radio 2, 27 October 2016.

ures, notably sanctions, which he portrayed as a 'failed policy' that did not work and boosted support for Putin and fuelled sentiment that the West was against Russia. Even more, he cautioned against the 'more kinetic' approaches raised by Johnson and the prospect of introducing a 'no fly zone' in Syria, as advocated by presidential candidate Clinton. Despite Brenton's acknowledgement of Russia's weakness, he warned that Putin, believing that the West was out to get him, was prepared to respond with armed force. Thus, in the former ambassador's perspective, the UK needed to be softer and more careful regarding Syria and Ukraine, which were the big questions for Moscow. Indeed, the former ought to be a point of co-operation, in his view, where a shared opposition to violent Islamist extremists provided good reason to work together (failing to recognise that this had been a major initiative by the UK, which had come to nothing – see below). Despite this, it was right, because of treaty commitments, to bolster NATO in Estonia and other parts of Central and Eastern Europe.

These somewhat informed perspectives were followed by contributions from the public, which urged the government not to 'goad' Russia, which was said not to be a 'natural enemy', and also noted the Russian contribution to the outcome of the Second World War and the need not to 'upset anyone unnecessarily.' The relative weakness of Russian military capability and the strength of British and Western quality over quantity was emphasized – but leavened with the caution that 'they have nuclear weapons, we have nuclear weapons', which meant that, in the end, a conflict would not occur. Overall, the contents of this discussion, despite the position of a former senior official in the UK diplomatic service, tended to reflect perspectives at odds with those of the government itself, as reflected in clear policy shifts since 2010 and during 2016, in particular. Those changes reflected a hardening position in face of unacceptable Russian action in Ukraine, Syria and other places, drawing to a close a quarter of a century of efforts to engage and build bridges with Moscow.

Another media perspective saw Russia far more clearly as a problem and a threat. World affairs specialist Tim Marshall explicitly pointed to Russia as an antagonist, in a 'back to the future' return to something like the Cold War – but, without the certainties and self-understanding of that era.[5] Now, Russia was 'acting strongly from a position of weakness,' he judged, throwing around cruise missiles and soft power. Putin had been undermining the UK and the West with 'soft power' and taking advantage of fixations with Brexit (and the EU's need to save itself) to assert itself in Syria, in particular, with hard power. In Marshall's astute view, this outward performance offered diversions that distracted brilliantly from Russia's weak, collapsed economy. However, that weakness, Marshall stated, made Moscow more

---

5   This Week, BBC 1, 3 November 2016.

dangerous than ever – having spent its 'peace dividend' on new military technology, rather than butter for a country with millions starving and in poverty. His views were reinforced by former UK Secretary of State for Defence Michael Portillo, who noted that Russia would have a fleet in the Mediterranean and that Putin had succeeded in a mission to put Russia back on the world stage. He, in turn, was echoed by Liz Kendall, an MP, who also agreed with Marshall and noted Russia's soft power with its propaganda broadcasting arm and its diplomatic impact in Africa.[6]

The passage of ships as a very visible projection of Russian military power threading their way through the English Channel was a prompt for renewed assessments of how the UK should relate to Moscow. There were, inevitably, mixed views. Some voices emphasised how dangerous Russia was and that the correct response for the UK would be to show understanding and, certainly, to avoid confrontation. In contrast, there was also a growing trend to see Russia as dangerous, but reaching the opposite inference – viz, the UK needed to stand up to Russia, where it could and where other action would not be irresponsible. This was also the emerging position of the government, following London's sharply being let down by Moscow in a somewhat wishful attempt to co-operate in a shared approach to Syria. This enhanced a position already emerging prominently in the context of strategic defence and security. This, the attempt at a joint strategy on Syria and the subsequent emergence of a harder line approach are set out in the following section.

Russia and UK Strategic Defence and Security

The then-Prime Minster, Cameron, introduced the *Strategic Defence and Security Review (SDSR) 2015* by suggesting that the world was a more dangerous and uncertain place than it had been in 2010.[7] However, little had changed between the reviews; the exception was Russian action, notably in Ukraine, which was of a kind not at all envisioned in the last review. Indeed, much of the analysis in *SDSR 2015* could have been in the first ever Strategic Defence Review (*SDR*) under the government of then-Prime Minister Tony Blair in 1998,[8] regarding the UK's position as an open, liberal, trading country that relies on open communications, a rule-based world, partnerships and

---

6   Ibid.
7   Securing Britain in an Age of Uncertainty: The Strategic Defence Review Cm 7948 Presented to Parliament by the Prime Minister by Command of Her Majesty London: The Stationery Office, October 2010.
8   The Strategic Defence Review, Presented to Parliament by the Secretary of State for Defence by Command of Her Majesty, London, The Stationery Office, July 1998. The 1998 SDR was the precursor to the more formal and regular SDSRs and, as such, the historic first attempt to take an overall strategic security review in the UK.

alliances, and, most of all, stability to prosper and be secure. However, while, in 2010, it was assumed that, amid the 'uncertainty' affecting the world, with international terrorism the most present danger, costs could be cut regarding conventional defence, both in retrospect and in light of Russia's aggression, that judgement appeared completely misplaced. The *SDSR 2015* revealed significant defence commitment decisions, which implicitly recognised that the government's emphasis on making cuts and savings in 2010 may have been an error. Moreover, the biggest mistake of them all, it could be said, was the misjudgement of Russia implicit in the 2010 assessment. Most of the commitments significantly to increase military expenditure were, at root, responses to Moscow's putting its military weight about, above all, Russia's aggression in Ukraine and its menace elsewhere, including around the British Isles.

The first and most prominent of the changes concerned the Queen Elizabeth Class Aircraft Carriers, which the government decided would be fully developed and fully deployed, in complete contrast with 2010. At that point, many commentators regarded the carriers as big budget white elephants inherited from the 1998 SDR. In 2015, both carriers formed the centrepiece of a new approach in which Britain's capacity to project influence around the world militarily was seen to be vital.

Decisions about the F-35 Lightning Strike Aircraft to be used on the carriers involved a second notable major shift. In 2010, it was envisaged that eight of these aircraft (previously known as the Joint Strike Fighter) would be purchased to come into service in 2023 on the one carrier operating. *SDSR 2015* reinforced the about-turn on the carriers, by committing to buying 42 aircraft to deploy by 2023, speeding up deployment, and, quite unexpectedly, committing strongly (though not absolutely) to purchasing all 138 of the aircraft for which the UK had originally signed a contract option with US maker Lockheed Martin. Both the carrier decision and the F-35 decision were responses to a world in which Russia had made old-fashioned power projection a contemporary and future need.

A third headline change from the retreat of 2010 was prompted by significant Russian activity around UK waters and airspace. This related to maritime patrol air capability. The *SDSR* announced that the US P-8 Poseidon Maritime Patrol Aircraft would be purchased to fill the gap left by the 2010 decision to scrap the Nimrod maritime patrol and submarine detection aircraft – which had just had a £ 4 million refit at the time it was abruptly and surprisingly scrapped. The decision to purchase the nine Boeing-made US aircraft was influenced, in particular, by Russia's probing of airspace and secret submarine missions, testing UK readiness and, at the same time, gathering intelligence. On the eve of the *SDSR* announcement, the UK had been obliged to call in French maritime patrol aircraft in an attempt to detect a Russian submarine suspected of spying on the UK nuclear submarine capability, which UK surveillance had lost. The P-8's roles were to protect the

Trident submarine nuclear deterrent fleet, and also to operate with the carriers, to carry out land surveillance and, if necessary, to perform air-sea rescue roles. As a matter of urgency, the UK also sought to borrow P-8s from the US, which aircraft would also be able to provide protection and support to US carriers, if needed (an added benefit and one of the influential factors in opting to buy the P-8 rather than other options) pending the arrival of the purchased aircraft. Finally, purchase of the P-8s to protect Trident also complemented a de facto decision announced in the *SDSR* that the UK's nuclear deterrent would be renewed, which was evident with the commitment to build four Successor submarines to replace the existing Vanguard fleet at a cost of £3.9 billion for the design phase and £31 billion over 20 years' development and implementation. The commitment to the nuclear deterrent was also a decision made easier by Russian actions in the world.

The new *UK National Security Strategy* (*NSS*) published jointly with the *SDSR*, placed cyber and intelligence capabilities centre stage, announcing massive new investment and major recruitment of new personnel. The biggest announcement among many was the innovative creation of a dedicated National Cyber Centre to be based at Cheltenham in Gloucestershire under the leadership of the UK Government's communications monitoring centre, the Government Communications Headquarters (GCHQ), already announced at GCHQ the week before by Chancellor George Osbourne, who explicitly justified the new Centre by the need to counter IS-Daeche.[9] However, very much in the unstated foreground shadows, the rapidly growing pressure from China and, especially Russia, in terms of cyber attacks was important. This involved both massive investment and a readiness to use offensive cyber capabilities.

The *NSS* reaffirmed the analysis of Britain's situation found in previous strategic defence and national security documents, including the previous *NSS* in 2010:[10] the UK was an open, liberal, trading country that relied on open communications, a rule-based world, partnerships and alliances for its security and prosperity. The reality was that little had changed and the analysis of the UK's position and the threats and challenges it faced remained broadly the same. The key changes concerned Moscow. Russia's brazen unlawful action in Ukraine and the tide of cyber attacks believed to be originating in Russia. There was a confident, front foot approach to security and the world, backed by significant new commitments and expenditure.

---

9   The Daily Telegraph 17 November 2015.
10   A Strong Britain in an Age of Uncertainty: The National Security Strategy Cm 7953 Presented to Parliament by the Prime Minister by Command of Her Majesty, October 2010.

The NSS contained eye-catching innovations. These were set out as part of a 'full spectrum' approach,[11] in which conventional defence was to be combined with intelligence, technical and scientific means, and security and police work to counter both terrorism and organised crime. The most radical step in a bold and wide-ranging NSS was the decision to create the dedicated National Cyber Centre as part of £1.9 billion new funding in this area. This reflected and significantly built on horizon scanning research that had already led to the decision by Cameron's Labour predecessor, Gordon Brown, to introduce cyber security as the 'thirteenth challenge' (the previous twelve owing to his predecessor as Prime Minister, Tony Blair) in the 2008 NSS:[12] the UK had become so dependent on networked digital technology, bringing enormous benefits, that it was vulnerable to attacks, which, in the worst scenario (albeit a very low probability, so long as the government and business remained vigilant), could result in the complete crippling of the UK, with banks not functioning, supermarkets not having food on the shelves and widespread social breakdown. Meeting that challenge and going beyond it was the new Centre's mission. Based alongside GCHQ at Cheltenham, the government's massive international eavesdropping, electronic communications centre, it would clearly complement some of GCHQ's monitoring work, focusing on the rapidly developing and changing digital world.

However, the new Centre was also to have quite radical roles. It was tasked to protect against attacks through development of secure networks both for government and the private sector. The last role was by far the most striking and radical, and represented a major change – at least in terms of open policy. The centre was given a role in conducting attacks as a means of deterrence against those identified as having conducted attacks, or to preempt those preparing to conduct cyber, terrorist, or other attacks – one of the key issues in preparing the *NSS* and the *SDSR* was to ensure the legal grounds for using offensive cyber operations.[13] In both cases, growing Russian attacks on UK cyber infrastructure lay behind these moves.

---

11   David Cameron, 'The Lord Mayor's Banquet 2015: Prime Minister's Speech', Prime Minister's Office, No.10 Downing St, 15 November 2015, at: https://www.gov.uk/ government/speeches/lord-mayors-banquet-2015-prime-ministers-speech, accessed 17 November 2015 ; Cameron, Prime Minister's Statement on Paris Attacks and G20 Summit', Oral Statement to Parliament, 17 November 2015, at: https://www.gov.uk/government/ speeches/prime-ministers-statement-on-paris-attacks-and-g20-summit accessed 17 November 2015.

12   Cabinet Office, The National Security Strategy of the United Kingdom: Security in an Interdependent World, London, The Stationery Office, March 2008 (hereafter UK NSS).

13   Research from a project involving the author informed this process: SNT Really Makes Reality: Technological Innovation, Non-Obvious Warfare and Challenges to International Law RCUK-DSTL Science and Security Programme Award: ES/K011413/1, Professors Guglielmo Verdirame and James Gow and Dr. Rachel Kerr, £239,398.59; see also http://www.paccsresearch.org.uk/snt-really-makes-reality-technological-innovation-non-obvious-warfare-challenges-international-law/.

The new *NSS* and the *SDSR* provided a positive context for the UK's – somewhat uncomfortably – allying itself to a new international strategy for handling IS/Daeche. The publication of the strategic documents and debate about them clearly provided a strong grounding for Cameron's announcement that he would call a vote in Parliament to back UK air strikes in Syria against IS/Daeche. The UK had aligned with, and helped to develop, a new international strategy on IS/Daeche and Syria that emerged in the weeks before the vote, following military engagement by both Russia and Iran to support the Assad regime. Despite the problems of Russian action in Ukraine, there was a sense that the common need to tackles IS/Daeche made it necessary to try a difficult arrangement involving Moscow's armed forces, given the run of major atrocities IS/Daeche, had committed, including the attacks in Paris, which sharpened attention and generated a greater preparedness to try what was otherwise a risky venture.

The strategy included new diplomatic initiatives regarding Syria's future, which also meant accommodating Russia and discredited Syrian President Bashar Assad. A necessary part of the strategy was to work with Russia and persuade it to target only IS/Daeche, rather than backing the Assad regime by hitting all opposition forces. To some extent, there were already signs of success in this respect, even before the UK formally joined the new approach, with Russian air strikes clearly appearing to make positive contributions prior to the British decision. However, a condition of Russia's involvement was, in effect, reluctantly to buy time for the doomed Assad regime and to negotiate a transitional period in which an official Syrian government would remain, even if arrangements were made over a period to time for Assad to give way to a new, diplomatically negotiated political arrangement for 'legitimate' government in Syria. Accommodating Russia and Assad on this was a necessary, but very uncomfortable, step for London, because of Moscow's illegal action in Ukraine and Damascus's criminal action against its own people, including mass murders and killing perhaps seven times more Syrians than IS/Daeche had, as well as Assad's already having 'lost' in the long-term.[14] However, the direct threat that IS/Daeche presented to the West made tackling it an overriding priority – and, so, working with Russia.

While the strategy had good prospects and coherence, it was not without risks. One of these was the proxy conflict between the Gulf States and Iran. Iran had committed 20-30,000 ground forces alongside Syrian government forces to bolster the government and these forces were acting implicitly in alliance with Russia's air intervention. Various Gulf States, including Saudi

---

14   The Daily Telegraph, 6 December 2015.

Arabia and Qatar supported IS/Daeche, either directly, in some respects, or by allowing private individuals significantly to support it. Although both Saudi Arabia and Iran formally supported diplomatic initiatives to end the armed conflict, their presence and their roles significantly complicated making diplomatic-political progress. Another concerned Turkey and the Kurdish forces spearheading action backed by US air power, especially if an implication might be an autonomous, or even, independent region.[15]

However, the biggest risk concerned Moscow's reliability. Having used co-operation with Iran and its diplomatic position through the UN to help protect Assad and delay his departure, Putin's forces increasingly attacked not only IS/Daeche and allied Islamist forces, but those of other movements fighting the government. Despite denials, it became ever more obvious that Russia was directing its attacks primarily at American-backed forces and others from what was called the 'legitimate' opposition to Assad's rule. By late 2016, Russian air attacks were destroying the rebel stronghold of Aleppo, provoking accusations of possible war crimes by the UK Ambassador to the UN at an emergency Security Council session, who then walked out (taking his French and American counterparts with him), accusations reinforced by the Foreign Secretary.[16] Moscow's approach showed little but contempt for any idea of a joint approach with Western countries.

Allegations of war crimes clearly stung Moscow. Past gross breaches of human rights standards in civil cases brought through the European Court of Human Rights had somewhat nonchalantly and quietly been acknowledged and compensation awarded by the court had been paid – while giving little heed to any need to operate by humanitarian standards.[17] However, Moscow reacted very tetchily to the British labelling of Russian action as potentially criminal. A Kremlin spokesman called Boris Johnson's backing of war crimes allegations, including, telling the UK parliament that 'the mills of justice grind slowly, but they grind small' – implying that the alleged crimes would not be forgotten and would, eventually, in forensic detail, be pur-

---

15   Of course, it should be noted that Turkey's position on an independent Kurdish region in either Iraq or Syria, based on the fear that a similar territory in Turkey would follow, was most likely misguided and unenlightened. It was far more likely that once an independent region – and certainly a state – were formed, irredentist pressures would diminish as the territory sought to establish itself and needed good relations with neighbours, therefore, ultimately working with the neighbours to quell independence impulses within a neighbouring country. In this sense, it was evident that, over time, the Republic of Ireland had worked with the UK to limit the effects of nationalist terrorism in Northern Ireland, while Slovenia's statehood, initially within the Yugoslav framework and eventually with full independent international personality, had served to manage and minimise nationalist pressures in both Italy and Austria.

16   The Guardian, 26 September 2016.

17   Vesko Popovski, "Terrorizing Civilians as a 'Counter-terrorist Operation'. Crimes and Impunity in Chechnya", Journal of Southeast European and Black Sea Studies, 7(3)2007, pp. 431-447.

sued.[18] A Kremlin spokesman accused the Foreign Secretary of 'Russophobic hysteria' and rejected the notion that Russian planes were in the area at all, even though Western surveillance left no doubt about the matter for UK and US officials. It was clear that, despite its brazen actions, Russia somehow felt that the British attacks impugned its honour – at a minimum, they played negatively on popular Russian self-images of Moscow's engagement. The potential damage to domestic support in a declining Russia and official sensitivity only encouraged British diplomacy in its calling a spade a spade.

The accusations of war crimes and the walkout from the UN Security Council were the first steps and a new, more hardline approach from London. This was made possible by two factors. The first of these was that Moscow's destruction of Aleppo and the evidence that accusations of war crimes and the walkout had piqued Moscow catalysed a crucial change in US diplomacy. In the British view, this was the key change in the personal perceptions of US Secretary of State John Kerry, who had led an international approach that had sought to eschew direct criticism of Moscow as far as possible, while relying on his own charisma and skill to co-operate with Russia in the fight against IS/Daeche and to pave the way for a 'legitimate' government in Syria. The evidence of Aleppo, war crimes allegations and the Security Council protest was judged by Britons to have forced Kerry to face the limitations, if not the clear failure, of his approach and his trust in co-operation with Moscow (despite their big differences in other areas) and endorse a new tack. From London's point of view, this gave considerable and welcome new scope to press Russia about its conduct.

The second factor boosting the British approach was the new Prime Minister, Theresa May. Having spent eight years as Home Secretary, May was very conscious of Russia's hostile activity against the UK. She was well aware of the daily intelligence about Russian espionage and cyber attacks on the UK, as well as Russian influence on certain parts of the British political elite – notably in her own Conservative Party, as well as Russian support for the right-wing UK Independence Party, led by Nigel Farage MEP (and similar support for other right-wing populist parties in Europe, notably the *Front Nationale* in France, led by Marine le Pen).[19] While cautious by nature, May was also intelligent and clear in addressing issues and being prepared to tackle them fearlessly and firmly.

For some years, the penetration of British politics had been understood, with the First Secretary of the Russian Embassy in London (who had links to the Russian security and intelligence apparatus via his father), described as a 'top-ranking' spy, at least,[20] facilitating the short-lived Conservative Friends of Russia group – it only lasted a few months after internal problems, culmi-

---

18   The Guardian, 12 October 2016.
19   The Daily Express, 1 June 2014.
20   The Guardian 30 November 2012.

nating with a crass, Kremlin-inspired homophobic attack on a Labour MP, Chris Bryant, Chair of the All-Party Parliamentary Committee on Russia.[21] This led to the resignation of Sir Malcolm Rifkind, an esteemed figure who had been Foreign Secretary and Defence Secretary in the 1980s and 1990s, who described the Bryant attack as the 'last straw',[22] while an unnamed former member of the group described it as comprising 'useful idiots' under Kremlin control.[23] That group, nonetheless had a successor, the Westminster Russia Forum, which automatically included the former group's remaining membership and continued, on whatever basis, to promote Russian positions. It is likely that those in security circles reporting to May would have advised her that the influence of Moscow within parts of her own party – and beyond it – extended far beyond the pro-Russian lobbying of this group – a far stronger 'Fifth Column' than had ever been possible in the Cold War. While her predecessor, Cameron, had perhaps been cautious in any dealings regarding this group, for fear of pressures from the right-wing of his party, above all on European issues, after the UK referendum on leaving the EU favouring an exit, there was no longer a fear of the damage that might be caused by figures such as these, promoting the interests of Russia both more broadly and also specifically in its desire to see the EU weakened, if not to disintegrate.

Coupled with May's mettle and the clear misconduct of Russia in Syria, a new, less-hamstrung approach to Moscow was evident – including the authority given to Royal Air Force pilots to shoot at Russian aircraft over Syria, if attacked. There was also a renewed focus on sanctions and the prospect of tightening the sanctions with new pressures, as the dominant analysis (contrary to the view of former Ambassador Brenton, cited above) was that sanctions had been highly effective and well targeted, a major cause of the economic pain Russia had suffered, even if this meant Putin turned to international provocations to distract his own population. This was all part of London's signalling to Moscow that previous shackles were off. However dangerous Moscow might be in its efforts to shake off economic and domestic weakness by acting provocatively on the international stage, it would have fewer ways out of the various strategic *cul-de-sacs* it had created for itself in the absence of significant Western blocking – other things being equal, that is. Those things, included, of course, the direction that American policy would take after the 45th President of the United States took office in January 2017.

---

21   Michael Weiss, 'In Plain Sight: Russia's London Lobby,' World Affairs, March/April 2013, at: http://www.worldaffairsjournal.org/article/plain-sight-kremlin%E2% 80%99s-london-lobby.

22   The Daily Telegraph 23 November 2012.

23   Weiss, 'In Plain Sight'

Conclusion

There was a marked change in the UK official assessment of, and position towards, Russia between the 2010 and 2015 National Security Strategy papers. However, while Russia was marked out explicitly as a potential threat in the 2015 assessment, London initially continued a somewhat flaccid and subdued stance towards Moscow until late 2016, when a harder approach emerged. This was, broadly speaking, the end of a quarter of a century attempt by London to build bridges with Moscow. The UK had made the strongest efforts to have a friendly, supportive and co-operative relationship with Russia since the end of the Cold War. At the same time, the two countries remained in deep competition and, in effect, covert confrontation – largely a result of the failure of some sectors in the Russian security apparatus fully to recognise the end of the Cold War, leaving the UK with little alternative but to engage.

Despite Britain's wooing Moscow for a quarter of a century and putting up with attempts at co-operation ignored, Russian state-backed murder in London and a string of other frustrations, it took not only the shameless annexation of Crimea, but even the subsequent violence in Eastern Ukraine to make London remove its official blinkers and renew its defence arsenal and adopt a stronger approach. Despite the firm responses to Russian mischief in Ukraine, there was still a willingness to seek co-operation over Syria. However, yet again, London's hopes were dashed in the disappointment of Russia's unforgiving air assault on Aleppo and the evidence of war crimes. Russian action in Syria, dovetailed with the emergence of Theresa May as a firm prime minister with a clear perspective on the need appropriately to counter Russia's hostile activity against the UK itself, whether seeking to penetrate the political and financial elite, buzzing British military aircraft and playing around the borders of British maritime waters, or attacking through cyber space.

Philip Remler

United States Narrative(s)

Summary

The predominant view in the U.S. holds that Russia is a power in decline; the U.S. sees Russia's aggressive actions in Ukraine and its spoiler role in many other issues as a Russian response to that decline. The predominant view holds that the U.S. and the West made a genuine, though flawed, attempt to integrate Russia into an emerging European security system and a rapidly globalizing economic system. Ultimately, this failed through clashing expectations: the West mistakenly expected Russia to want to integrate with the West and adopt its values; Russia mistakenly expected the West to recognize it as the world power it felt entitled to be, with the type of world influence it enjoyed during the Cold War. There is recognition that some of what alienated Russia stemmed from flaws in U.S. and Western policy, but there are no U.S. regrets for other Western actions that most inflamed Russian opinion: from halting genocide in Bosnia and Kosovo to supporting the aspirations of Arabs and Ukrainians alike to call repressive and corrupt leaderships to account.

The predominant U.S. narrative includes a post-Soviet history of continuous Russian bullying of its neighbours, paired during the Presidency of Vladimir Putin with increasing authoritarianism and rejection of liberal democratic values, along with a religious- and ethnic-based rejection of common human rights. The narrative sees Russia joining other countries such as China in seeing "Western" values as a tool for maintaining Western dominance of the current world order. Based on events in Ukraine, the U.S. narrative fears that for Russia, these rejected values include the post-World War II consensus on interstate relations, codified in the Helsinki Final Act, which has kept the peace in Europe for 70 years.

The Range of U.S. Narratives: Non-Mainstream Views

In late 2013, with the Euromaidan already in progress, I interviewed senior officials, former officials, and analysts from a wide range of U.S. government institutions and think tanks in connection with the Network project on threat perceptions. Not one of them considered Russia to be a major threat, including those whose portfolios included a focus on Russia. Most considered Russia to be a power in decline, capable of no more than playing a spoiler role to act out its resentment over no longer occupying the position it enjoyed in the bipolar Cold War world. Just one official saw Russia as part of a larger threat: a consensus of authoritarian governments, most importantly China, that saw the international order as stacked against them, and viewed the values of liberal democracy not as universal values, but as a Western ideology designed to cement Western dominance over that world order. But Russia was just one among those governments, and distinctly less important than China.

The Russian annexation of Crimea and forcible placement of puppet separatist regimes in the Donbass has given rise to numerous books and articles that brought to prominence a broad spectrum of narratives that were mostly not new, but which were the province of specialists when less attention was paid to Russia. The spectrum ranges from full-throated Cold-War philippics to vehement apologias for Russian actions and admiration for Vladimir Putin as a leader.

Many of the more vehement narratives are outside the mainstream or predominant narrative. For example, the dire warnings of politicians such as John McCain, or writers such as Anne Applebaum and Edward Lucas (and though the latter is English, he reaches an American audience) stress that Russia retains of a Soviet view of the world in which great powers dominate the smaller, balance of forces dictates right, and expansion and domination are the main goals. In this view, the wily Russian leader (this is invariably personalized) is outplaying the American side, either through his intellectual superiority to President George W. Bush, or through the passivity and indifference of President Barack Obama, or through a willingness to play dirty in ways that Western leaders cannot match, whether by corrupting Western politicians or poisoning opponents.

On the other extreme, Professor Stephen F. Cohen, who has made numerous media appearances (but whose book on the subject is not yet available as of this writing), holds that the United States provoked a crisis with Russia by acting with triumphalism as the victor in the Cold War, deliberately humiliating Russia and expanding the Western sphere of influence to take advantage of Russia's weakness, not recognizing that, as Putin put it in 2007, a spring compressed far enough will spring back. In Cohen's view, Russia acted to defend its interests as any power would, and it is the U.S. that missed the chance to turn Russia into a real partner – to the great disadvantage of the U.S., as demonstrated, he maintains, by the rise of the Islamic State and its terrorist attacks in Europe.

What is striking is the extent to which the proponents of these narratives (those who are old enough, that is) are saying the same things now that they were saying during the height of the Cold War. Those who were hawks a generation or two ago remain hawks now. At the other end of the spectrum, Cohen wrote, in a book published in 1986, that the main American problem in dealing with the USSR was "Sovietophobia," which prevented the U.S. from partnering with the Soviet Union – using the same terms he now uses to regret that the U.S. is not partnering with Russia. A certain consistency has been the hobgoblin of many American commentators on the USSR and Russia, and even the legendary George Kennan's opposition to NATO's 1997 enlargement echoed his opposition a half century earlier to its creation.

That does not mean that both extremes are entirely devoid of merit. With regard to the hawks, it is a fact that the current leadership of Russia received a Soviet education based on Marxist-Leninist dialectic, which imposes a particular way of analyzing the world. Likewise, many in the leadership (including President Putin) are alumni of the KGB, which also possessed a strong corporate culture and a common outlook. It is entirely natural that these formative experiences left their mark. With regard to the second extreme, the U.S. has often reacted to traumatic events in emotionally satisfying but ultimately irrational and counterproductive ways: for example, reacting to Pearl Harbour through the internment of Nisei, or to 9/11 by invading Iraq. McCarthyism – which Cohen broadens and refocuses as "Sovietophobia" – fits this description. But making a few valid points does not substitute for a holistic and multi-dimensional view.

Another narrative that received wide attention was the *realpolitik* critique of John Mearsheimer and several others such as Walter Russell Mead and Stephan Walt. In this view the West, carried away by the victory of liberal democracy over communism (the "end of history," as Francis Fukuyama put it), forgot about the basic security needs of a land-based state surrounded by flat, hard-to-defend frontiers. As Robert Legvold sums it up (Return to Cold War, 2016, p. 17) "The United States and its European allies, charmed by the notion that the age of *realpolitik* had passed, assumed that extending the institutions underpinning Western Europe's democratic peace to the Soviet Union's former empire was both constructive and in tune with the times. Russia disagreed, and it ended in the Ukrainian crisis." Mearsheimer called it the West's fault, and in particular that of the "liberals," the polar opposites of the "realists" (But Mearsheimer's argument has some factual issues: Henry Kissinger might be surprised to learn that by Mearsheimer's definition he is a "liberal," not a "realist," since he supported NATO enlargement in 1994, when it first came up before the U.S. Congress in the NATO Revitalization Act. Russia was supposedly defending its geopolitical position when it went to war in 2008 with Georgia, which might be therefore surprised to learn that its border with Russia, which features mountains higher than Mont Blanc, is flat).

Russia has been and will probably remain an issue in the U.S. presidential campaign of 2016. Hillary Clinton appears to subscribe to the mainstream view, adding some campaign rhetoric about the danger Vladimir Putin personally represents. Donald Trump appears to belong to the Marine Le Pen and Viktor Orban school of those who admire Putin as a strong leader with whom one can make advantageous deals. And there has been some play about Trump's campaign manager, who used to flak for Putin's protégé Yanukovych.

The mainstream narrative can be exemplified by two books: the short book by Legvold (op. cit.) and a longer one, still unpublished, by William Hill, who is serving on the Reflection Group for this project. Hill's book, No Place for Russia: European Security Institutions since 1989 (Woodrow Wilson Center/Columbia University, 2017), is a detailed examination of the approaches taken in the West and Russia to "find a place" for Russia in the emerging post-Cold-War security architecture of Europe. Reading these books is reminiscent of reading Christopher Clark's The Sleepwalkers, about the outbreak of the First World War: none of the great powers wanted a war, but their interests were fundamentally different, and they misread one another's intentions and red lines.

Legvold says – and by implication Hill agrees – that Russia and the West made an effort to find a "place for Russia" in post-Cold-War Europe, but that a number of factors prevented this from taking place by creating friction between Russia and the West. Legvold lists three:

1. Internal developments in Russia, especially the "reforms" that led to the oligarchization and criminalization of Russian society, discrediting democracy. Legvold does not include the Chechen wars in this list, but their brutality and atrocities clearly had an effect on American views.
2. Russia's heavy-handed bullying of its neighbours, including in the Baltics and in the separatist wars and tensions in Moldova, Ukraine, Georgia, and Azerbaijan.
3. Finally, the growing U.S.-Russian differences over the Balkan wars and in how to react to them. Legvold believes these contributed significantly to the Russian view that America habitually ignored international law, and made it certain that Russia would interpret NATO enlargement as an effort at encirclement.

The American narrative tends to look at Russia through the prism of these factors. While there is general revision of Washington's initial enthusiasm for the "Washington Consensus," and a recognition of the harmful aspects of the U.S. assistance effort in Russia, which included technical assistance on many of the privatizations that led to the economic anarchy of the 1990s, it is also true that American popular culture in the 1990s was permeated by clichés of the "Russian mafia" and the "Wild East." The two Chechen wars, especially the first, which began in late 1994, cemented the view of a military that made up for its incompetence by its extremes of brutality. For many Russians, democracy equalled anarchy in the 1990s, but this was invisible to Americans; and Vladimir Putin's rollback of democratic freedoms, especially after the Beslan terrorist attack of 2004, was seen in the American narrative as the replacement of democracy with the kind of authoritarian rule that Americans associate with aggressive and expansionist foreign policies.

Russia's actions toward its neighbours were a continuous source of friction with the U.S., cementing into the U.S. narrative a view that Russia was driven by the loss of its empire. Russia's bullying intruded on the U.S. consciousness in a number of places – including the Baltics, Moldova, and Ukraine; but the most salient events occurred in Georgia, a country that was a favourite of the George H.W. Bush, Bill Clinton, and George W. Bush administrations alike. Georgian President Eduard Shevardnadze, though vilified in Russia, was a hero to many in the U.S. for his role in ending the Cold War and the reunification of Germany. Russia supported separatist rebellions in Abkhazia and South Ossetia, and its military bases in Ajara and Javakheti were associated with separatist tensions. In the midst of Georgia's civil war, U.S. Secretary of State James Baker, who visited Tbilisi and saw the lawlessness there, expressly requested that the CIA help train a presidential bodyguard service to protect his friend Eduard. The 1993 murder of the officer assigned to this task, Freddie Woodruff, was widely seen as a warning from the Russian security services not to meddle in "their" turf. Russian-linked assassination attempts against Eduard Shevardnadze followed in 1995 and 1998. Russia's vilification of Shevardnadze was exceeded only by its vilification of the man who ousted him, Mikheil Saakashvili. Vladimir Putin, deeply immersed in the Georgia dossier, often revealed his personal animosity toward the erratic Saakashvili, who reciprocated in kind, and Russia pursued a path – including embargoes, border closures, and transit bans – that led directly to the war of 2008. Even as Vladimir Putin called George W. Bush to express support after the 11 September 2001 terrorist attacks, the issue of Georgia came between them: Putin, engaged in the second Chechen War, likened the 9/11 attacks to his problem with the Chechens and their refuge in Georgia's Pankisi Gorge. Georgia is a thread that runs through the predominant U.S. narrative of tensions with Russia over Ukraine.

The Balkan Wars, too, or rather their reflection in the Russian narrative, form part of the basis for the U.S. narrative. While there has been much revision in U.S. thinking on such issues as the Washington consensus, the U.S. role in Russian privatization, and the unilateralism of the 2003 Iraq war, there are no second thoughts over the U.S. intervention in the Balkans to prevent genocide in Bosnia (1995) and Kosovo (1999). The U.S. political establishment had been traumatized by its failure to prevent the 1994 genocide in Rwanda, and after the Srebrenica massacre (1995) demonstrated to the U.S. the genocidal intent of the Serb leadership under Milosevic and Karadjic, the U.S. reversed its policy of leaving that conflict to the Europeans to resolve and imposed its own peace in a forceful way. The extremely negative U.S. view of Serbian actions, including the conviction that Milosevic, Karadjic, et al. were war criminals who had committed crimes against humanity, ensured that Russia's support of the Serbs in Bosnia and in Kosovo a few years later helped to shape the U.S. impression of a Russia whose commitment to democracy and human rights was contingent, at best.

Russia, as we know, takes a different view of events in the Balkans, and Russian writers and interlocutors have frequently cited the NATO bombing campaign of 1999 as a turning point in Russia's view of the U.S. and the West. This criticism, however, simply has no resonance in the mainstream American view. To the U.S., the Russian position, seen as support for war criminals, remains incomprehensible.

The Role of NATO Enlargement in the U.S. Narrative

NATO's continued existence after the end of the Cold War, and its enlargement, are often cited in the Russian narrative as a principal cause of today's tensions, but the U.S. narrative rejects this contention. To be sure, NATO was created as the foremost expression of the U.S. policy of containment of the Soviet Union (over the objections of the author of the containment policy, George Kennan). Over the course of the Cold War, however, NATO came to embody all U.S. security interests and commitments in Europe. The end of the Cold War did not change that: the extinction of an opponent – the Soviet Union – and its replacement by a partner – Russia – did not mean, for most American foreign policy thinkers, that NATO had lost its purpose and relevance. Indeed, one could argue that, given the strong and vocal misgivings of Margaret Thatcher and François Mitterrand about German reunification, the United States was constrained to recommit itself to NATO as a means of reassuring the United Kingdom and France, who may still have believed that, as NATO's first Secretary General Lord Ismay quipped, the purpose of NATO was to "keep the Americans in, the Russians out – and the Germans down."

Ironically, while Russia found NATO enlargement so alienating, it was also strongly opposed by the U.S. military establishment. U.S. military thinkers in the early 1990s believed that only "net exporters" of security should join the alliance, and the countries of the former Warsaw Pact were all "net importers." The clear fear of former Warsaw Pact members, on the other hand, was that if a new Iron Curtain were to descend on Europe, they wanted to be on the right side of it this time. The Clinton Administration came down on their side, believing that the reforms needed to join NATO – reforms such as civilian control of the military – would help make the transition to democracy irreversible. The Clinton Administration in any case viewed Russia as unaffected by an enlarged NATO, since it was no longer an enemy or even a rival, but a partner.

The task of selling this policy to the American people was made easier by Russia's often aggressive, bullying and heavy-handed behaviour toward its new neighbours. A strong coalition of cold-war hawks and pressure groups (including ethnic diasporas) on behalf of the Visegrád Group of former Warsaw Pact countries brought before Congress incidents of aggressive Russian behaviour, some of which we have already mentioned: in Georgia, support for and military intervention on behalf of separatists in Abkhazia and South Ossetia and the perceived use of Russian military bases in Ajara and Javakheti to support proto-separatist movements, and support for the attempt by Zviad Gamsakhurdia to overthrow President Shevardnadze by force; in Azerbaijan, support for the 1993 coup by Surat Huseynov and military support for all sides in the Karabakh conflict; in Moldova, support for and military intervention on behalf of separatists in Transdniestria; in Ukraine, political support for separatists in the Crimea; and in the Baltics, support for "Russophone" proto-separatist movements.

In the mid-1990s Russia undertook additional operations that intruded on the American consciousness. One was the August, 1995 assassination attempt, widely linked to Russia, against Georgian President Eduard Shevardnadze. The alleged perpetrator was a former security chief who had fled to Russia; the Russian authorities denied they knew his whereabouts even as he appeared repeatedly on Russian television. Another event that impressed itself on the U.S. was the brutal and bloody war in Chechnya, which undermined the Western view of Russia as a budding liberal democracy. Authors such as Anatol Lieven may have drawn the lesson from that war that Russia was harmless because its army was inept and incapable (Chechnya: Tombstone of Russian Power, 1998). But looking at it from Riga or Vilnius, the lesson was the opposite: that even when incapable of defeating an opposing fighting force, the Russian military was capable of and willing to flatten entire cities, kill thousands of civilians, and displace hundreds of thousands more. Spurred by such factors, there was widespread U.S. support for NATO membership for Poland, Hungary and the Czech Republic, which acceded in 1997.

To be sure, there were certainly relics of Cold War thinking in the U.S., as expressed, for example, in the writings of lobbyist Bruce Jackson, who was influential during the administration of George W. Bush. Along with Ronald Asmus, a former Deputy Assistant Secretary of State during the Clinton Administration, Jackson co-authored a study titled "The Black Sea and the Frontiers of Freedom" (Hoover Institution, 2004), which advocated enlarging NATO to include all other Black Sea littoral states (including Ukraine) plus Armenia and Azerbaijan, with the express purpose of encircling Russia and limiting its influence in the "wider Black Sea region." It is clear that Russian analysts and policymakers took note.

The U.S. narrative notes efforts by the U.S. and the West to include Russia and make it feel it belonged. The inclusion of Russia in the G7 to form the G8 took place at a time when Russia's per capita GDP was roughly one fifth that of Canada's. Russia was offered a place in NATO's Partnership for Peace in 1994 (along with many other former Soviet and Warsaw Pact nations). The NATO-Russia Founding Act was adopted in 1997, and the NATO-Russia Council was established in 2002. Both Legvold and Hill note that none of these ever took off as effective ways of integrating Russia, and believe the West shares some of the blame for that.

Hill notes that the U.S. and especially Russia believed that Russia would become a full partner in European security through an institutionalized CSCE, but that this process was stymied both by the unwieldy expansion of the organization to include all the new post-Soviet and post-Yugoslav states, including their quarrels with one another; and by the intense suspicion with which many of the former Soviet and Warsaw Pact states viewed Russia. In addition, the security partnership offered by the West through the OSCE was sometimes seen by Russia as an infringement into the sphere of influence it wanted to retain from Soviet times: Western attempts to share mediation and in some cases peacekeeping responsibilities in the Karabakh, South Ossetia, Abkhazia, Transdniestria, and Chechnya conflicts were resented, discouraged, and sometimes sabotaged by Russia.

The U.S. narrative generally recognizes that following 9/11 Russia offered co-operation to U.S. efforts in Afghanistan by permitting transit. Russia also expressed a willingness to co-operate with the U.S. on counter-terrorism, though U.S. officials involved with the exchange expressed disappointment with the limited extent to which such co-operation actually materialized. It is also generally recognized that U.S. unilateralism in Iraq was a blow to all forms of co-operation and raised suspicions on the Russian side; so that by 2005, for example, Russia was pushing for an end to U.S. access to Manas Air Base, in Kyrgyzstan, for its Afghanistan logistics. The U.S. mainstream narrative recognizes that the U.S. withdrawal from the Anti-Ballistic Missile (ABM) Treaty in 2002, as well as its failure to ratify the Comprehensive Test Ban Treaty (CTBT) and the Adapted Conventional Forces in Europe (A/CFE) Treaty, were negative steps that may have prompted Russia to withdraw from the original CFE Treaty and to violate the 1987 Intermediate Nuclear Forces (INF) Treaty.

Legvold (p. 106) cites examples of attempts by the Obama administration to "reset" co-operation with Russia, including proposals to co-operate on ABM development, the establishment of a U.S.-Russian Bilateral Presidential Commission (a reprise of the Gore-Chernomyrdin Commission of the 1990s), and the (failed) attempt to ratify CTBT. The U.S. supported the OSCE in creating the "Corfu Process" to discuss President Medvedev's sketchy proposal for a new security dialogue. None of these efforts bore fruit, and Legvold concludes that neither side took co-operation seriously and unambiguously enough to make it work. Another writer (not American, but published in the U.S.), ascribes the failure to mistaken expectations: the Obama Administration expected the reset to improve Russia's behaviour on the world stage, while Russia expected the reset to mean the West would recognize Russia's great power status and sphere of influence (Bobo Lo, Russia and the New World Disorder, London and Washington, 2015).

It is also the case, however, that Obama's reset faced an uphill battle in any case, given that Russia took a decided turn toward authoritarian governance, and Putin's election campaign in 2012 featured accusations that the U.S. was sponsoring a "colour revolution" in Russia. Even before the Ukraine crisis, Putin cancelled a visit to the U.S. in May, 2012; and in August, 2013 Obama cancelled his own visit to Moscow scheduled for the following month. Soon thereafter, Putin kicked off the chain of events leading to the Ukraine crisis: on 3 September, Armenian President Serzh Sargsyan, having been summoned to Moscow by Putin, announced that he would not be signing an Association agreement with the EU, but would instead join Russia's customs union. By December 2013, when I interviewed a series of U.S. officials, not one of them mentioned the "reset." The attempt to reset relations, which got off to a rocky start when Secretary of State Hillary Clinton handed Sergei Lavrov a button marked "overload" (peregruzka) instead of "reboot" (perezagruzka), was officially dead.

The Ukraine Crisis

With the Arab Spring, the United States consistently looked favourably upon the efforts of people to change otherwise unchangeable, sclerotic and repressive regimes. Since Iraq, however, there has been a wariness about intervention, and the chaos that followed the death of Mu'ammar al-Qadhafi in Libya, the hard choices in Syria, and the re-emergence of a military regime in Egypt have led to questioning whether the survival of a repressive dictator might not be better than his exit from the scene.

That questioning has by and large *not* affected the mainstream American narrative on Ukraine. The U.S. foreign policy establishment has heard the Russian narrative – that a Western- and American-backed coup ousted the legitimate president of Ukraine, leading the people of Crimea and the Donbass spontaneously to rise up against the new, illegitimate regime that wanted to pull Ukraine into NATO. The U.S. rejects that narrative.

In the U.S. view, NATO was irrelevant to the issue, since there had been no developments on Ukrainian accession since NATO's Bucharest Summit in 2008, when all plans were put on hold. The relevant actor was the EU, which offered an Association Agreement to Ukraine, among others, as a way of improving relations with the EU's neighbours without holding out the prospect of EU membership. Russia viewed this as an incursion into its sphere of influence, and summoned the leaders of both Armenia (September, 2013) and Ukraine (November, 2013) to Moscow, putting the choice as an either-or decision. Both Serzh Sargsyan and Viktor Yanukovych acceded to Putin's demands, Yanukovych in exchange for a $15 billion aid package and guarantees on gas pricing. In the U.S. view, this provoked protests by a populace that just wanted a normal life, but whose hopes had been extinguished by a corrupt deal. The U.S. supported the protesters, but rejects the assertion that it was involved in a coup that ousted Yanukovych. In the U.S. view, the leaked transcripts of a conversation between Assistant Secretary of State Nuland and Ambassador Pyatt show that the U.S. was offering advice to the Maidan opposition, but nothing more.

In the U.S. narrative, Russia – possibly feeling a loss of face from these events – decided to punish Ukraine and did so with a military operation, first in Crimea and then in the Donbass. The U.S. foreign policy establishment is concerned that the annexation of Crimea through that military operation will undermine the Helsinki consensus that has kept the peace in Europe, the more so in that it was paired with a high-powered propaganda effort promoting the idea, made explicit by Putin, that the international order as currently constituted is inherently stacked against Russia. That returns us to the threat presciently perceived by one informant in the 2013 project mentioned at the beginning of this report: that a "bandwagon" of authoritarian states, including Russia, was rejecting the norms of liberal democracy and post-war documents regulating interstate relations, charging that these were in reality an imperialist imposition designed to maintain Western dominance. In the U.S. view, this is perhaps the most dangerous long-term legacy of the current crisis in Ukraine. For this reason, the Minsk process may "manage" – though not resolve – the conflict in the Donbass, but the unresolved Crimea precedent is likely to keep sanctions in place for the foreseeable future.

Policy Options

Outliers such as Stephen Cohen criticize the U.S. sanctions regime as ineffective, and therefore argue that they should be abandoned. Outliers on the other side also criticize them as ineffective; they demand more robust action, such as the sanctions that were previously imposed on Iran. Both miss the point that is perhaps unspoken but nonetheless drives this particular U.S. policy: sanctions, which produce the desired effects on a country's behaviour only after years or decades of rigorous imposition – and often not even then – are not intended to change a country's behaviour in the short term; rather they are an expression of displeasure that goes beyond mere words but falls short of actual war.

President Obama was confronted with this choice by the occupation and annexation of the Crimea. There were three basic options: issue a condemnation that imposes no penalty; reverse the occupation by military means, using whatever force might prove necessary; or impose sanctions to punish Russia for its unacceptable actions, without the unrealistic expectation that they might reverse Russia's actions. Since the first two courses were unsustainable with the American electorate, the Obama administration chose the third. The debate within the U.S. is whether to retain that policy or move to "option 2½," which would involve accelerated military assistance to Ukraine to prevent further incursions from Russian-backed forces, recognizing that this would risk a wider war.

That said, future options for the U.S. depend on how the narrative develops its evaluation of Russian intentions. As Legvold puts it (op. cit. p. 35), a salient characteristic of the Cold War was that the sides were opposed not just in interest, but also in *purpose*. There was little point in seeking a real mutual understanding until the leadership of one side or the other changed. The personalization of the confrontation has led to a tendency to define America's problem with Russia in two words: Vladimir Putin. Voices have been raised against this, however, and the U.S. is grappling with the question of whether it has a Russia problem or a Putin problem. If the analysis remains personalized, it is likely that steps will not be taken to alleviate the current confrontation.

On the other hand, if the "official" narrative comes to de-emphasize Putin and devote its attention to real problems the U.S. has with Russia as a country, that would argue in favour of transactional compartmentalization: understanding that there are areas in which the U.S. will continue to express its displeasure with Russia by inflicting punishment; areas in which co-operation will remain impossible; and other areas in which co-operation can proceed as and when they are in the U.S. interest. The analogy would be to U.S.-Soviet relations: in the 1980s the U.S. continued to support efforts against the Soviets in Afghanistan, to inflict pain for an invasion that was viewed as unacceptable behaviour; but at the same time it negotiated and concluded significant arms control agreements.

A recent article by Thomas Graham, a former U.S. State Department and National Security Council Official, argued in favour of a transactional relationship with Russia, noting that "On some issues, such as strategic stability and nonproliferation, U.S.-Russian cooperation is essential," but warning not to choose "a policy based on a search for grounds for cooperation." In its efforts to prevent Russian aggression against its neighbours, Graham reminds us that, "The best barrier to Russian expansion, as history shows, is strong, capable, successful states along its borders," implying that statebuilding among Russia's neighbours is the best containment policy (Thomas E. Graham, The Sources of Russian Conduct: Kennan's Long Telegram needs an update for Putin's Russia," in: The National Interest, August 24, 2016).

Legvold (p. 38-40) has compiled a list of areas, derived from various sources, in which co-operation has continued, those in which it has ceased, and those in which new co-operation might be contemplated to defuse the current crisis:

Continuing:
- 2010 New START Agreement is still implemented
- Nuclear agreement reached with Iran
- U.S. and NATO forces transited Russia from Afghanistan (until May, 2015)
- Space programs

Ceased:
- Most arms control initiatives, including:
  - Advancing from New START
  - Cooperative Threat Reduction (Nunn-Lugar)
  - Nuclear Security Summit
  - Missile defence co-operation
  - Dealing with other nuclear confrontation lines (e.g., India-Pakistan)
- European security
- Military Exchanges
- Energy efficiency co-operation
- Arctic (despite some co-operation, it is becoming militarized)

New initiatives:
- Follow-up on the European-Atlantic Security Initiative (EASI)
- Northeast Asia dialogue
- Cyberwarfare security
- Dialogue over U.S.-Russian interaction in the former Soviet space
- Dialogue on activities outside the Middle East to combat Islamic State
- Dialogue on incident prevention in Ukraine

Even the most elementary co-operation, however, will be problematic. As we know from Schelling's game theory, if two persons are chained together at the edge of a cliff, with one to be released if the other surrenders, the best strategy for either is to dance closer and closer to the edge of the cliff, taking ever greater risks of falling off and killing both – until either both fall off or one surrenders. Co-operation requires stepping back from that sort of game. It is not clear that such a course is politically sustainable at present in either Moscow or Washington.

Annex

European Security – Challenges at the Societal Level

Acknowledgements

This project was encouraged by the 2016 German OSCE Chairmanship and jointly sponsored by the Austrian Federal Ministry for Europe, Integration and Foreign Affairs, the Finnish Ministry for Foreign Affairs, the German Federal Foreign Office and the Swiss Federal Department of Foreign Affairs. The OSCE Secretariat provided administrative and financial monitoring. We express our sincere gratitude for this support. In particular, we would like to thank Gernot Erler, Special Representative of the German Federal Government for the 2016 OSCE Chairmanship, who first proposed a project based on reports of national security policy narratives. We would also like to express our gratitude to the Geneva Centre for Security Policy and the Russian International Affairs Council as well as their staffs for hosting one workshop each, the latter with generous support from the Friedrich Ebert Foundation. And we are grateful to the representatives of sixteen member institutes of the OSCE Network of Think Tanks and Academic Institutions for contributing to this report by elaborating narrative reports and other analyses. Finally, we express our gratitude to the members of the project's reflection group – Nadezhda Arbatova, Hüseyin Bağci, Serena Giusti, William Hill, Kornely Kakachia, Dzianis Melyantsou, Kari Möttölä, Barend ter Haar, Marcin Terlikowski and Monika Wohlfeld – as well as to all other scholars and governmental officials who discussed studies on narratives and draft reports at the two workshops in Geneva and Moscow.

---

1   Working Group: Wolfgang Zellner (principal drafter), Irina Chernykh, Alain Délétroz, Frank Evers, Barbara Kunz, Christian Nünlist, Philip Remler, Oleksiy Semeniy, Andrei Zagorski.

In the wake of the current confrontation between Russia and the West, will the nations of Europe govern their interactions by rules and principles, as the signatories of the Helsinki Final Act hoped, or by the conjuncture or clash of national interests, unmitigated by a code of behavior? If by rules and principles, will those reflect shared values? Or are the values once deemed universal shared, in fact, only by certain elites? If a clash of interests prevails, can Europe contain the ensuing struggle and make the competition a non-zero-sum game? Or will each nation in Europe be faced with a series of stark choices between conflict and concession, winning and losing?

Europe – by which we mean here the OSCE area – faces a multitude of challenges, some, such as terrorism or climate change, have external origins; and some pertain to our living together on the European continent. Among the latter is the Ukraine crisis, which clearly shows that the Helsinki Consensus is being challenged – not because it has been disavowed, but because each side in the clash between Russia and the West claims that the other has broken it. Other challenges, such as the rapid growth of populist, nationalist and xenophobic forces in the face of the migration crisis, are symptoms of strain. Confrontations between sets of values are played out both within societies and between them.

As a result, the institutional foundations of cooperative security in Europe and the rules and principles they represent are rapidly disappearing. Both Russia and the West are starting to prefer deterrence to cooperative security. This spirit is also beginning to pervade economic relations and inter-societal interactions. Other countries increasingly see this confrontation as a threat to their own security. Attempts to restore a normative approach to international governance – rules and principles, whether based on shared values or not – would appear to require a significant lessening of current tensions first.

This report, therefore, argues that interim rules of the road in the security, economic and social fields, based on current realities and currently shared interests, are needed to help reduce those tensions: a *modus vivendi* that allows the sides to retain their principled positions on the European order, and how they believe it is threatened; but that also allows for the mitigation and containment of existing conflicts. This will not produce as much stability as a norms-based regime, and may result in less human security for individuals, but it can pave the way for serious discussions that can lead to a return to norms and principles as a guiding force for the European order.

The ideas in this paper are based on fifteen national narratives produced by institutions affiliated with this Network and which will be published separately. The narratives show that though in several countries – e.g., Russia, the United States, and the United Kingdom – societies perceive the standoff in mutually exclusive terms, the populations of many other counties have views that diverge strongly from the "Western" or "Russian" narratives. The narratives identify numerous shared interests on which to base an interim *modus vivendi*: on global and strategic issues and transnational threats, on conflict resolution in Europe and the Middle East, and on economic issues.

Our narratives generally recognize the need for a program of urgent action aimed at resuming dialogue and seeking cooperation, structuring multiple lines of dialogue as a starting point for broader intergovernmental cooperation, and agreeing on some urgent measures without political conditions and linkages. In light of recent dangerous incidents involving military forces, these should include an agreement in the NATO-Russia Council on avoiding military incidents and accidents and engaging in further dialogue on military risk reduction. Measures should also include dialogues on economic and social matters and the beginning of what will probably be a protracted dialogue on re-establishing a shared understanding of the principles of the Helsinki Decalogue.

At the same time, the narratives recognize that progress on resolving the Ukraine crisis will be a major factor in permitting the success of these measures and that failure to resolve that crisis will render most of them – and especially the attempt to re-establish norms – problematic. The OSCE has contributed greatly with the Special Monitoring Mission, but urgently needs to develop further operational capacity to make a greater contribution to the full implementation of the Minsk Agreements.

Key Recommendations

We recommend agreement on a Code of Conduct for Facilitating a Diplomatic Process including elements such as:

–   lowering the level of confrontation by avoiding steps that raise tensions and taking agreed de-escalatory measures;
–   strengthening communication by de-escalating rhetoric and discouraging hate speech, maintaining channels of communication at all levels, conducting a dual dialogue: both on issues where agreement is possible and on issues where no agreement can be expected soon; and encouraging academic and other exchanges to mitigate contradictory and mutually exclusive narratives; and
–   taking measures to re-establish cooperation by avoiding conditionality on cooperation, working together on climate change, terrorism and other global or transnational issues, consulting with partners throughout the world to encourage their involvment, and publicizing the willingness of political leaders to cooperate.

We recommend creating a more connected economic order by measures including:

- developing a package of economic and environmental confidence-building measures to counter the tendency toward autarky that has been strengthened by the use of economic sanctions by all sides.

We recommend working on re-establishing a shared normative order through initiatives including:

- analysis of historical narratives on Western-Russian relations,
- initiating a dialogue on norms at the societal level, and
- utilizing existing networks of young leaders to help shape future interactions.

Introduction

Europe[2] is passing through a period of unprecedented challenges in terms of scope, complexity and speed. They are generated from within and from outside of Europe and challenge Europe's cohesiveness, integrity and competitiveness. Its competitiveness is challenged by ongoing shifts in the global distribution of power in an increasingly polycentric world. Its cohesiveness is severely tested by mounting global challenges and transnational threats, including climate change and transnational terrorism and a decreasing political ability to absorb inflows of refugees and migrants.

Europe's integrity is endangered by disputes over the European order and deepening institutional fragmentation, within both multinational groupings and individual societies. Societies are increasingly entrenching themselves behind fault lines, particularly those between Russia and the West.[3] But fault lines are also emerging *within* the Euro-Atlantic and Eurasian communities. Societies are often tempted to shield themselves from perceived external challenges through nationalism, isolationism and protectionism instead of addressing them through cooperation and openness. The challenges Europe is facing now are unlikely to disappear any time soon. Rather they will shape Europe's agenda for years to come.

While acknowledging numerous other fault lines affecting the OSCE area, this report concentrates on the divisions between Russia and the West. The reason is that Russian-Western relations represent the backbone of European security. There will be no resolution for the open and protracted conflicts nor agreement on an inclusive European order without cooperation between Russia and the West.

The purpose of this report is not to assign blame, but to understand where we are and why, and what needs to be done to manage those divisions.

---

2   When speaking of Europe, we mean the 57 OSCE participating States.
3   By "Western states", we mean all states that are members of or are associated with the EU and/or NATO.

Based on its analysis, the report strongly advocates the resumption of a comprehensive dialogue between Russia and the West. While such a dialogue should be independent from the current crises, it is evident that it can only be productive to the degree that progress in crisis resolution is achieved, particularly regarding the Ukraine crisis. On the other hand, more dialogue will facilitate progress in crisis resolution. The argument that a business-as-usual approach to relations with Russia is unwarranted does not preclude extraordinary dialogue and fails to address the fact that the challenges we are facing are unprecedented and require extraordinary means.

Dialogue should lead to what the report calls pragmatic transactional cooperation, that is, cooperation starting from the current realities. In chapter 3, the report proposes a number of urgent steps to be carried out within the OSCE and beyond. In addition, it proposes a number of projects focused on the link between the societal and the governmental level, to be implemented by the OSCE Network of Think Tanks and Academic Institutions (cf. section 3.2).

Narratives for a Europe in Crisis
The role of narratives on the current crisis of European security is emphasized by a 'competition of narratives' within a European order shaken by 'the return of geopolitics' and 'the resurgence of geo-economics' between Russia and the West (as organized politically within NATO and the European Union) with the participation of in-between actors.
As a concept for analysis and policy, narrative may refer to material, institutional and ideational drivers of actorness. From the strategic point of view, narrative is a means used by policy makers to construct a shared meaning of the past, present and future of international politics in order to shape the behavior of domestic and international actors. Publics regularly internalize and rationalize the world in the form of narrative and media may exert a greater impact on public perceptions than government.
From the discursive point of view, narrative is an identity-driven and identity-reproducing process, whereby nations, leaders or people strive to connect their roles and destinies with internal and external developments. As a result, narrative tends to be a widely used and recognized story of the past.
Narrative and policy belong together and proceed in parallel. Narrative is used to validate or legitimate policy to domestic and international audiences and those messages may not necessarily be identical, but may be tailored to serve a function or purpose. The need for narrative within governments and societies is at its greatest when there is a change underway or expected in policy. As interpretations of developments in the Euro-Atlantic and Eurasian region, narratives serve to rationalize and validate strategies and actions in a formative period of international security.
Kari Möttölä, Finland between the Practice and the Idea: the Significance and Change of Narrative in the Post-cold War Era. (Paper prepared for publication in the context of the OSCE Network Study Group: European Security – Addressing Challenges at the Societal Level).

The report is the outcome of intensive exchange and discussions among representatives of sixteen institutes from all regions of the OSCE area that participate in the OSCE Network. Our joint research and the discussions were supported by two workshops held in Geneva and Moscow in May and October 2016.

The report builds on 15 studies on national security policy narratives written by the members of the group. In analyzing the differences and shared views among Russia, Western countries and the countries that cannot be attributed to either "side", it focuses more on the link between the interstate and the societal level and less on the purely intergovernmental politics that are usually the main object of comparable reports. Therefore, it deals only peripherally with issues such as arms control or violent conflicts, but focuses on aspects that are more directly felt by citizens. We have chosen this approach because the current conflicts and problems run much deeper than intergovernmental politics and have reached the societal level. Suspicion and estrangement between societies have again reached levels not seen since the end of the Cold War. As a consequence, it has become much more difficult to re-establish cooperative politics, because re-creating confidence at societal levels is more difficult than at inter-governmental levels, where things can be repaired quickly if there is political will.

An important finding from the studies conducted is that the narratives we have identified do not exactly match the standard Russian and Western security narratives, which are almost mutually exclusive and lay blame for all evil on the other side. The debate over Russia reveals very different approaches. There are countries such as Austria, Italy and France where perceptions of closeness and even friendship with Russia are prominent. Switzerland, deeply anchored in the West, takes positions, but largely avoids blaming sides. And there are other countries, such as Georgia, the United Kingdom and Ukraine, where people feel fundamentally threatened by the Russian Federation. On the other hand, narratives underlying even official discourses in a number of countries allied with Russia, such as Belarus and Kazakhstan, reveal remarkable differences from the Russian mainstream narrative. What unites almost all narratives is the shared objective of pragmatic cooperation among Russia, the Western states and those countries that belong neither to Euro-Atlantic nor to Eurasian institutions.

1. The Challenges Ahead

The challenges ahead are numerous, complex and difficult to address. The situation in the OSCE area is characterized by a number of major fragmentation lines as well as external challenges that can roughly be sorted into four groups: fragmentation and divisions within and between societies; fragmentation within the integration structures; conflicts in Russian-Western relations; and negative influences from outside.

Divisions and Authoritarianism within Societies

We start from the assumption that long-term and more fundamental political change is driven by societal forces. Under the heading of society we understand all strata of the population of a country apart from the sphere of institutionalized politics – ideally parliaments and governments. Thus, society includes a broad variety of associations of any kind from business networks and trade unions, via churches, sports clubs, and cultural and scientific associations to non-governmental organizations.

In most countries within the OSCE area, we observe a deepening of domestic fragmentation lines and the strengthening of populist, nationalist and xenophobic forces whose main desire is to cut their countries off from global developments. In some countries, these forces, by exploiting disconnects between ruling establishments and populations, have influenced the formation of governments or even assumed political power. Political forces of this kind represent a serious danger to a free and open Europe.

More people perceive threats and harbor suspicion and even hatred than at any time since the end of the Cold War. Because it is necessary for political leaders to secure the support of their electorates before they can repair ties at the intergovernmental level, any return to cooperative politics has become more difficult.

Fragmentation within the Integration Structures

The European Union (EU) is the most sophisticated integration structure in the OSCE space. Its development is key for the whole of Europe, and the EU-Russia relationship is a major pillar of the European order.

Currently, the EU's internal disagreements are so serious that they amount to a comprehensive crisis. No recipe has yet been found for the deep socioeconomic North-South divide within the EU. With Brexit, the EU will lose one of its strongest member states. A substantial move backwards towards disintegration can no longer be ruled out. Such a development would harm the whole of Europe and can be in nobody's interest. Against this background, the influx of refugees is seen by many as an unbearable burden.

NATO is also facing significant challenges in relation to the conflict in Syria, where different member states are pursuing different and even conflicting strategies. Moreover, the latent dispute over transatlantic burden-sharing is serious in times of scarce resources.

The Eurasian Economic Union (EAEU) has not yet become a driver of economic cooperation among its member states. Trade among them has been in steady decline. Western sanctions on Russia and Russian counter-sanctions, Russia's withdrawal from free trade with Ukraine and the extension of EAEU membership to Armenia and Kyrgyzstan have contributed to the erosion of the Euro-Asian Customs Union. The Ukraine crisis has triggered political concerns among member states over Russia's role and, most fundamentally, has revealed the fact that their national interests suffer severely from the confrontation between Russia and the West. Neither EAEU nor Collective Security Treaty Organization (CSTO) membership is seen by these states as a solution for these concerns. Particularly in the context of the current crisis, Russia's allies are emphasizing their multi-vector foreign and security policies and seeking to expand their relations with Euro-Atlantic institutions to balance their relations with Russia.

Russian-Western Relations

Relations between Russia and the West are at their lowest point since the end of the Cold War. Security relations soured in the wake of NATO enlargement, disputes over arms control, the Kosovo conflict and independence, and Western interventions in Iraq and Libya. As manifested by the conflict over Ukraine's association with the EU, economic integration issues are now part and parcel of the highly securitized dispute over the European order.

These developments are reinforced by a widening gap in how the actors understand the underlying norms and values of the European order, while mounting controversy at interstate level is complemented by deepening estrangement between societies. Russia no longer sees itself as part of the Euro-Atlantic community of states and, instead, seeks to protect itself from the Western policy of promoting democracy and human rights, often confused with a policy of regime change and interference in the internal affairs of sovereign states.

At the same time, Russia's involvement in the Ukraine crisis has raised concerns in the West, especially among Russia's neighbors, that Moscow is pursuing a revisionist policy that seeks to revise the post-Cold War European order. This has moved Russia's neighbors, which have recently become members of the EU and NATO, to seek credible reassurances from the Alliance and to move towards a deterrence posture vis-à-vis Russia.

As a result, we are witnessing a further deepening and hardening of the fault line between Russia and the West and a rapid dismantlement of the foundations of cooperative security in Europe, which have been in place since the end of the Cold War. The British narrative speaks of the end of an attempt over a quarter of a century to build bridges and of "deep competition and, in effect, covert confrontation". To be sure, current developments do not replicate the historical Cold War, which was a global and antagonistic ideological confrontation pursued by orderly assigned camps. However, they are increasingly reminiscent of Cold War behavior, in which the "other" was framed in a black and white manner as the only one bearing guilt for the conflict, and had to be removed before a resolution could be found. This kind of essentialist approach is a really alarming sign.

Two developments have had a salient impact on Europe: The change in global economic and power structures, and conflicts and instability in Europe's vicinity.

Rates of growth in Europe – the EU as well as wider Europe – are generally low, while a number of emerging countries are growing much faster. Europe can thus be said to be losing ground, at least in comparative terms. A new wave of protectionism would further complicate the situation. At the same time, Europe depends increasingly on global developments and decisions over which it has less influence. Europe, as well as its major constituent parts, has not yet found a way to deal with this.

At the same time, climate change and large-scale disintegration and violent conflict in neighboring regions have had a number of consequences for the OSCE region, among them the increasing danger of transnational terrorism and violent extremism, as well as more refugees. It is undeniable that conflicts in these regions are having a direct impact on Europe, far more so than in the past. There is little hope that these conflicts can be resolved in the foreseeable future. Just decreasing their intensity would be a success.

The complexity and interconnectedness of today's conflicts have a number of consequences. Changes in one area can have substantial implications for completely different areas. Whether the USA and Russia cooperate or do not cooperate on Syria has an impact on their general relations as well as on conflicts in Europe. There is always the possibility of sudden, nonlinear changes in the quality of conflicts, for better or for worse. Thus, governments and populations have to learn to exercise governance in the face of a hitherto unknown level of uncertainty. The prime task is to deal with the situation in a cooperative manner.

2. Russia and the West – Differences and Shared Views

In analyzing the relations between Russia and the West, we are looking for convergences and divergences in perceptions to find possible platforms for cooperation. We start from the understanding that Russian-Western disputes are only one part of the larger problems that plague the OSCE space. We believe that patiently overcoming these divisions and shaping cooperation between Russia and the West serves the interests of all OSCE states and that failure to cooperate will make appropriate adjustments to the current challenges an increasingly hard mission. For achieving sustainable and pragmatic cooperation in the OSCE space, dialogue is indispensible.

We have started by analyzing the issue of *principles and norms*, followed by *interests and assessments*, and come, finally, to *institutions and instruments.* Each of these three sub-chapters deals with security, economic and normative issues.

2.1 Principles and Norms

One of the characteristics of the current turbulent period is that the behavior of governments is less norm-guided than it was in more stable times. Violations of international law and related accusations have become common.

Security. Nobody in the OSCE area openly questions the validity of the Helsinki principles governing relations among the OSCE participating States. However, there are substantially and increasingly different interpretations of what specific principles imply and what their mutual relationship is. This concerns most of the ten principles, particularly those of sovereign equality (I), refraining from the threat or use of force (II), the inviolability of frontiers (III), the territorial integrity of states (IV), non-intervention in internal affairs (VI), respect for human rights and fundamental freedoms (VII), and equal rights and self-determination of peoples (VIII).

The commitments to democracy based on human rights and fundamental freedoms, prosperity through economic liberty and social justice, and equal security for all nations, expressed in the 1990 Charter of Paris for a New Europe and reconfirmed on many occasions thereafter, among others, in the 1999 Charter of European Security and in the 2010 Astana Commemorative Declaration, are increasingly disputed. Russia and some other states, including countries in the West, differ from the mainstream Western understanding of political principles, leaving an increasing normative gap.

According to the prevailing Western narrative, the Russian government has seriously broken international law in Crimea and through its involvement in the conflict in Eastern Ukraine, calling into question the whole European order. In a number of countries, for example, Germany and the USA, there is concern that Russia might broadly reject the Helsinki consensus of a rule-based European order. From a Finnish point of view, the Helsinki and Paris order is in serious crisis, but not yet necessarily broken. For its part, the Russian narrative says that Western countries have broken and undermined international law with a number of military interventions and attempts at regime change from Kosovo to Libya. Russia sees itself as having pushed for a rule-based European order with its European Security Treaty initiative, which Western countries were not ready to discuss seriously. An additional asymmetry is that Russia perceives its conflicts with Western states as a global issue, whereas the West sees relations to Russia predominantly as a regional question.

194

From a more specific security policy perspective, the 2010 Astana vision of "comprehensive, co-operative, equal and indivisible security"[4] is in jeopardy. While cooperative security has remained the official concept of the OSCE and no state has yet formally renounced it, the practical behavior of most states shows that they currently rely more on deterrence than on co-operative security. Correspondingly, two of the three pillars of the OSCE arms control regime are either politically dead (Treaty on Conventional Armed Forces in Europe / CFE) or urgently need modernization (Vienna Document on Confidence- and Security-Building Measures 2011), while the Open Skies Treaty is still functioning.

The expectation prominent in the early 1990s that a comparatively quick norms transfer to the transition countries would lead to more cohesion and, thus, to stability, has largely failed. The question remains whether this failure is temporary or long-term in nature. The answer to this question, which is not yet apparent, has fundamental consequences. In the first case, a rule-based order remains a long-term option; in the second case, it will be very difficult to achieve.

Historical optimism makes us believe in the first option. The long-term objective of a norm-based European security order – a security community – should be maintained. However, for the time being, and this means a period of undefined duration, it remains a remote goal. The normative consensus between Russia and the Western countries is not stable enough to build concrete politics upon. Consequently, cooperation has to be based on more concrete interests to achieve a critical minimum of stability and cooperation. From the perspective of some countries, this is not new. In Kazakhstan, the prevalent view is that norms are not so decisive. Also in the French narrative, the perception that one should follow a *realpolitik*-based approach, focusing on interests, plays a prominent role.

Economy. In the 1975 Helsinki Final Act, the expectation was expressed that economic cooperation would foster stability and security: "Convinced that their efforts to develop co-operation in the fields of trade, industry, science and technology, the environment and other areas of economic activity contribute to the reinforcement of peace and security in Europe and in the world as a whole."[5] This is echoed by the 2003 "OSCE Strategy Document for the Economic and Environmental Dimension", which assesses itself as "an important step forward in developing our efforts to intensify economic and

4   OSCE, Summit, Astana 2010, Astana Commemorative Declaration. Towards a Security Community, para. 2.
5   CSCE, Summit, Helsinki 1975, Helsinki Final Act, chap. Co-operation in the Field of Economics, of Science and Technology and of the Environment, 1st sentence.

environmental co-operation among the participating States and thus to ensure comprehensive security and stability in the OSCE region."[6]

While statements like these are still fundamentally valid, they need differentiation. *Weak economic interdependence*, such as the simple exchange of goods, can achieve only little in creating stability and security. But this is precisely what we have in the relationship between Russia and Western countries. Moreover, *asymmetric interdependence*, where one partner is more dependent on the other, can even be used to exert political pressure with economic sanctions or other trade restrictions. Thus, the belief that economic interconnectedness will *automatically* lead to more stability has been seriously challenged.

Values and norms can unite or divide societies as well as states. While principles and commitments are codified in international documents, the body of norms and values on which different societies agree is constantly changing. Within the OSCE area, we observe quite different social and governance structures and value systems. Consequently, there are – beyond the level of official documents – quite different sets of domestic values and different perceptions of right and wrong.

Summary. Contrary to the dominant expectation in the 1990s, there is no normative consensus among Russia, Western and other countries in the OSCE space that would provide a sufficient basis for practical politics. That does not mean that norms and commitments do not play any role at all. Neither does it mean that the problem can be reduced to a lack of appropriate implementation. It *does* mean that the normative consensus among the participating States is so weak that it no longer sufficiently informs policy-relevant decisions. For a norm-based organization, such as the OSCE, this is a fundamental problem that the 57 participating States have not yet really addressed.

This sober finding has two principal consequences: *First*, at the present stage, cooperation among states should be primarily based on shared interests and assessments. This will not produce as much stability as a norm-based regime. It will also produce less human security for individuals and increase the risk of human rights being relativized in view of powerful interests. *Second*, societies, states and the OSCE itself should start to deal with normative issues in a serious manner. At the state level, this concerns the principles and norms of the Helsinki, Paris, Istanbul and Astana *acquis* that should not be renegotiated. Rather, their interpretation and application under the current conditions should be discussed.

At the societal level, norms dialogues should be conducted with the aim of mapping the currently existing normative structures, their divergences as

---

6   OSCE, Ministerial Council Meeting, Maastricht 2003, OSCE Strategy Document for the
     Economic and Environmental Dimension, pt. 4.1.

well as their convergences, and discussing how a future common normative basis might look. In Recommendation C we make a corresponding proposal.

2.2 Interests and Assessments

European order. The core of the dispute between Russia and Western countries is the disagreement over the European order. As evidenced by, among other things, the Ukraine crisis, there is no longer a consensus on the principles, instruments and institutional framing of such an order. Historically, the Helsinki Final Act represented a compromise on the European order relevant for the period up to 1990. *De facto* European frontiers, including those of Eastern Germany, were politically recognized, irrespective of historical territorial claims. Since it was clear which bloc controlled which frontiers, the spheres of interest were clear-cut and rather well respected during the Cold War.

Currently, we have neither a functioning cooperative order nor one that sets rules for competition, since one of the security blocs that formed the basic structure of the Cold War has disappeared. Some argue that this implies that all European states should be free to choose the organizations they wish to join. Others believe that indivisible security dictates a natural privilege of interest in certain spheres. The competition between these two visions is the core of the dispute. This competition without rules leads to instability and violent conflict. If Europe wants to regain lasting stability, states have to elaborate a shared understanding of a set of rules governing the European order on the basis of the Helsinki and Paris principles. Finding a proper starting point for such a process would, in itself, mark a major step forward.

The dispute over the European order rests on the fact that efforts to create a sustainable inter-linkage between Russia *and* the West, in the sense of a durable, cooperative and resilient connection between these two elements, have failed, at least for the time being. Discussions about the integration of Russia *into* NATO were not fruitful. What was actually attempted was establishing a special relationship between Russia and the Western integration structures. The NATO-Russia Council and the EU Four Common Spaces are the most important examples. However, although not completely unsuccessful, these efforts have not resolved the problem.

Russia has started to build up its own integration structures, namely the *Collective Security Treaty Organization* (CSTO) and the *Eurasian Economic Union* (EAEU). These institutions may be quite different from their Western counterparts and serve different purposes. What matters is that they exist.

The boundaries of the Russian and Western sets of integration structures are not clearly delineated. They overlap as far as countries are concerned which are not, but eventually may (and, in some cases, desire to) become part of either or both of them. Consequently, there is competition in one form or another for the states that have not yet made their choices.[7] This produces a dangerous tendency to treat such countries as objects of policies pursued by European powers, rather than as sovereign states that should make their own choices.

This concern is reflected in the security policy narratives of the countries involved. In Belarus, for example, Russia-West détente and a convergence between EU-based and Russia-led integration projects is perceived as an important precondition for mitigating the consequences of the current confrontation. In Kazakhstan, the growing competition between the leading powers is increasingly seen as a threat to their national interest. The vital importance of maintaining high-level political contacts, even in difficult times, is also emphasized in the security policy discourse of other countries, such as Finland. Switzerland, supported by a number of states, has initiated the "economic connectivity" debate to transform a spheres-of-influence thinking into a win-win situation.

Politico-military situation. The dispute over the European order has been widely securitized and, to a certain degree, re-militarized. The war in Ukraine is the most visible evidence. Both Russia and the West currently prefer deterrence to cooperative security. This manifests itself in the increased number and size of military exercises, including those conducted on short notice and close to borders, as well as risky maneuvers by vessels and aircraft, which can lead to unintended incidents, with a considerable potential for escalation. Therefore, it is long overdue that Russia and the NATO states start to discuss these issues in the NATO-Russia Council.

Most military measures taken by the various sides aim at increasing the readiness of armed forces or at relocating them to a limited degree. The overall figures of military equipment, however, have remained comparatively low and no general build-up, rearmament, or arms race has yet been observed. Neither side has enough military capabilities to start "large-scale offensive action" on a continental scale. What *is* possible, however, is geographically limited war, such as in Ukraine, as well as unintended war. Hybrid warfare, cyber attacks and other attempts to undermine societal resilience add to the picture. Taken together, for the time being, we are observing a limited militarization including some risk of re-nuclearization. The military situation can become more dangerous if it remains unchecked, but it is a symptom, not the cause of the dispute.

Threat perceptions. The fluid situation of a limited militarization is reflected in the fact that a number of governments harbor stronger threat perceptions than their populations do. Thus, significant majorities of the populations in such diverse countries as Belarus, France, Italy, the Netherlands and Switzer-

---

7   Cf. Back to Diplomacy, Final Report and Recommendations of the Panel of Eminent
     Persons on European Security as a Common Project, November 2015.

land rate military threats as low. However, in a more recent poll (February / March 2016), 48 per cent of Germans perceived Russia as a threatening country, whereas only 25 per cent of Russians saw Germany as threatening.[8] At the same time, Russian public opinion polls recorded an unprecedented surge of fears of a possible war with the US during the culmination of fighting in Ukraine at the end of 2014 and early 2015. More than the general public in many countries, governments and international organizations have started to allude to more or less explicit security concerns. In the communiqué of the NATO Warsaw Summit of 8-9 July 2016 we read: "Russia's aggressive actions, including provocative military activities in the periphery of NATO territory and its demonstrated willingness to attain political goals by the threat and use of force, are a source of regional instability, fundamentally challenge the Alliance, have damaged Euro-Atlantic security, and threaten our long-standing goal of a Europe whole, free, and at peace."[9] And the 2015 National Security Strategy of the United Kingdom states about Russia that one "cannot rule out the possibility that it [Russia] may feel tempted to act aggressively against NATO Allies."[10] Conversely, we can read in the "Concept of the Foreign Policy of the Russian Federation" of February 2013: "Russia maintains a negative attitude towards NATO's expansion and to the approaching of NATO military infrastructure to Russia's borders in general as to actions that violate the principle of equal security and lead to the emergence of new dividing lines in Europe."[11] It is, however, striking that states such as Belarus or Kazakhstan avoid identifying specific threats, but express their concern in more general terms such as an "increase in competition between leading powers."

The situation is significantly different in countries, such as Georgia or Ukraine, where threat perceptions about Russia are most prominent, both among the public and in governments. In general, we observe that there is a gap in threat perceptions between those countries that are situated close to Russia and those that are further away. Among the latter, perceptions also differ significantly between governments and populations. However, the longer the divisions between Russia and the West exist, the more threat perceptions spread among the broader population.

---

8 Körber Stiftung, Russland in Europa, Annäherung oder Abschottung. Ergebnisse einer repräsentativen Umfrage von TNS Infratest Politikforschung in Deutschland und Russland, Hamburg 2016, p. 7.

9 NATO, Warsaw Summit Communiqué, Issued by the Heads of State and Government participating in the meeting of the North Atlantic Council in Warsaw 8-9 July 2016, para. 5.

10 HM Government, National Security Strategy and Strategic Defence and Security Review 2015. A Secure and Prosperous United Kingdom, Cm 9161, Presented to Parliament by the Prime Minister by Command of Her Majesty in November 2015, pt. 3.20.

11 Ministry of Foreign Affairs of Russia, Concept of the Foreign Policy of the Russian Federation, Approved by the President of the Russian Federation V. Putin on 12 February 2013, para. 63.

Economy. The fragmented picture of European economies is a direct consequence of the countries' unequal abilities to adapt to globalization and the different results of economic transition. Countries such as Poland, the Czech Republic, Slovakia and Hungary have become integral parts of the international production chain. Accordingly, the convergence between these countries and those from the old West is deep, although differences in political culture and identity remain.

Apart from that, the economic exchange between the EU countries and the countries from the post-Soviet space has mostly remained at a rather simple level: Raw materials, most prominently hydrocarbons, are exchanged for machinery, cars and other manufactured goods. The comparison of these two cases shows the direct impact of economic and societal factors on the interstate level: Whereas in the first case, we have *deep interdependence* in the sense that the two elements – the old and the new EU states – cannot be separated without destroying the whole, the second case is characterized by *weak and asymmetrical interdependence* that makes it easier to use economic tools, including trade barriers and sanctions, as instruments in political disputes, provided the political will is present to accept the resulting economic costs.

Competing interests in economic integration have been a significant source of conflict in the case of Ukraine. And while politics can influence economic transition processes only modestly and over the long-term, it can directly instrumentalize economic vulnerabilities for political purposes. Although it is exaggerated to say, as some experts do, that economic warfare has replaced military warfare, this contains an element of truth. As a result, it is possible to start a negative, disintegrative, economic-political spiral by political means: The exploitation of economic weaknesses by one side can be followed by attempts by the other side to reduce its own vulnerabilities. This can only be achieved by reducing the connectedness between economies and societies and leads ultimately to a policy of isolation and autarky.

A responsible European stability policy must counteract such tendencies and strengthen interconnectedness to the point at which stability is achieved by strong interdependence. Economic relations must be calculable on a long-term basis. Tendencies towards economic warfare must be contained by new economic confidence-building measures. In Recommendation A, we propose the elaboration of such a set of economic and environmental CBMs.

Perceptions of shared interests. Against the background of the current tensions, it is encouraging how many interests shared by Russia and Western countries have been identified in the narrative reports. Strategic issues, such as the New START Treaty, and cooperation on space matters and Iran, are mentioned in the U.S. paper; nuclear non-proliferation in the Dutch and Kazakhstani papers. Cooperation on transnational threats – terrorism, "Islamic State", cybercrime and climate change – is mentioned in most reports, including those on France, Germany, Italy, Kazakhstan and the Netherlands. The same is true for cooperation on Libya, Syria and the Middle East (France, Germany). However, conflicts within the OSCE space – Ukraine, Nagornyy Karabakh – are also mentioned as objects of cooperation (Germany). Finally, economic cooperation is mentioned in the narrative reports on Ukraine, France, Italy and Kazakhstan and the Dutch report explicitly mentions potential relations between the EU and the EAEU. Altogether, the main focus of perceptions of shared interests is on global issues and transnational threats, on conflict resolution in Europe and the Middle East, and on economic issues.

Summary. While the fault lines between Russia and the Western states are undeniably deepening, a more careful analysis of the situation shows that this process has not yet become irreversible. Even under the presently strained relations, there is an impressively long list of shared interests that allow for and necessitate cooperation. Thus, Europe should engage in pragmatic cooperation in as many fields as possible.

2.3   Institutions and Instruments

Towards a New Compromise on the European Order

The long-term strategic task is to restore consensus on a sustainable and rule-based European order. This may take a long time. The relevant dialogue has not yet even started, pending a settlement of the Ukraine conflict. Therefore, from a mid-term perspective, it will be necessary to agree on a *modus vivendi* that would allow for mitigating and politically managing existing disputes and conflicts.

This part starts by outlining some obstacles on the way ahead, then sketches alternative scenarios for Europe that require different kinds of political orders. Subsequently, it attempts to describe the problem structure of a new European order, followed by a proposal to develop a *Code of Conduct for Facilitating a Diplomatic Process.*

Obstacles on the Way ahead

First, political leaderships of most states are overwhelmed by urgent practical issues from Brexit to Syria and Ukraine. This makes it difficult to address the more fundamental question of the European order.

Second, zero-sum game calculations and unilateral approaches prevail on many sides. There is not yet enough readiness to seriously address the relevant issue of the European order. However, attempts to change the conditions to one's own advantage and only then to negotiate will likely have no success.

Third, any consensus on a sustainable European order would require a respective normative basis. However, there is no readiness yet to reopen the issue of reaching an agreed interpretation of the Helsinki and Paris principles in order to achieve a shared interpretation adjusted to the new landscape without renegotiating them.

Fourth, multiple external factors aggravate the difficulties of creating a European order.

Approaching the starting point for a process towards a shared understanding of the principles of the European order makes it mandatory to work on each of these areas of difficulties.

Alternative Futures for Russian-Western Relations

There is a wide spectrum of imaginable alternative options for shaping future relations between Russia and the West, ranging from containment to minimal or selective cooperation, *pragmatic transactional cooperation*, through developing a security community.

A strategy of one-sided or mutual containment, accompanied by an increasing remilitarization and nuclearization of security relations, does not find support in any of our 15 narrative reports. It is evident that this approach would ruin Europe and would represent a danger for the rest of the world.

A somewhat milder version could be called a *strategy of neglect and minimal or selective cooperation*. Cooperation would be limited to some key economic areas, such as trade with hydrocarbons, whereas other areas could be the subject of sanctions. This would be accompanied by at least a limited remilitarization. This option also received no support in the narrative reports.

A third option would be a *strategy of pragmatic transactional cooperation*. This kind of cooperation starts from the current realities, whether one likes them or not, and looks for as many possibilities for cooperation as possible. This approach got support in almost all of the narrative reports, reflecting the security policy discussions in, among other countries, Belarus, the Netherlands, Finland, France, Germany, Italy, Kazakhstan and the United States. However, the level of confidence in the potential of such a strategy varies significantly: While the Ukrainian perception expects equal or even growing confrontation with Russia and does not see a viable option for a win-win situation, the Finnish narrative aims at restoring common security based on the OSCE principles. The proponents of *pragmatic transactional cooperation* see a comparatively large spectrum of possible areas of cooperation, from economic issues to addressing transnational threats to resolving conflicts in Europe (cf. para. 2.2).

The option of introducing a new *Yalta-type order* by clearly delineating and observing a sphere of influence for Russia in Eastern Europe or that of returning to a *Vienna Congress-type concert of European powers* governance system, strongly favored in the Russian mainstream thinking, does not find any significant support in other countries.

Finally, there is the *Astana vision of a norm-based security community*, which was not mentioned as a realistic option in any of the narrative reports.

The more cooperation between Russia and the West, the more a new compromise on the principles governing the European order is needed.

Problem Structure of a New European Order

We are still far away from having solutions for a new consensus on the European order. Our governments have not yet started a substantial discussion on the issue. However, it is possible to discuss the structure of the problem.

The European order should rest on the Helsinki principles, but cannot simply copy the bipolar Helsinki order. The key element of this historical order was the legitimation of existing frontiers, which, under the Cold War conditions of opposing, stable military blocs, made it possible to legitimize the existence of three groups of states – Western, Eastern and neutral and non-aligned (NN) states. Thus, the status of each state was defined and the different spheres of interest were largely respected.

Today's situation is much more fluid in every respect. The status of a number of states is not clearly defined. They may be interested in cooperation with this or that side or with both. According to Helsinki Principle I, they have the right to choose which to join. Various integration organizations compete over them using various means. In this situation, the key issue is the relation between different emerging integration structures. In addition, external states, such as China, influence the OSCE space. The historical bipolar reflex tells us: either we or they. A modern approach would think in terms of overlapping memberships and rules governing cooperation and competition.

Principle I of the Helsinki Decalogue stresses "sovereign equality, respect for the rights inherent in sovereignty" and includes the following text: "They [the participating States] also have the right to belong or not to belong to international organizations, to be or not to be a party to bilateral or multilateral treaties including the right to be or not to be a party to treaties of alliance; they also have the right to neutrality."

Apart from the recognition of the neutral and non-aligned states, this principle did not play a major role for the Helsinki order until this order was transformed by the dissolution of the Soviet Union and the Warsaw Pact and the reunification of Germany. But Principle I could play a major role for a future European order. The formula "to be or not to be a party to bilateral or multilateral treaties" means free choice. At the same time, the OSCE participating States have committed themselves to "bearing in mind the legitimate security concerns of other States"[12] while implementing this freedom of choice. This is only possible if there is no pressure to decide to join this or that side and if the necessary framework is in place. This requires contact and dialogue between all integration structures and, particularly, between the EU and the EAEU and the NATO and the CSTO / Russia, joint rules of behavior, and the elaboration of a framework that allows individual states to participate in the treaties in which they want to participate without losing their cooperation with others.

Whereas the Helsinki order was adapted to a bipolar world, the prime challenge for a new European order is to govern integration issues in an inclusive and flexible manner that avoids falling back on the inherited patterns of bipolarity.

Code of Conduct for Facilitating a Diplomatic Process

The Panel of Eminent Persons' 2015 Report "Back to Diplomacy" called for a "robust process of active diplomacy" with the "ultimate aim [...] to reestablish security on a co-operative basis"[13]. There is no alternative to such a political process apart from ongoing crises, escalation and war. However, starting a process towards a cooperative order requires at least an agreed starting point and an overall objective, both in terms of the dos and the donots, and there must be a mental mindset guiding the process. Elements of such a starting point can be formulated in a kind of Code of Conduct that does not necessarily have to be a written document, but can also be expressed in the form of a series of statements.

Such a Code of Conduct would aim at lowering the level of confrontation, strengthening communication among the sides, and setting up guidelines for cooperation.

Measures to lower the level of confrontation could include:

- The sides – governments and different societal actors alike – should deliberately avoid any steps that might raise the level of confrontation. In principle, this means reacting sub-proportionally to any step by the other side that is perceived as unfriendly.
- The sides should agree on deliberate de-escalatory steps. Such steps can also be taken by relevant societal actors, such as religious denominations or economic enterprises.

---

12 OSCE, Code of Conduct on Politico-Military Aspects of Security, 3 December 1994, DOC.FSC/1/95, para. IV.10.
13 Back to Diplomacy, quoted above (note 7), pp. 5 and 14.

Measures to strengthen communication could include:

- The sides should de-escalate their rhetoric, discourage hate speech and stop attempts to frame the other side as an enemy with whom no solution can be found. It should be clear that the partner at state level is the current government in office and not any future government that might be seen as better.
- The sides should maintain as many channels of communication as possible at all levels. Sustainable cooperation will need related public diplomacy efforts.
- The sides should conduct a dual dialogue both on issues where agreement can be achieved and on issues where agreement cannot be expected soon. The first line of dialogue serves to frame platforms for cooperation, whereas the second serves to avoid misperceptions arising from disputed issues.
- Governments could turn to academic or other societal bodies to deal with contradictory narratives and adjust visa regimes to facilitate such contacts.

Measures to re-establish cooperation could include:

- The sides should cooperate wherever possible, on any given subject, at any level, be it state or society. Unnecessary conditions for cooperation should be avoided.
- The sides should cooperate on climate change, terrorism and other global or transnational issues. In doing so, they should include science and education, as well as other societal fields, to the maximum extent possible.
- The sides should consult on their cooperation with third partners in neighboring regions as well as on a global level.
- Political leaders should communicate to their populations their willingness to cooperate.

A Code of Conduct of this kind shapes the mindsets in the direction of cooperation, based on compromises.

Creating a More Connected Economic Order

Currently, we are observing two major characteristics in economic governance beyond the rules of the World Trade Organization (WTO). *First*, despite the existence of two different economic integration vehicles, the EU and the EAEU, there are no formal political ties between these organizations. *Second*, the re-emergence of economic sanctions in the Russian-Western relationship underlines the need for mechanisms guiding states' economic behavior in case of interstate conflicts.

Relations between the EU and the EAEU. These two organizations are very different in every respect – their objectives, the instruments available and performance. This is frequently used as an argument against dialogue and relations between these two bodies. However, the Ukraine crisis has shown that this line of argument is counterproductive. Among other factors, it was the lack of communication that contributed to creating the conditions for the conflict. Thus, the EU and the EAEU, as well as their member states, should enter into a dialogue with the objective of exploring the kinds of relations that *are* possible. Such an approach is supported by a wide range of states, including Belarus, Germany, Italy, Kazakhstan, the Netherlands, and Russia. The dialogue should include wider issues related to economic affairs, such as the freedom of movement. It should also include relations to third states, such as China. Discussions could be kick-started in the OSCE framework, i.e. in the OSCE Economic and Environmental Forum and in the Permanent Council's Economic and Environmental Committee.

Economic confidence-building measures (CBMs). Both in the Ukraine conflict and in the 2016 dispute between Russia and Turkey, economic sanctions and counter-sanctions have played a prominent role. Thereby, this instrument is back on the table on a scale not seen in Russian-Western relations in three decades. The necessary condition for sanctions is a certain economic connectedness, the sufficient one is weak interdependence, meaning that the connectedness does not go far enough and/or is of an asymmetrical nature. At least in part, economic sanctions have been used as a replacement for military measures. To stimulate the discussion, this report proposes the elaboration of an initial package of OSCE economic and environmental CBMs (cf. Recommendation A).

Working on Re-Establishing a Shared Normative Order

Any notion of a security community, but also of a cooperative European security order, requires the existence of a shared normative basis. Currently, no sufficiently firm joint value base on which to build practical policies exists. Norms are not only not shared, but different and diverging norms are used as political weapons in an attempt to violate and humiliate the political 'enemy'. Thus, when we speak about the option of re-establishing a cooperative European order, we implicitly presuppose not only the termination of such norms manipulation, but also and, much more profoundly, the reversal of the trend of a divergent normative development in favor of a convergent one.

Restoring the OSCE States' damaged value base is a long-term project with uncertain success. Despite and just because of this fact, a number of steps should be started.

First, States should stop misusing norms disputes as political weapons.

Second, civil society actors should initiate norms dialogues at the societal level. In Recommendations B and C we make proposals for such dialogues.

Third, it is urgent that the OSCE, as a norm-based organization, start to deal with the fact that its presupposed shared normative basis has broadly disappeared.

Working on norms is difficult and will not produce results soon. However, it is an indispensable task in view of the objective of a new consensus on a cooperative order in Europe.

3.   Recommendations

We offer two sets of recommendations. *First*, addressing the governments of the OSCE participating States with a Program of Urgent Action (3.1), which summarizes the most important steps that should be addressed immediately. The *second* set concerns recommendations to be implemented at the societal level by the OSCE Network of Think Tanks and Academic Institutions.

3.1   Program of Urgent Action

In view of unpostponable global and regional challenges, the states in the Euro-Atlantic and Eurasian area should agree on a Program of Urgent Action that serves the following goals:

–   Sending a clear signal that the states are ready to resume dialogue and look for options for cooperation.
–   Structuring the different lines of dialogue and thus defining a starting point for broader intergovernmental communication.
–   Agreeing on some urgent measures without political conditions and linkages.

It is clear that the key issues will have to be dealt with between the EU and Russia, NATO and Russia, and at bilateral levels. Both the Council of Europe and the UN Economic Commission for Europe (UNECE) can also play a constructive role. The OSCE can make significant and, in some areas, crucial contributions. It is not important in what form a Program of Urgent Action is agreed, formally or informally. What is important is that there be a clear shared understanding among the key actors. Such a program could have the following elements.

A. Measures to Normalize the Situation

States should send some clear public political messages that they *do* want to resume political dialogue and explore options for cooperation. Such messages can take different forms:

–   Concerted public statements of political leaders represent the easiest option.
–   A Code of Conduct for Facilitating a Diplomatic Process (cf. para. 2.3), whether informally agreed or formalized, would represent a more elaborate variant.

Whereas questions of form can be flexibly handled, it is key that states consistently send the same message – returning to political dialogue and cooperation.

B. Structuring the Dialogue

The argument of 'no business as usual with Russia' has become ineffective. On the one hand, global and regional challenges do not wait until states agree on something. On the other hand, dialogue is key for resolving conflicts including the one in and around Ukraine.

The necessary dialogue will be conducted along different lines: Some elements have to be discussed between the EU and Russia, others in the NATO-Russia Council, still others in the OSCE, and some other issues are on the agenda of ad-hoc arrangements, such as the Normandy Format. The key stakeholders should come to an informal or formal agreement on an inclusive and structured dialogue that is transparent about what is discussed where and with whom. This dialogue structure is the starting point of broader intergovernmental communication on the options for a pragmatic transactional cooperation.

C. Politico-Military Issues

States should quickly agree on some immediate steps and, at the same time, create the space for further exchange.

–   States should conclude, in a timely manner and in the framework of the NATO-Russia Council (NRC) – an agreement to avoid military incidents and accidents including measures to be taken if they should occur.
–   States should initiate, also in the NRC, a high-level political as well as military-to-military dialogue on further options for risk reduction and stabilization through measures of confidence- and security-building and arms control.

These measures should be accompanied by discussions among the 57 states in the OSCE Forum for Security Co-operation, including on the modernization of the related OSCE instruments (Vienna Document 2011).

D. Conflict Resolution

The relevant states should agree on substantial progress in the implementation of the Minsk Agreement and on further strengthening the OSCE's crisis prevention and conflict management tools.[14]

– It is evident that substantial progress in the implementation of the Minsk Agreement, of its security as well as of its political parts, would significantly facilitate a positive development in other areas, while failure would leave larger questions open. Therefore, progress in resolving the Ukraine crisis is key.
– The deployment of the Special Monitoring Mission (SMM) to Ukraine has shown that the OSCE can operate a mission of this size. However, it has also become clear that the SMM brought the OSCE to the limits of its capacities. Therefore, there is a need to further strengthen the operational capacities of the OSCE, including by innovative means. The OSCE Permanent Council should establish an Informal Working Group to elaborate proposals.

E. Economic and Environmental Matters

The overall objective in this area is to create a more connected economic order in the Euro-Atlantic and Eurasian space. While key tasks need to be carried out by the EU, the EAEU and Russia, the OSCE can also contribute.

– The EU and the EAEU should upgrade their technical talks to the political level and explore what kind of relations, contacts and joint activities are possible. Related discussions can be kick-started and accompanied by debates in OSCE bodies.
– The OSCE should elaborate a set of economic and environmental confidence building measures (cf. 3.2, Recommendation A).
– The OSCE should modernize its 2003 "OSCE Strategy Document for the Economic and Environmental Dimension" adapting it to the current needs.

---

14   Another working group of the OSCE Network of Think Tanks and Academic Institutions, chaired by Ambassador Philip Remler, has recently published the Study "Protracted Conflicts in the OSCE Area. Innovative Approaches for Co-operation in the Conflict Zones".

F. Conducting a Norms Dialogue

Even if cooperation is primarily based on interests, norms continue to matter. Therefore, states and societies in the Euro-Atlantic and Eurasian area should make efforts to re-establish their severely damaged norms base. This should include a number of normative dimensions:

- States should work on re-establishing a shared understanding of the principles of the Helsinki Decalogue including their mutual relationship.
- States should also work on restating a common understanding of the basic norms of human rights, democracy and the rule of law contained in the Paris Charter and follow-on documents.
- States should also make efforts towards a joint understanding of the norms guiding "comprehensive, co-operative, equal and indivisible security" (Astana Commemorative Declaration).

Finally, states should work on any other relevant normative issues. Norm dialogues must include civil society actors in a multitude of formats. Norm dialogues have a long-term perspective. But they are essential for laying the ground for re-establishing a shared understanding on the European order.

G. Conducting an Inclusive Trans-Societal Dialogue

As the populist movements in many regions of the OSCE area have shown, political mobilization and divisions have long since reached the societal level. In the same way, addressing these challenges in a cooperative manner will only be successfully achieved by a comprehensive approach including all relevant strata of society. As a consequence, all relevant lines of discussion must also be conducted at societal levels. Track 2 and 1.5 formats can parallel intergovernmental talks. Sometimes, they can address issues that are still too sensitive for intergovernmental treatment. And trans-societal debates can put aspects on the agenda that have been neglected by governments. Together, discussions at societal levels represent not only a supplement to intergovernmental talks, but also a value in themselves.

3.2 Proposals for Concrete Action by the Network

The following recommendations concern activities of the OSCE Network of Think Tanks and Academic Institutions that, *first*, serve and support the political process towards a shared understanding on the basics of a future European order and, *second*, focus on the societal level.

A. *Elaborating a Set of Economic and Environmental Confidence-Building Measures*

We recommend elaborating a set of economic and environmental confidence-building measures for the OSCE space.

Historical lessons learned as well as more recent studies provide evidence that, although economic connectedness and interdependence raise the cost of confrontation and violent conflict, they do not automatically prevent a conflict, particularly when political or security stakes are perceived by parties as outweighing economic costs of confrontation.

Most recent experiences, gathered in the context of the Ukraine crisis, have confirmed that in the course of a confrontation, economic interests and interdependence do not prevent the countries concerned from applying sanctions and counter-sanctions of various sorts, including economic ones.

Discussing economic confidence-building measures leads to the conclusion that sanctions do not contribute to building confidence but, rather, highlight the vulnerability that results from interdependence and thus militate for autarky. We believe it is unrealistic to suggest banning sanctions as a policy instrument. However, a set of measures can help not only to (re-)build trust and confidence among states and businesses, but may also be instrumental in arresting, at an early stage, conflict-prone developments that can, at some point, lead to the application of sanctions.

In its diverse dimensions, the OSCE offers various tools, better known as "mechanisms", allowing the participating States to raise specific concerns and committing the relevant states to responding to them, with a view toward identifying the eventual problems that may result from taking certain decisions, and searching for cooperative solutions before the problems escalate. However, no such preventative mechanism exists in the economic and environmental dimension of the OSCE.

We recommend setting up a Network working group which would be tasked to:

- Explore the merits of setting up a mechanism for bilateral and/or multilateral consultation on economic and environmental issues that raise concern of individual participating States and may affect their interests.
- Consult relevant stakeholders on the issue.
- Assess the feasibility of establishing such a mechanism within the OSCE.
- Study measures that may be required to avoid the abuse of such a mechanism or its interference with other existing cooperative mechanisms, for example between the EU and individual countries or within the WTO.
- Elaborate a food-for-thought paper for consideration by the participating States that can be presented at a side event at the 2017 OSCE Ministerial Council meeting in Austria.

B. Analyzing Historical Narratives

We recommend analyzing historical narratives and elaborating recommendations on how to deal with historical narratives in a non-confrontational manner.

Narratives are sets of perceptions and beliefs that shape collective actors' expectations and, thus, frame their decision-making corridors. Historical narratives are sets of perceptions and beliefs coming from the past, related to the past and transmitted up to today that contribute to shaping actors' expectations. (Historical) narratives are not necessarily "objective", "rational" or free of contradictions – quite the contrary. Their relevance is that they exist and impact actors' expectations. The Study Group could establish a working group of historians with the following tasks:

-   Identify historical narratives on Russian-Western relations that are still relevant for the present stage and analyze their development.
-   Compare different sets of historical narratives shared by certain groups in the OSCE area and elaborate key differences and agreements.
-   Elaborate recommendations for governments, international organizations and foundations on how to deal with historical narratives in a way that does not undermine cooperation in Europe.
-   Elaborate recommendations on how to further organize a meaningful discussion process on (historical) narratives.

The working group should recruit itself and cooperate with the Council of Europe, in particular with respect to the project on "Educating for diversity and democracy: teaching history in contemporary Europe" and initiatives such as "Historians without Borders" or the Polish-Russian Working Group on Most Difficult Issues.

A report could be presented at a side event at the 2017 OSCE Ministerial Council meeting in Austria.

C. Conducting a Norms Dialogue at the Societal Level

We recommend creating a dialogue format for reflection on a common normative basis, starting with the mapping of the status quo. Participants should be representatives of the generation that will shape interstate and intersocietal relations in about ten years.

The conflict between Russia and the West is not only occurring on an intergovernmental level. Rather, we are back to levels of suspiciousness and estrangement between societies we thought were long gone. In this sense, the current conflict is both an inter-societal and an intra-societal conflict. The various narratives collected are ample proof of this assessment, which is confirmed by polls on a regular basis.

Thus, overcoming the current crisis takes more than intergovernmental measures and expert discussions. We strongly believe that it is necessary to continue and to intensify people-to-people contacts at all levels. Before reaching a consensus on a shared normative order, more knowledge about different views and beliefs is required, as is a better understanding of the factors and events that have created these views and beliefs.

Therefore, we suggest working on the question of what chances exist for a common normative basis for a future European order beyond cooperation based on common interests and transactional advantages.

This dialogue format should bring together younger experts, officials and interested citizens. The participants will have a double role: Working towards a better understanding among each other and, thus, among the various societies in the OSCE area, but also contributing to shaping opinions within their own societies and professional communities. By making use of the opportunities offered by social media, individuals' impact on opinion formation has grown tremendously. This opens up a path for new approaches.

To that end, an OSCE-wide dialogue format could be created aiming at:

–   Mapping currently existing norms bases within societies of the OSCE area.
–   Discussing what a future common normative basis may look like.
–   Serving as dialogue "ambassadors" within their own societies.

A report could be presented at a side event at the 2017 OSCE Ministerial Council meeting in Austria.

Disclaimer

In the preparation of this report, valuable advice and various contributions were given to us by a Reflection Group of members of the OSCE Network of Think Tanks and Academic Institutions. Nonetheless, the views set out in this report are solely those of the authors. They do not necessarily reflect the views of the institutions they represent.

Drafting Group Members

Irina Chernykh
Kazakhstan Institute for Strategic Studies under the President of the Republic of Kazakhstan, Almaty

Alain Délétroz
Geneva Centre for Security Policy (GCSP), Geneva

Frank Evers
Institute for Peace Research and Security Policy at the University of Hamburg (IFSH), Centre for OSCE Research (CORE), Hamburg

Barbara Kunz
Institut français des relations internationales (Ifri), Paris

Christian Nünlist
Eidgenössische Technische Hochschule (ETH) Zürich, Center for Security Studies (CSS), Zurich

Philip Remler
Carnegie Endowment for International Peace, Washington, DC

Oleksiy Semeniy
Institute for Global Transformation, Kyiv

Andrei Zagorski
Primakov National Research Institute of World Economy and International Relations (IMEMO), Moscow

Wolfgang Zellner
Institute for Peace Research and Security Policy at the University of Hamburg (IFSH), Centre for OSCE Research (CORE), Hamburg

Reflection Group Members

Nadezhda Arbatova
Primakov National Research Institute of World Economy and International Relations (IMEMO), Moscow

Hüseyin Bağci
Middle East Technical University (METU), Ankara

Serena Giusti
Sant'Anna School of Advanced Studies, Pisa

William Hill
National War College (NWC), Washington, DC

Kornely Kakachia
Georgian Institute of Politics (GIP), Tbilisi

Dzianis Melyantsou
Belarusian Institute for Strategic Studies (BISS), Vilnius

Kari Möttölä
Network for European Studies (NES), University of Helsinki, Helsinki

Barend ter Haar
Clingendael – Netherlands Institute of International Relations, The Hague

Monika Wohlfeld
Mediterranean Academy of Diplomatic Studies (MEDAC), University of Malta, Malta

About the Authors

Prof. Hüseyin Bagci is Professor at the Middle East Technical University (METU), Ankara, and Chair of the Department of International Relations.

Prof. Ali Serdar Erdurmaz is Associated Professor at the Department of Political Science and International Relations, Hasan Kalyoncu University, Gaziantep, Turkey.

Prof. Serena Giusti is Assistant Professor at the Sant'Anna School of Advanced Studies, Pisa.

Prof. James Gow is Professor of International Peace and Security at the Department of War Studies, King's College, London.

Barend ter Haar is a Dutch diplomat and currently Senior Visiting Research Fellow at the Netherlands Institute of International Relations Clingendael, The Hague.

Dr Kornely Kakachia is Director of the Georgian Institute of Politics (GIP), Tbilisi.

Dr Barbara Kunz is Research Fellow at the French Institute of International Relations (IFRI), Paris.

Prof. Kari Möttölä is a retired Finnish diplomat and currently Visiting Scholar at the Network for European Studies (NES), University of Helsinki.

Dr Christian Nünlist is a Senior Researcher at the Center for Security Studies (CSS) at the Eidgenössische Technische Hochschule Zürich, and head of its think tank team "Swiss and Euro-Atlantic Security".

Ambassador Philipp Remler is a retired U.S. diplomat, a former Head of the OSCE Mission to Moldova, and currently Research Fellow at the Carnegie Endowment for International Peace, Washington, DC.

Dr Oleksiy Semeniy is Director of the Institute for Global Transformations (IGT), Kyiv.

Prof. Andris Spruds is Director of the Latvian Institute of International Affairs and Professor at Riga Stradins University.

Prof. Andrei Zagorski is Head of the Department for Disarmament and Conflict Resolution at the Primakov National Research Institute of World Economy and International Relations (IMEMO) and Professor at the Moscow State Institute for International Relations (MGIMO-University), Moscow.

Dr Wolfgang Zellner is Deputy Director of the Institute for Peace Research and Security Policy at the University of Hamburg (IFSH) and Head of its Centre for OSCE Research (CORE).

Benno Zogg, MA, is a researcher in the "Swiss and Euro-Atlantic Security" Team at the Center for Security Studies (CSS) at the Eidgenössische Technische Hochschule Zürich.